D0699744

Single Point of Failure

Single Point of Failure

THE TEN ESSENTIAL LAWS OF SUPPLY CHAIN RISK MANAGEMENT

Gary S. Lynch

John Wiley & Sons, Inc.

This book is printed on acid-free paper. ♾

Published by John Wiley & Sons, Inc., Hoboken, New Jersey.
Published simultaneously in Canada.

For general information on our other products and services, or technical support, please contact our Customer Care Department within the United States at 800-762-2974, outside the United States at 317-572-3993 or fax 317-572-4002.

Wiley also publishes its books in a variety of electronic formats. Some content that appears in print may not be available in electronic books.

For more information about Wiley products, visit our Web site at *http://www.wiley.com.*

Library of Congress Cataloging-in-Publication Data:

Lynch, Gary S. (Gary Scott), 1958–
Single point of failure : the ten essential laws of supply chain risk management / Gary S. Lynch.
p. cm.
Includes index.
ISBN 978-0-470-42496-4
1. Business logistics. 2. Risk management. I. Title.
HD38.5.L963 2010
658.5'03–dc22

2009026530

Printed in the United States of America
10 9 8 7 6 5 4 3 2

I dedicate this book to the future generations that now must manage the risk created by prior generations. To my children Christopher, Robert, Colleen, and Brian; my daughter-in-law Katie; my nieces and nephew, Brian, Jennifer, Matt, Tracey, and Katie; to my best friend's children, Eden and Erika—I wish you well, for you are the ones who have to tame the risk parasite, a new world of uncertainty, one that is moving faster than anyone's ability to understand. Finally, I dedicate this book to all those who protect and serve our great nation—thank you.

Contents

About the Author xi

Preface xiii

Acknowledgments xvii

Introduction Getting to the Truth 1

Chapter 1 **The Laws of the Laws** 9

Laws of the Laws
Risk Management Defined
Law of the Laws #1: Everyone, without Exception, Is Part of a Supply Chain
Law of the Laws #2: No Risk Strategy Is a Substitute for Bad Decisions and a Lack of Risk Consciousness
Law of the Laws #3: It's All in the Details
Law of the Laws #4: People Always Operate from Self-Interest
Indirect and Secondary Impacts
What Can You Conclude?
Notes

Chapter 2 **Law #1: If You Don't Manage and Lead Change, You Have to Surrender to It** 31

The Risk Wake-Up Call—Planned Change, Unplanned Consequences
We Can't Change the Past, but . . . Can We Change the Future?
Can You See the Icebergs Ahead?
Notes

Chapter 3 **Law #2: The Paradigm Should Destroy the Parasite: Begin by Defining the Paradigm, Not by Fighting the Parasite** 61

The Paradigm in Action
Why Does the Organization Need to Identify a Supply Chain Risk Paradigm?
Beware! The Paradigm Can Shift without Notice
If the Shoe Fits
Notes

Chapter 4 **Law #3: Manage Your Business DNA in a Petri Dish of Evolving Risk** 87

Expanding the Risk Awareness Universe
Know Your Business—Know Your Surroundings
The Keys to Your Risk Kingdom
Your Operation's Complete Footprint
Your Action Plan
Notes

Chapter 5 **Law #4: In Supply Chain Risk Management, Demand Trumps Supply** 115

Everyone's Customer
Building Your Demand-Based Strategy
Market and Client Factors to Consider
Notes

Chapter 6 **Law #5: Never Set Up Your Suppliers for Failure** 143

Supply Chain Risk Management Program
Sourcing Strategies That Create More Risk, Not Less
Trust but Verify
Notes

Chapter 7 **Law #6: Managing Production Risk Is a Dirty Job: Focus on Managing the Endless Risk of Manufactured Weakest Links** 173

Going Global with the Production of Risk
A New Collaborative Effort
Why Is Production So Critical?
Part Two of the Double Whammy: Labor
Notes

Chapter 8 **Law #7: The Logistics Risk Management Rule: Managing the Parts Does Not Equal Managing the Whole** 199

What Is Logistics Risk?
Cargo and Warehouse Theft
The Piracy Risk
What's at Risk?
Single Points of Failure and Aggregate Risk
Supply Chains Don't Survive on Product Flows Alone; Information Flows Are Essential
In the End It's All about the Priorities and Economics
Notes

Chapter 9 **Law #8: Mitigation: If Supply Chain Risk Management Isn't Part of the Solution, It Will Become the Problem** 225

Now What Do I Do?
Enter the Risk Intelligent Supply Chain
Economic Change—A Catalyst for Redefining Resiliency Management
Predisruption
At Time of Disruption
Postdisruption
What Is Risk Mitigation?
Notes

Chapter 10 **Law #9: Financing: The Best Policy Is Knowing What's in Your Policy** 249

Insurance and Its Role in Supply Chain Risk Management
Background on Insurance in the Supply Chain Risk Area
Current Insurance Solutions and Their Limitations
Introducing Supply Chain Insurance: Approach and Challenges
Corporate Customer Benefits Arising from Supply Chain Insurance
Conclusions
What Does the Future Hold?
A View from the Insurer's Side
Notes

Chapter 11 **Law #10: Manage the Risk as You Manage Your Own: Your Supply Chains Are All Interdependent but Unique** 279

Questioning Old Assumptions
Personal Laws of the Laws

Index 287

About the Author

Gary S. Lynch, CISSP, is an internationally recognized expert on risk management issues. He is an author and Global Leader of Marsh's Supply Chain Risk Management Practice. He also leads Marsh's Global Pandemic Response Center. He works as a management consultant, specializing in helping senior executives solve complex risk issues. He has developed critical thought leadership and solutions around emerging risk issues, including supply chain risk management and financing, information protection strategies and schemes, value chain risk strategies, pandemic preparedness, and IT risk.

Lynch has contributed to the World Economic Forum (WEF) Global Risks Report and participated on a China European Institute & Business Studies/WEF panel on risk with directors and CEOs from privately owned Chinese-based organizations. Lynch has been a speaker on pressing global business risk issues for organizations such as Asia Pacific Economic Cooperation (APEC), Risk and Insurance Management Society (RIMS), the World Customs Organization (WCO), and the Wharton School, Center for Risk Management and Decision Processes. He also is a member of the advisory board for the New York Institute of Technology's Center for Risk.

Lynch has held client-facing leadership positions over sixteen years:

- Managing Director and Global Practice Leader, Supply Chain and Risk Intelligence, Marsh
- Partner, Booz Allen Hamilton
- Partner, Ernst & Young
- Research Director, IT Risk, Gartner Group

He has also held senior management positions over seventeen years:

- Chief Information Security & Continuity Risk Executive, Prudential
- Corporate Informaion Security Executive, Chase Manhattan Bank

Lynch is the author of *At Your Own Risk: Creating a Risk-Conscious Culture to Meet the Challenge of Business Change*, published by John Wiley & Sons in May 2008. He has appeared on Bloomberg TV, CNBC Asia Squawk Box, NBC Nightly News, and ABC. Lynch has been published in the *Wall Street Journal, Financial Week, CEO Magazine, Financial IT Decisions, CIO Insights, The Asset* (Asia Pacific), *Business Review Weekly, Institute of Internal Auditors* (Information Security Management & Assurance), *Information Security* magazine, *Knowledge at Wharton*, The Conference Board, and *Computerworld.*

Lynch is a member of the National Association of Corporate Directors (NACD). He received a commendation from the U.S. Secret Service for his 9/11 disaster response and support activity and was awarded the Silver Medal of Valor by the Nassau County Fire Service, New York.

Preface

Have you ever stopped for a moment to think about what is needed to produce the products you depend on? Critical drugs like blood thinners, polyethylene (plastic)-based products such as syringes, isotopes for medical imaging, or milk-based baby formula? Or maybe your livelihood depends on your ability to transport products, your customers having access to your online order entry system, or the timely receipt of parts from your suppliers on the other side of the world. But because of a product contamination, failure of a key supplier, labor strike, trade credit squeeze, earthquake, pandemic, software glitch, project mismanagement, or some other adverse event—what you depend on is simply not available.

Ironically, as this book was on its way to print, that was the case for a select group of patients with rare genetic disorders. According to a *Wall Street Journal* article, Genzyme Corporation, the biotech company that produces Cerezyme and Fabrazyme (enzyme replacement drugs), had to shut down a critical node in its supply chain—the main U.S. manufacturing plant. The identification of a suspected virus in a vat used to make Cerezyme was the suspected cause. Company officials stated that this *single point of failure* would cause shortages over the next few months, while analysts were estimating the potential lost revenue from the shutdown to range from between $100 million and $300 million.[1] A virus, an unplanned event that suddenly threatened the well-being of the patients as well as the financial stability of the organization, had halted this supply chain.

The occurrence of a single point of failure, the breakdown of any given product, information, and/or cash flow caused by a process or resource (e.g., people, technology, physical, or relationship) failure

[1] David Armstrong, "Genzyme Shuts Down Plant Tainted by Virus," *Wall Street Journal*, June 17, 2009.

at any given point in global interdependent and interconnected supply chains may interrupt the flow of goods and cause systemic failure. Ask yourself:

- What do I depend on?
- What are these single points of failure and how will my organization be impacted by a failure at different points in the supply chain?
- How do you recognize whether or not you are exposed (and to what degree)?
- Who is responsible for understanding and managing this risk?
- When and where are you most exposed?
- Why should you invest time, resources, capital, and management attention to address these risks?
- And, most important, what can I or my organization do about it?

These are just a few of the questions that I set out to address when I began this book and that you need to keep in mind as you read forward.

When I began the journey, I found that many of the people with whom I interacted globally struggled to define, understand, and articulate the concept of supply chain risk management. All acknowledged that it was important and that they should be addressing the risk—but most weren't sure if they really were addressing it and they couldn't concisely define who *owned* the problem. In many instances, they didn't know where to start.

So with the help of dozens of experts from industry and academia located around the globe, I set out to define a common language, a shared context, and comprehensive framework to help better understand and manage supply chain risk management. I documented the lessons learned as well as the lessons not learned. This is just the beginning of the journey, and after I completed the manuscript, I realized that I had only begun to scratch the surface. There was so much more to address: enterprise resource planning systems and supply chain technologies, environmental risk and regulations, geopolitical challenges, climate change, and compliance to name a few. I will save those topics for another time. I share with you the countless challenges, practical experience, and the frustration faced by so many senior managers—risk, procurement, logistics, operations, security, product quality, distribution, compliance, manufacturing, finance, and even directors and senior officers. The issues are not unique to any industry, geography, company, function, or individual. But what is unique is the supply chain itself. Richard Steinke, Executive Director of the Ports of Long Beach, stated, "if you have seen one supply chain . . . you've seen one supply chain."[2] I would add to his comment that if you've seen it—look again—that supply chain and associated risk has probably changed. Simply put, organizations rely on dozens, if not thousands, of virtual supply chains in which the participants and the paths are constantly reshuffled.

So let's begin the journey together and acknowledge that there is no end point and that we will be forever learning, improving, and hopefully reducing the risk to the supply chains that we depend on so heavily to deliver what we value the most.

[2] The Asia Pacific Economic Cooperation workshop on Trade Disruption, Singapore, 2008

Acknowledgments

Over the past few years, I was fortunate to work alongside many brilliant and experienced professionals from a variety of private industries, public organizations, and geographies. All were concerned about the mounting supply chain risk issue. It was their concern that motivated me to write this book. I'd like to recognize some of the many people who have help me assemble *Single Point of Failure.* Unfortunately, contractual obligations of my day job force me to maintain client confidentiality so, for the most part, I regretfully am unable to publicly share their names or the employer's names. However, I silently want to extend a special thanks for their contribution, confidence, and, most of all, countless real-world stories of the near misses and failures they experienced while trying to manage the forever changing supply chain risk parasite.

Single Point of Failure would not have been possible without the participation, writing, and mind-share from a group of individuals that share my passion to raise awareness to this escalating concern. Nick Wildgoose, Supply Chain Global Product Manager, Zurich Global Corporate, thank you for taking time out of your incredibly hectic schedule to provide the extensive content that led to the creation of the chapter on risk financing. I would like to thank Ben Tucker, Managing Director, Property Practice and Paul McVey as well, Managing Director at Marsh Property Claims for sharing his many, many years (I promised I wouldn't tell) of experience managing complex business interruption and property-related claims. I would like to extend my gratitude to Paul Ranta and the Corporate Responsibility Team at Nike for their contribution—I appreciate that you took the time to discuss your "war stories," daily challenges, and evolving strategies. Thank you, Kate Meyers, Senior Manager, Global Corporate Media Relations; Caitlin Morris, Director of Stakeholder

Relations; Mark Loomis, Manager, Corporate Responsibility, and, of course, Paul, Sustainability Manufacturing Operations. Thanks for bringing it all together and helping me understand the daily risk challenges of operating in so many different cultures and political systems. Craig Bartol, Nike's Global Risk Manager, thank you for your insight with regard to the learning challenge and the need to apply lessons learned to continuously improve the overall risk management program. As I began the process of creating this book, several people were instrumental in shaping my thinking. Gary Mucha, Senior VP of Business Integration and Performance Excellence—thanks for challenging my thinking and driving the concept of the "risk paradigm." David Nadler, Vice Chairman, Marsh & McLennan Companies, and an expert on organizational behavior—thank you for your insights on the changing business climate and the need for intelligent, collective, technology driven, and socially engineered risk problem solving. Rajeev Kadam, Vice President of Olam International Ltd.—your explanation of risk was spot on; I will carry it forward in my global travels. James Irwin, Global Tamiflu Product Manager, Roche—I appreciated your early insights and perspective on the "people" element of managing complex risk. The research you and your organization provided early on was helpful in formulating the content in the chapter on the demand driven supply chain. Bob Murphy, VP of Operations, Rockwell Automation, thank you for agreeing to share your 30-plus years of experience and insight; your passion for execution is what moves many of these concepts and constructs off the paper and onto the shop floor. Your view of managing supply chain risk management within a given corporate culture was enlightening.

I would also like to express my gratitude to Karen Avery, Managing Director and Head of Business Continuity, for your valuable insights, perspective, and the eleventh-hour proofing; Drew Staniar, a 30-year consumer packaged goods expert and SVP, Marissa Antonio, and Marc Cerro, all colleagues of mine on the Marsh Supply Chain Risk Management Solutions team; Matt Enuco for your early writing and ideas; and Colleen and Brian Lynch for sacrificing the time to proof the many revisions of the chapters.

This book represents the beginning of a journey, one with many twists and turns I experienced while trying to create this material. Yes, even I was substantially impacted by change as the financial crisis took hold; it forced me to dispense with the early writings, push back the delivery schedule, and start over. So let me end the acknowledgments by saying thank you to John DeRemigis and Judy Howarth at John Wiley & Sons, Inc. for being so patient and supportive. I'd also like to thank Michael Thomsett for helping me write this book. Michael, your patience and support (let's not forget your ideas) made this happen. Finally, I'd like to thank Myriam Carayannis, my executive assistant at Marsh, for running interference, working the network and calendar, and basically keeping me from jumping off the ledge. Thank you!

P.S.: I forgot one more acknowledgment—to the crew at the Chester Starbucks in New Jersey and Liz and the gang from the 44th Street Starbucks, thank you for the caffeine kick and the conversations. I knew I could count on a visit to get the words flowing again whenever my engine stalled. Please, keep your supply chain resilient; it's part of my critical infrastructure!

back the timeline, schedule and start over. So let me extend the acknowledgments by saying thank you to John DeCarlo and Judy Howarth at John Wiley & Sons, Inc. for being so patient and supportive. I'd also like to thank Michael Thomsett for helping me write this book. Michael, your patience and support (let's not forget your ideas) made this happen. Finally, I'd like to thank Miriam Campanini, my executive assistant at Marsh, for running interference, working the phones and calendar, and basically keeping me from jumping off the ledge. Thank you.

Plus, I forgot one more acknowledgment, to the crew at the Chester Starbucks in New Jersey and Liz and the gang down the Fifth Street Starbucks, thank you for the caffeine kick and the conversations. I knew I could count on a visit to get the words flowing again whenever my brain stalled. Please keep your supply of them well in stock; it's part of my critical infrastructure.

Single Point of Failure

INTRODUCTION

Getting to the Truth

It's not what you look at that matters, it's what you see.
—Henry David Thoreau

One thing that never ceases to amaze me, after 30 years of working for or with dozens of organizations, is that there are so many conflicting beliefs about the true objective of that organization. This is especially true when it comes to managing and prioritizing the risk to the lifeline of that organization—the supply chain.

Most of you know what I mean. If you ask three people in your organization to describe the objective of their business, you are going to get three different answers. The marketing manager might tell you that the objective of their business is to get the product visible to the greatest number of customers; accountants might say they are in the business of controlling budgets and preparing payroll; and the mail-room clerk might explain that he is in the business of sorting and delivering mail. All have a functional view of their organization, and their actions typically extend to only what they can see, feel, or touch.

These disparate points of view overlook a key reality: The sum of parts enable the whole, but only if the objective is the same and the incentives and penalties are aligned with the agreed-upon objective.

This is especially true when managing supply chains and supply chain risk. Everyone in the corporate hierarchy, from top to bottom, as well as anyone that comes in contact with the supply chain, has a role and specific responsibilities when managing risk to the flow of goods, services, information, and cash. However, the effectiveness and efficiency of supply chain risk management is totally dependent on understanding the organization's value proposition (through the customer's vantage point); product, information, and cash flows that support the creation of value; and the functions and resources that are used to support critical flows. Once this is understood then the strength of each individual link in the chain as well as the strength of the connection between the links must be assessed. (see Exhibit I.1).

To achieve this objective, the strength of the individual and connected links must be in proportion to the value being protected. Hence, the need to understand the hierarchy from the value to the resources used to support the creation and delivery of value. This applies to all those you've entrusted to be part of your chain; they must manage the risk to the links with the same degree of diligence. The responsibility for managing risk to the supply chain extends far beyond the accountability of anyone's function. But those responsible for designing and maintaining the strength of the links, that is, mitigating the risk, must do so by first agreeing on the value and then on the risk appetite. Once the risk expectations have been set, then the goal is to establish a common risk-conscious culture throughout the extended supply chain—one that provides clear incentives and penalties, and one that is not ruled by individual operating paradigms or static views of the risk profile. This is rarely the case.

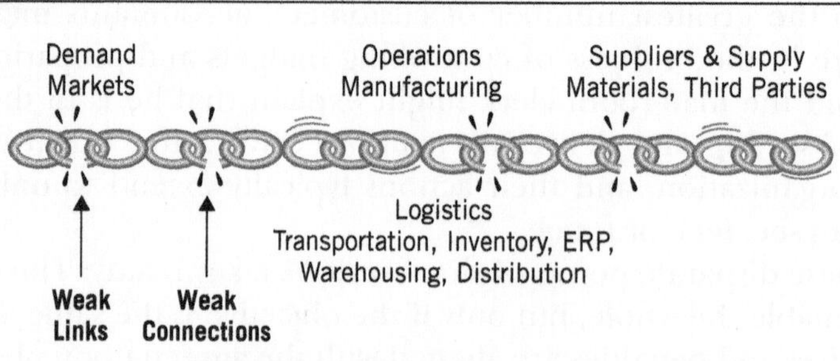

Exhibit I.1 Supply Chain Hierarchy

The fact that so many people have not given serious thought to this reality is of great concern because it allows risks to permeate the organizational culture and behavior on all levels—internally (the organization) and externally (third parties). "It's not my job" is a common answer to concerns raised about any number of problems, existing or anticipated, not due to the fault of the individual but merely inherent in functionally designed organizations, especially those with more than 1,000 employees. How many times have you heard "It's not in my job description," "It's beyond my pay grade," or "I think that's someone else's responsibility"? Unfortunately, our global economy is now dependent on far-reaching, interconnected, and interdependent supply chains—with an infinite number of *single points of failure.* The market, these "chains," and all of the resources now exist in a world where extreme volatility has become the *norm*—where we witness wild fluctuations in energy, material, and commodity prices; geopolitical instability; increasing numbers of natural and weather-related events; and a constantly changing trade credit and financing market.

This extreme volatility directly impacts the supply chain by constantly shifting the network configuration, whether through a change to terms from cash payments to suppliers prior to shipping (versus a traditional letter of credit) or a change to the distribution strategy for which warehouses service customers. The need for financial discipline and rigor with regard to supply chain risk management and investment has never been greater. The days of rocky rides on roller coasters are over. Globalization has placed organizations on a supersonic rocket and launched them into deep space where many of the risks are unknown. We are now reaching a critical juncture, one that was highlighted by the World Economic Forum's Global Risk Network in its "2008 Global Report on Risk." For the first time, supply chain risk was identified as one of the top global risks. *Single Point of Failure* analyzes how the failure of one link, the failure of the interconnected links, and an abrupt shift in demand or supply (extreme volatility) could cause systemic failure. The book also describes why this growing problem is not isolated to a single company, industry, or country. I am hoping that you will gain insight from this book. After reading it, I believe that everyone will change their opinion and point of view and say, "It *is* my job" and believe that they really need to think about their own role in managing risk and promoting a risk-conscious culture.

I've broken down the discussion of supply chain management into ten basic laws. These are universally applicable to all supply chains and to all participants, on one or more levels. These are not academic concepts, theories, or mathematical formulas; they are the operational basis and management principles that define whether your organization's supply chain risk program succeeds or fails. I begin by setting some ground rules in Chapter 1, "The Laws of the Laws." This chapter demonstrates the basic truths and practical realities about supply chains and supply chain risk management and defines common assumptions and the initial rules everyone needs to have in order to succeed. For example, you cannot expect others to manage the risk to the supply chain unless there is something in it for them—incentive or penalty. I refer to this reality as "people always operate from self-interest." So when an organization pressures its suppliers to cut costs, then they should expect the people of that organization to do so in a way that does not significantly impact their financial well-being. A cost cut to an already laser-thin supply chain will most likely result in a change to the risk profile, including the level of quality, service, and security. The balance must be struck between your risk appetite or tolerance and the opportunity offered by change. But one fact is certain: Everyone will operate from his or her own self-interests! I provide examples of this throughout the book, where best intentions turned into catastrophic single points of failure.

If the operating premise is wrong, so will be all subsequent efforts to fix these problems. While this might seem obvious as a mere statement, application proves that it is not quite so obvious. Without any doubt, you will be able to locate numerous examples of inefficient, expensive, and perhaps even dangerous systems within your organization, which have grown from a lack of definition in the first place.

As I expand into each of the ten laws, I apply "The Laws of the Laws" to each of the focused areas of discussion. I provide you with statistics, surveys, case histories, real-life examples, and conversations from organizational leaders who have experienced not only successful supply chain operation but, of equal value, have gone through the expensive disaster of systems that have failed.

The purpose to this book is to focus narrowly on supply chain risk management as an expansion of my previous book, *At Your Own Risk* (John Wiley & Sons, 2008), where I addressed issues broadly for the risk-conscious culture of organizations. I use the term "supply chain" to distinguish a specific and comprehensive value chain described in my previous book—the flow of products/services, information, and cash. One important note: I use the term "supply chain" because of its universal acceptance (and, quite frankly, because of the way search engines are designed). However, this term is somewhat limiting. The supply chain represents the ecosystem of flows, relationships, infrastructure, labor, assets, technology, and process that drives the business. For most, it is the business—excluding the market and clients. As the supply chain concept evolved over the past decade, so did the opportunity to improve productivity, eliminate overhead, and speed the flow of goods and services.

Supply chains and supply chain management have matured and now represent the "business network" or "value chain" needed to support the innovation, creation, manufacturing, assembly, distribution, service, and disposal of product. So I will use the term "supply chain" as commonly accepted terminology and as a way of keeping everyone on the same script—one of the lessons I learned is the importance of common and standardized language to facilitate timely and accurate communication. My first book included detailed discussions and many, many examples of change and its impact; understanding the functional paradigms that served as the root cause for a certain decision (the way a function such as procurement or the external suppliers view their role in supply chain risk management); and consciousness as the beginning element of an action plan. While I discussed the supply chain in this context, the previous book was designed as an overview of the problems and solutions for operational risks.

This book shows you how everyone is involved in the supply chain itself, often on several levels at one time; how the footprint (the network) of the chain is exposed to an infinite number of constantly changing threats; how weak links in that chain represent threats and vulnerabilities (to profitability, continuity, safety, and health); and how those threats and vulnerabilities can be managed, reduced, and eliminated. This book is designed to address the concerns of executives responsible for overall operations; managers at divisional or even departmental levels (supply chain, procurement, logistics, risk management); employees; subcontractors (manufacturers and producers, outsourcing centers, and vendors, for example); and department or section leaders involved in day-to-day operations or in specialized projects. In other words, because everyone participates in numerous supply chains, everyone needs to be aware of common problems and what it takes to support a pervasive, risk-conscious, and common supply chain risk philosophy.

Of course, the best-known examples of supply chain begin at the beginning—those industries that are closest to the raw materials or source of value. These industries include mining and minerals, energy, agriculture, and forestry. Without the natural resources—farms, fields, mines, rivers, animals, trees—there would be no opportunity to create value and enable the dependent industries, such as transportation, utilities, communications, life sciences, retail, chemicals, medical, and financial, to name a few. So, as we move upstream, closer to the source, the importance of managing risk becomes exponentially more important. On the other side of the equation, and equally important, is the demand, the market, and customers (and their organizations) whose chains touch the customer, patient, or the end buyer. These organizations wake up every day, relying on others' chains to support the brand. Their chains are just an extension of others' chains; however, they bear the burden of the brand risk. When those in the agricultural chain fail to manage risk and the result is melamine-contaminated infant formula, the hospitals and retailers are the ones on the front line with the media and the public.

This view of supply chains and supply chain risk management is referred to as the demand view—without the demand, there is, of course, no need for supply. Therefore, when we look at supply chains and their outputs, we must look at them in the context of the customer and markets or demand side of the equation (downstream). As customer needs constantly evolve, and in many instances change in unpredictable ways, the supply chain must be ready to respond by rapidly expanding or contracting capacity, especially in times of great volatility and tight financial markets. The decisions to do so have significant risk implications as described in this book. My point in *Single Point of Failure* is to demonstrate that those same lessons also have universal application, and their solutions have universal appeal. So a contract manufacturer in an overseas product factory actually is not dealing with unique or segregated problems; the processes at that plant exist as part of a complex supply chain, and an enlightened manager recognizes that the level of risk passes from there all the way up the chain—from the manufacturing floor in Taiwan to the customer in New York. Marketing manager, accountants, and mail room supervisor all face the same issues (as well as those who are directly engaged with the operations of supply chain such as logistics, procurement, production, and transportation personnel); they may not have the same name or involve the same control demands, but the concept is identical. All processes consist of a series of steps and functions that equate to a chain. **But it takes only a single weak link, the *single point of failure*, for the entire chain to fail; so the risk-conscious culture must be agile, resilient, sustainable, and adaptable**. This premise applies everywhere and to everyone, and the simple truth of this problem cannot be ignored.

More alarming, perhaps, is the very real possibility that a supply chain could contain many weak links and failure can (and will, based on Murphy's Law) happen at the worst time, in the worst conditions, and more than once—such as a pandemic. This book looks at how the aggregate risk is often overlooked and the planning assumptions used by many organizations are flawed (not to mention inefficient and possibly misleading). It only takes one, but you may confront several of these problem areas. Unfortunately, my experience is that risk strategies usually assume the best-, not the worst-case scenario. The truly successful supply chain is one in which the potential worst-case single points of failures are assumed and that decisions about the supply chain are structured on the anticipation of potential future failure points. When you are able to continue keeping a supply chain up and running even in an environment of rapid and complex change, then you have mastered the principles I bring up in this book.

Remember, *believing* that all is well may be a self-deception. You need to continually analyze and evaluate the risks to your supply chains and business networks, determine and learn from the root cause of problems, and decide whether you have the proper philosophy, culture, and systems in place to identify, measure, mitigate, and finance risk. Good business strategy dictates that you must:

- Remain agile to avoid risk
- Be resilient to respond, adapt, and absorb risk
- Develop methodologies that are sustainable to scale and maintain risk solutions

I address risk from several points of view: demand, supply, production, and logistics, to name a few—and always from the angle that the customer uses, which I call the "demand lens." Anyone who wants to stay in business needs to adopt this organizational world view, and the most successful enterprises historically are those that have recognized this reality early enough to ensure that risk did not overcome them on the road to success.

CHAPTER 1

The Laws of the Laws

Laws are like cobwebs, which may catch small flies, but let wasps and hornets break through.

—Jonathan Swift,
"A Critical Essay upon the Faculties of the Mind," 1709

The time is far in the future. A commercial space towing ship, the Nostromo, *makes an unscheduled stop at a remote planet, where one of the crew members is attacked by a parasite. A horrible scene in which the parasite bursts through his chest sets up the rest of the story in which each crew member meets a horrible death until only one remains. As it turns out, the encounter was intentional. The creature, a perfect killing machine, was known to authorities months before and they wanted to use the ship's crew to bring one of them back so it could be weaponized. The crew, of course, had no idea.*

—Synopsis of the movie *Alien*

The lesson we can learn from *Alien* is profound and has many aspects. One lesson, perhaps, is that if you find yourself in an unknown situation, assume the worst case and don't get too close to the unknown danger. Another is that if you don't know your real mission, disaster is likely to follow. *Alien* is all about risk, the unknown single point of failure, and the consequences of operating in an undefined environment. The movie should be required watching in every organization and in every business school.

Have you ever considered the possibility that the premise on which you built your organization might not be valid anymore? It is a profound suggestion not only because the answer might startle you, but because the question does not occur to many of us. Poor Ripley, the sole survivor in *Alien*, thought she was towing ore and had no idea that she was really set up as bait for the perfect killing machine alien creature. And like the movie itself, the lessons have a lot to say about the nature of risk in today's organization.

Risk is a parasite that resides in every process.

We have lost the association of risk as a threat or even as a negative. Risk itself has become meaningless. Terms like "risk management" and "risk expert" have normalized the concept of risk as a parasite and as a very real threat, not only to profitability and brand but often to an organization's ability to survive. Much new risk has been introduced—threats once not relevant now impact global supply chains with greater frequency and consequences. Thanks to globalization, the risk parasite can quickly weave its way through the logistics, sourcing, and production processes that support these long-tailed supply chains. The parasite can lie dormant in these processes, undetected by the organization. Then an event unleashes the parasite, creating a single point of failure, a broken link in the chain. The catastrophic outcomes can affect any stakeholder in the supply chain regardless of geographical or organizational boundaries. The trigger, large or small, can result in the same outcome. No longer can we distinguish between low-probability/high-impact events and everyday incidents. Whether an explosion at a natural gas plant or the availability of a single part, today's interdependent and lean supply chains as well as a fiercely competitive global marketplace leave little space, or time, for error.

Consider, for example, that an explosion in western Australia in the summer of 2008 to an Apache Energy gas line significantly threatened global commodities supplies because Rio Tinto and Alcoa, two major miners in the region, lost power to their mines. Or, in another case, the shortage of components for windmills (which have 8,000 components) and solar panels has been hampering the growth of alternative energy. Even the failure of a single ingredient, such as osteoblast milk protein (melamine), in the food and dairy supply chain, can be far-reaching. In a recent case, melamine was added to the product and allegedly killed eleven; sickened another 296,000; bankrupted Sanlu Group, a major Chinese dairy company; and caused significant negative global media attention to Fonterra Co-operative Group Ltd, a joint partner of Sanlu Group and a major contributor to the global dairy supply chain. The parasite was released; as a result, globally interconnected supply chains were idled. The release of the parasite is not limited to natural hazards or events that affect only physical assets. In June 2009, the Venezuelan government ordered Coca-Cola Company to withdraw its Coke Zero beverage from the country, citing unspecified health risks.[1] No organization is exempt from the parasite and most have experienced its wrath—ExxonMobil Corporation, Fonterra Co-operative Group Limited, Rio Tinto Group, Gazprom, Cadbury Schweppes plc, Apache Energy, Wal-Mart, General Motors Corporation, Baxter, Intel, Petróleos Mexicanos (PEMEX), Microsoft, Toyota, and Mattel—to name only a few.

I think of the risk parasite as a metaphor to remind me how to address existing vulnerabilities and anticipate future challenges throughout the supply chain before they become catastrophic. The risk parasite knows no boundaries. It resides in every resource and attaches to every process flow. However, often an organization divides its supply chain risk defenses against the threat of a parasite by organizational functions. A security issue is treated by the Security Management group, an environmental issue by the Environmental, Health and Safety group, and an IT risk issue by the IT Risk group. Each function has its own assessment techniques and standards for measurement, as well as its own turf. However, the risk parasite does not distinguish between functions and locations. When the parasite is attached to the process, it can take on any form and easily travel up- and downstream in the supply chain. Unlike each of these groups, this invasive parasite has freedom of movement.

But risk management is not separate and distinct; the effective approach is to think of the supply chain risk management process as part of the supply chain network. It is an overlay to the major processes of the network: sourcing (material requisition, third-party management), logistics (transportation, distribution, warehousing, inventory management, IT/ERP), and production (manufacturing,

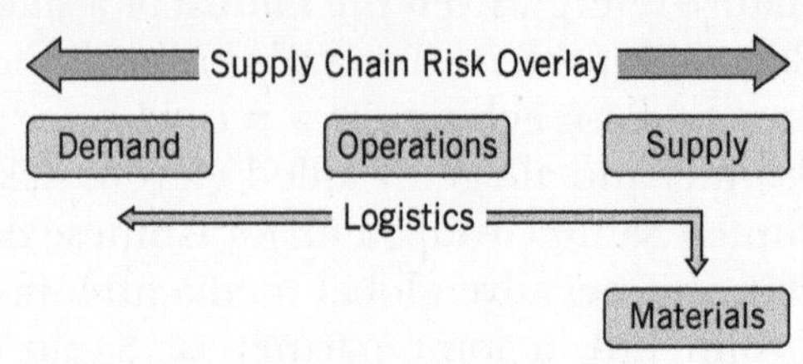

Exhibit 1.1 Supply Chain Risk Overlay

assembly, subassembly). Refer to Exhibit I.1 in the Introduction. Simply stated, an effective supply chain risk strategy is one that is holistic and mirrors the supply chain network design and cash, information, and product flows, not just the functional design. The risk strategy is discussed further in later sections.

The strategic supply chain risk overlay shown in Exhibit 1.1 identifies and minimizes the impact of potential single points of failure, improves quality, protects critical data, and makes the supply chain more efficient. The risk parasite is a negative but realistic metaphor; the solution is to manage the whole body of the supply chain by identifying and removing, containing/isolating, or reducing the effects of the risk parasite.

Laws of the Laws

This book is organized into a series of laws that apply to everyone along the extended supply chain. However, before proceeding, I want to provide you with a brief set of questions about the nature of your business network, the value your organization creates, the supply chain relationship, and a definition of risk.

Questions to ask yourself before you proceed:

- How does my business create value and what role does the supply chain play in that process? Can I visualize the risk, worst-case scenarios, and impact at various points throughout the supply chain, as well as identify the point of maximum impact (i.e., maximum exposure)?
- How do my customers, investors, business partners, and other key stakeholders view and define supply chain risk, if at all? What are their expectations? How do they measure success and failure? Do they even consider these critical issues?

- What impact does my ability to manage supply chain risk have on protecting brand, ensuring margins, moving cash, and generating revenue to assure long-term growth?
- Who in my organization is responsible for the management of supply chain risk? Who at my third-party providers is responsible?

A good starting point for any challenge is to understand the context in which the solutions must be implemented. What are the practical realities of the culture, behaviors, and intangibles that cause the solution to succeed or fail? Most people know these unwritten rules, whether they are budgeting an expansion program, introducing a new product, eliminating manufacturing defects, or heading up a quality control team. This premise leads to four specific precepts that I call the Laws of the Laws. These specific points are articulated below and reflect how most of them successfully attack the parasite based on the unique culture of your organization. The ten laws of the supply chain risk process you find in the following chapters all have to address these four basic precepts on some level, and often on several levels.

Risk Management Defined

Before getting to these precepts, I have to start with the basic definition of *risk management* itself. There are many definitions in use and the meaning varies depending on your role. During my travels through Singapore, I ran into Rajeev Kadam, Vice President of Olam International Ltd., a global leader in the supply chain management of agricultural products and food ingredients. Rajeev articulated a simple but concise definition of risk.[2]

Risk has two essential components:

1. Uncertainty
2. Exposure to uncertainty

We face risk when both uncertainty and exposure are present.

Consider an example: A man jumps from a sixty-story skyscraper. According to our definition above, there would be no uncertainty if the man were to jump off the building without a parachute. His chance of survival would be zero. However, if the man were to jump with a parachute, then there would be some degree of uncertainty about whether the man would live or die. The jumper faces risk because he is personally exposed to the uncertainty of the parachute failing to open. We could begin to calculate this uncertainty.

Suppose you are watching this event as a bystander from the pavement below this tall building. Are you facing any risk even if there is uncertainty in this event? The answer is no, because you are not personally exposed—unless the jumper is your relative, or has borrowed money from you, or you have a coffee shop on the pavement where he may crash land.

We could continue with this example but I am sure you understand the point. Uncertainty can be difficult to calculate, especially when the exposure is not understood or realized. This, by far, is the most fundamental challenge of supply chain risk management—organizations not knowing or understanding how exposed their supply chains are to uncertainty, or to how much.

You need to define exposure to uncertainty in terms of impact: the cost of the loss, and what that loss means in terms of stakeholders, your brand and reputation, and even to the basic ability to provide your goods and services to your customers. With this definition in hand, I can now introduce the practical realities, or the Laws of the Laws, to guide you with the execution of your own supply chain risk management. Consider these four precepts.

Law of the Laws #1: Everyone, without exception, is part of a supply chain.

Law of the Laws #2: No risk strategy is a substitute for bad decisions and a lack of risk consciousness.

Law of the Laws #3: It's all in the details.

Law of the Laws #4: People always operate from self-interest.

The following will expand on these four precepts.

Law of the Laws #1: Everyone, without Exception, Is Part of a Supply Chain

It was a revolutionary innovation in assembly line automobile production when a major manufacturer decided to give any individual on the line the power to stop the process if he or she saw a flaw.

Before that, without the vested interest, the theme "It's not my job" allowed visible flaws to proceed through the line even though dozens of assembly line workers saw the flaws. Because "It's not my job" was the cultural rule, several points prevented diligence on the assembly line:

- Pointing out quality and safety defects was seen as criticizing a fellow line worker.
- Delaying the process reduced shift output and was seen as a negative.
- Pay was based on units produced and not on quality.

All of these flaws added to supply chain problems rather than solving them. In the 1980s, Toyota Motors first employed *jidoka*, the concept of empowering workers to stop an assembly line to prevent defects. The goal was to make it possible for everyone, at all critical points, to understand their role in the greater goal of supply chain value creation and, when appropriate, participate. This idea flew in the face of assembly line standards set by the Ford Motor Company, where once the line began to move, *nothing* was allowed to stop it:

> At every stage of the assembly line, Toyota employs devices allowing workers to stop production to correct defects. Such devices may be as simple as a rope strung above the assembly line, or a button that can be pushed. In other cases, it is sophisticated monitoring software such as Activplant's Performance Management System, which can alert operators to problems with equipment or robots in real time.[3]

The concept of allowing individual assembly line workers to bring the whole line to a grinding halt because they see a flaw is culturally revolutionary. It is also diligent, a method for gaining participation among key stakeholders—the employees—and preventing and correcting flaws many steps before end-users discover problems after purchase. By changing the broad assumption to "It *is* my job" and doing away with the self-interest of the individual or even of the shift, assembly line workers were given a sense of ownership in the end-result quality of their product. They recognized their individual contribution and were empowered to the end goal of producing the highest value to the customer. Toyota acknowledged early that workers were not just part of the supply chain, they *were* the supply chain. If they failed, the supply chain failed.

This is a relevant example of how supply chain risk thinking usually works versus how it should work. The Toyota example demonstrates why there can be no shortcuts and everyone is part of the whole. Before the institution of *jidoka*, an assembly line worker might fear punishment for making waves, not to mention the antagonism of fellow workers, notably those on whom the whistle had been blown. The observation that "There can be no shortcuts" can be expressed in another way: "Without diligence, no supply chain can be expected to work."

A point of view worth adopting is that performance based on diligence is the only acceptable operating method. Diligence is a means for assigning responsibility for all of the pieces that add up to the whole. An auto assembly worker is trained to recognize that any flaws make the singular product defective. Stopping the line to correct existing flaws and prevent new ones is essential. You can apply the same thinking to anyone's home life. The necessities—food, shelter, energy, safety, transportation—do not simply appear on their own. The household pays for all of these necessities, but the family also relies on food growers, stores, and transportation facilities; on home builders and designers; on financial institutions for credit; on an endless range of experts required to maintain the property; on utility companies and energy generation as well as raw materials; on infrastructure at local and national levels that creates roads for vehicles; as well as on auto manufacturers and mass transit facilities. This primary residential supply chain is complex and far-reaching, involving all aspects of commerce and government not only in one country but internationally. It requires incentives and the consciousness and empowerment of all those involved—that is, to hit the stop button when someone witnesses something wrong. The personal supply chain is an excellent model for beginning to develop an appreciation of the basic law. Imagine trying to find shortcuts for provision of food or shelter.

It would have a snowball effect and cause great suffering and loss throughout the supply chain. Supply chain risk management begins with awareness, a consciousness that everyone is part of an endless stream of supply chains, which are linked together by relationships and configured according to needs. Ask yourself the following:

- What are the products and services I rely on—for health, energy, food, water, my livelihood?
- Where am I exposed to uncertainty? Who have I entrusted to create and deliver high-quality, safe, and risk-free products?
- Do I understand the basics of these supply chains—who and what's involved? Is there transparency into critical interdependencies and do I have confidence that those touching the chain are managing the risks?
- What adjacent and interdependent supply chains are required to satisfy my needs (transportation, communications, energy, shipping, trucking, and so on)?
- How will delays or disruption in these supply chains affect me and my business if the product is unavailable for a day? A month? Permanently?
- Do I understand the financial, brand, regulatory, and strategic impacts of a risk being realized?

Whatever products your organization sells or what services it offers, your role is an essential part of the supply chain, and potentially of other supply chains within the organization. Be ready—you will need to be able to continually measure value and impacts and prioritize risk within your supply chain.

We are living in the age of interdependency; small ripples upstream cause tidal waves downstream.

Numerous examples in today's world involve seemingly small glitches causing large consequences. In one such example, jellyfish caused a reactor to shut down. PG&E Corporation, California's largest utility company, silenced its Diablo Canyon 2 reactor and was forced to operate another reactor at 50 percent capacity when a rapid influx of jellyfish reduced water flow to pumps. This is not the only case. Globally, jellyfish have caused hundreds of millions of dollars in damage to fisheries, seabed mining operations, ships, and other industrial operations.[4]

It's not always a material issue. Look at what happened in 2008 and 2009 with the market-wide credit meltdown. In the past, you might have trusted your "establishment institution" to protect your assets, if only on the premise that they were experts in managing other people's money. After the meltdown, in which many of those banks and brokerage firms went broke or were bought out at bargain-basement prices, it became obvious that you could not merely assign risk to the experts. It was *your* risk as well, and it had been your risk all along. They were merely custodians of your assets. You were always part of the supply chain involving capital, credit, investment, money management, market risk, and even basic evaluation of companies. The fact that the brokerage firm did not do its job (assuming that included protecting clients against market risk) does not exclude anyone from the supply chain, or from its very real risks. You owned the risk, you were exposed to uncertainty, and you felt the pain.

We all know that now, of course. But in the future, how can you better protect yourself and reduce these market risks? Some fundamental changes may include self-directing most of your money and using outside experts for advisory help only (risk ownership); distributing capital among several management resources, such as banks, brokerages, or mutual funds (risk diversification); and improving knowledge about the range of risk activities of a firm. For example, is your brokerage firm holding billions in mortgage obligations? If so, what are those risks (risk education, measurement, and transparency)? Ultimately, you are responsible for risk itself (risk accountability). The same is true for the management of supply chain risk—seeing, understanding, measuring, and mitigating or financing. One fact is certain—everyone, without exception, is part of a supply chain.

Law of the Laws #2: No Risk Strategy Is a Substitute for Bad Decisions and a Lack of Risk Consciousness

The main theme for the second Law of the Laws is that almost all adverse impacts can be traced back to a bad decision somewhere in the chain. Bad decisions are made without accurate or relevant information (uninformed decisions), significantly influenced by emotion and not made fast enough. One case of an organization not moving fast enough was that of Intel's Pentium FDIV bug. The Pentium FDIV bug caused errors in certain floating point division operations. According to Intel, a few missing entries in the lookup table used by the divide operation algorithm caused the bug. The flaw was discovered by a professor at Lynchburg College, who subsequently reported the issue to Intel. Intel would later admit that it had been aware of the flaw during testing but did not take action. This was bad decision making by Intel. It had knowledge of the bug but chose not to manage the risk fast enough. While many independent estimates found that the bug would have negligible effect on most users, public outcry ensued. Intel offered to replace flawed Pentium processors on the basis of requests in response to mounting public pressure that brought a huge potential cost to the company.

This makes the point that in protecting yourself and your organization against the risks inherent in the supply chain, you need to develop a strategy to support effective and efficient risk decision making (intelligence gathering and tracking, monitoring, filtering, surveillance, and analysis) to keep things flowing and to engage all others in your supply chain; for knowing how to prevent potential losses; and, of course, to respond if and when a loss or delay does occur. You need to understand interdependencies, pain points, impact of failure at each link, and alternatives to ensure free flow of information, products or services, and cash. No one can plan for everything; understanding how big an impact the issue might present and gauging an appropriate response can help you navigate around *most* losses.

Only by recognizing that everyone is part of the supply chain and that risk decisions will be part of standard operations can you expect yourself to effectively take the needed steps. Being resilient, agile, and ensuring against insurable losses is only a small aspect of the larger, more enlightened, and more progressive approach. Other behavioral attributes of good risk decision making include education, awareness, and training; critiquing and learning from failures and near misses; and understanding motives, incentives, and penalties.

A well-recognized supply chain risk management case that shows the benefits (and consequences) of good risk decision making involves a major supplier to Nokia that produces semiconductors for Nokia phones. The company suffered a severe fire at its plant in Albuquerque, New Mexico, on March 17, 2000. Smoke spread throughout the facility and contaminated wafers in almost every stage of production, destroying millions of chips in just a few minutes. Consequently, production of cell phone chips intended for Nokia and Ericsson was halted. Nokia quickly realized that the disrupted supplies would prevent production of some four million handsets and could impact 5 percent of its annual production. The team quickly ascertained the availability of alternate sources for the parts. Nokia responded by working with existing suppliers to ensure that Nokia operations would continue with minimal interruption.

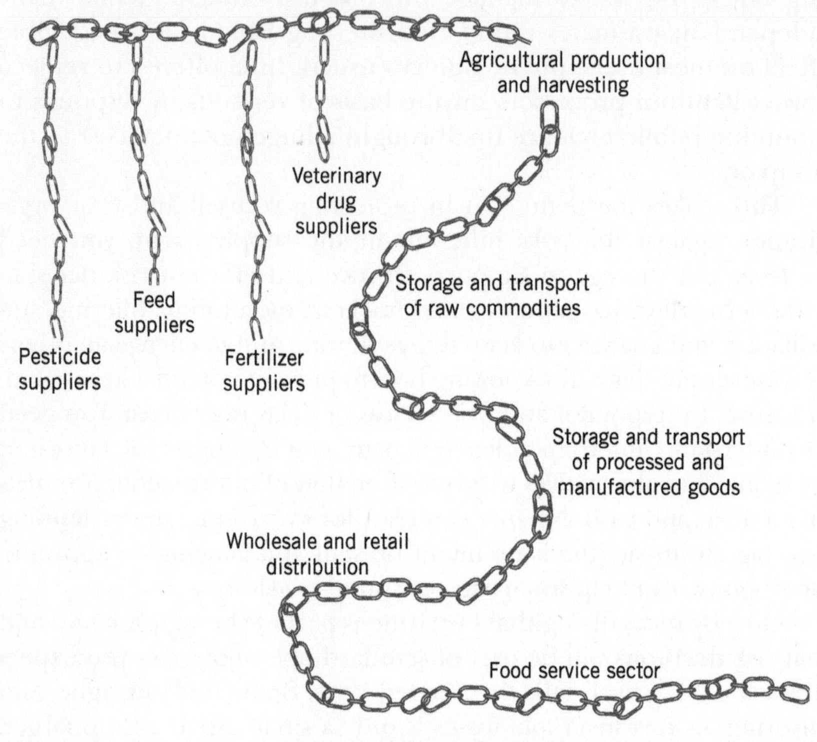

Exhibit 1.2 Food Supply Chain

When it was clear that the much-needed chips were significantly delayed, lower-level employees at Ericsson did not communicate the news to their bosses. The head of the consumer electronics division did not learn of the problem until several weeks after the fire. By the time Ericsson realized the magnitude of the problem, it was too late and it lost market share to Nokia. If Nokia were to follow the Band-Aid approach, it would have stopped after the disrupted supplier had recovered. However, it took further action following this event. Nokia developed a series of visibility systems to track major shipments of all of its major suppliers. It also established a risk management assessment for each of its major suppliers and created contingency plans for disaster planning at each location. Then, suppliers were trained in all of these planning elements. Finally, Nokia reevaluated its entire supply chain network to avoid single sourcing any major component, and it integrated these plans into its global sourcing strategies.[5]

Law of the Laws #3: It's All in the Details

What risks to your supply chain are you worried about the most? In my travels, I often hear a response from executives such as "I'm doing business in China and I am worried about risk to my supply chain." But to truly understand the risk we will have to revert to our definition of risk—uncertainty and exposure to uncertainty. In the case of the food supply chain, what precisely is the fear of the executive? Is it the uncertainty, the threat of a pandemic or snowstorm? Or is it the exposure to uncertainty, the vulnerabilities that apply to an organization's specific supply chain, such as poor worker hygiene practices by upstream factory workers during processing and materials handling. Or maybe it's poor temperature and expiration date control in wholesale and retail distribution or the food service sector. Exhibit 1.2 illustrates a few of the many risks that exist throughout the extended food supply chain.

The point is that the details are needed to understand and manage risk in the flow of products, services, information, and cash. Broad generalizations can be costly by over-allocating resources to the wrong priorities. The specifics must be articulated—the financial, brand, strategic, and compliance impacts, and acquisition, deployment, and maintenance investment to manage the exposure. Exhibits 1.3 and 1.4 represent the cost of the each threat to the organization and the potential investment areas.

Scenario	Impact
Threat Scenario 1: Unclean processing and materials handling	$$$$
Threat Scenario 2: Contamination of goods	$$$
Threat Scenario 3: Poor temperature and expiration control	$$

Exhibit 1.3 Threat Scenarios

Law of the Laws #4: People Always Operate from Self-Interest

We are all aware of what we need and want as a greater priority than the more abstract "greater good." The functional organizational construct exacerbates the issue. Everyone is categorized and incentivized into their function—armed with a checklist and motivated by an

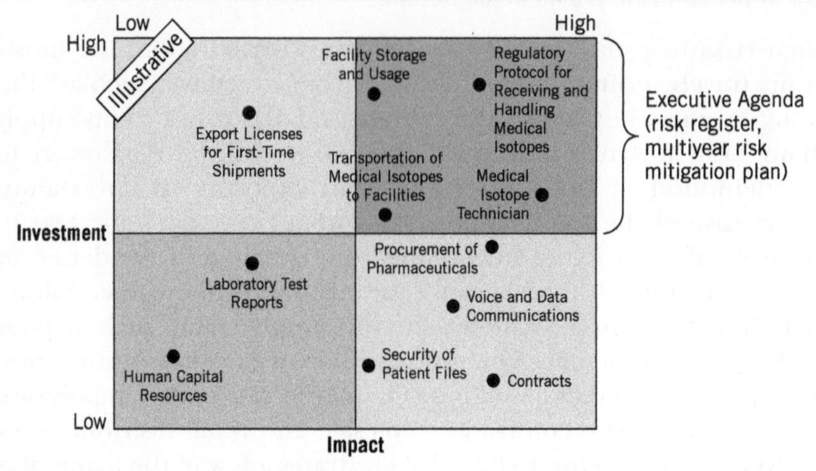

Exhibit 1.4 Specific Resource Risk Prioritization

evaluation system that teaches them to think about the parts, especially the parts in their own organization, rather than the whole.

Managing Risk of the Parts Is Not Equal to Managing Risk of the Whole

In behavioral science, one theory that describes how people think is called the Tragedy of the Commons. This theory, first published in 1968, makes a point by illustrating how people act in a given situation. In this game theory, many individual herders share a single piece of land where all are entitled to graze their stock. A paradox develops because each individual perceives maximum benefit by grazing as many cows as possible, but over-grazing will destroy the pasture for everyone. Any individual herder who adopts the long-term view and reduces grazing so that all can benefit ends up losing not only immediate profits but the entire pasture along with everyone else.[6]

The concept that people work from self-interest is not new. While the Tragedy of the Commons expressed this idea with a story everyone could understand, the problem has been recognized since ancient times. As one Greek writer stated it long ago:

> . . . people tend to devote a very small fraction of time to the consideration of any public object, most of it to the prosecution of their own objects. Meanwhile each fancies that no harm

> will come to his neglect, that it is the business of somebody else to look after this or that for him; and so, by the same notion being entertained by all separately, the common cause imperceptibly decays.[7]

The problem is universal, and the closest anyone can come to overcoming it involves cultural and systemic supply chain changes. The previously cited example of *jidoka* in the Toyota assembly line is one method for achieving this, but it involves more than simply giving individual participants the right to stop the assembly line or giving people a sense of ownership in the process.

The education of participants or stakeholders in the supply chain requires providing a *clear line of sight* from beginning to end and creation of a real sense of the big picture, allowing people to overcome their narrow view of their own jobs and enabling them to contribute to the organization's value proposition. They must understand the concepts of value, flows (product, service, cash, information) impact, and exposure (hence the earlier questions about the business). Problems in supply chain processes occur in big companies with complex international interdependencies, but they also happen to every small to medium-size business, individual, and family.

This reality can bring home the crucial importance of group thinking rather than self-interest. In the Toyota example, it was necessary to overcome the concept that an employee would get into trouble by pointing out defects created by someone else, or would bring anger on themselves by reducing output for the shift. Even union members have often tended to think in terms of "us versus them" when it comes to management, making it even more difficult to create a real team approach within the supply chain. If management is prevented from taking steps to reduce defects and, in many cases, from even communicating directly with workers without a union representative present, the challenge can make success close to impossible.

In another real-life example, the procurement manager of a technology manufacturing company was told to cut material costs by 5 percent for the coming year, after cutting material costs by nearly 26 percent in the two prior years. His compensation was based on this 5 percent target and, although not explicitly stated, the security of his job was dependent on meeting this objective. He responded by notifying suppliers that they needed to figure out how to cut 8 to 10 percent out of the cost structure. As has been said, it rolls downhill. He informed the suppliers that they needed to comply or "lose the relationship." Of course, the suppliers in turn communicated the message to their material suppliers, contractors, and job shops. As is typically the case, as the message moved farther upstream—the greater the impact and the smaller the shop. Many of the upstream suppliers were able to cut costs by 1 or 2 percent without cutting corners, but those last few percentage points meant they had to do something drastic.

I liken it to the difference in the repercussions between a magnitude 5.0 and 6.0 earthquake. When moving up the scale, the increase is not linear but rather exponential, or in the case of the Richter scale and earthquakes, it's a tenfold increase when moving from 5.0 to 6.0. This kind of consequence is an accurate business-model emergency, or what I call ER, which means "exponential repercussion." I checked back with the procurement manager several months later and asked him if there were any negative consequences of the squeeze. He told me that most of the suppliers conformed to his requests and the net reduction turned out to be about 5.5 percent. However, he went on to say that the company was now beginning to notice a significant decrease in quality measured by the increased number of customer complaints. The increase in the number of returns was believed to be linked to use of subpar materials. Their investigation revealed that materials were being sourced from another geography. I thought to myself, *What other risks lie beneath and how did these vendors cut so much cost out of an already thin margin chain?*

Operating in Self-Interest Yields Short-Term Gains and Long-Term Risk

In every supply chain, the supply chain and operations managers face four constant pressures. These pressures establish their perspective and motivations toward supply chain risk management actions. The four pressures are:

1. Continuously improve the velocity of cash (time between receipt of money for goods and payment of money to suppliers).

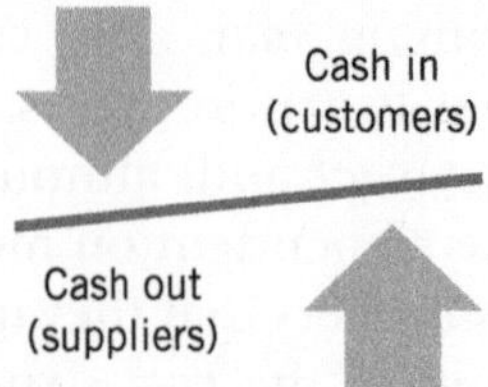

2. Continuously improve operating margins—cut costs and expenses.

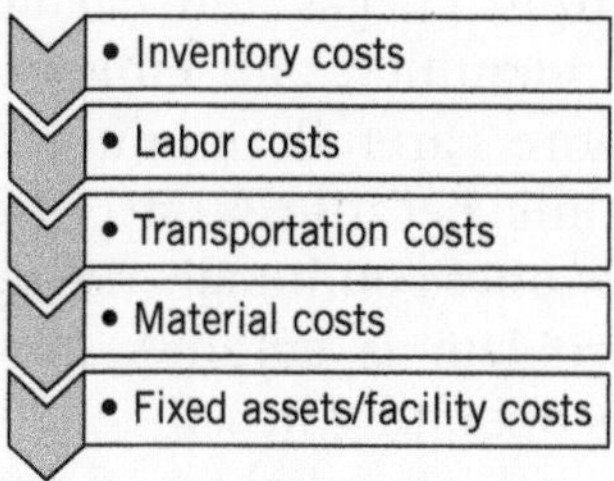

3. Always comply with service-level agreements, plus other legal and regulatory obligations.

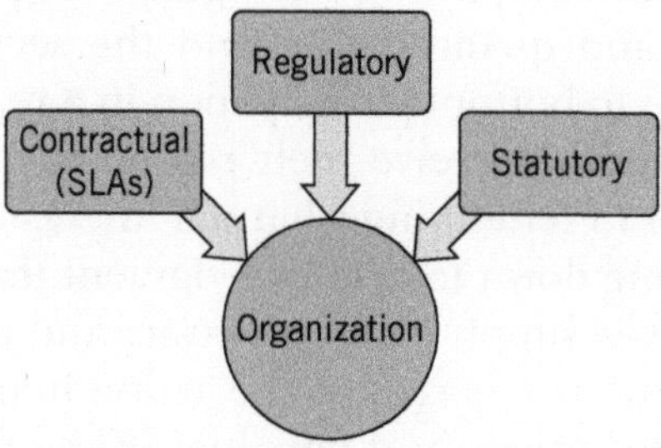

4. Always have product for the customer (i.e., never have a stock out/no inventory).

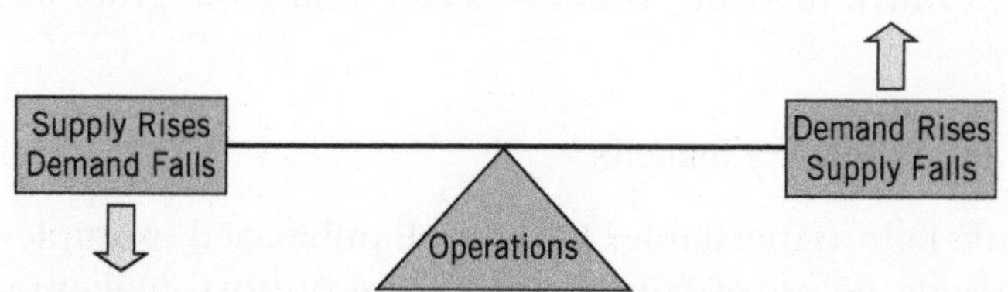

- Customer needs are constantly changing in unpredictable ways. The supply chain must be ready to respond by either expanding or contracting.
- Corporations must consider how customer demand would change as a result of a pandemic and what the new operating realities are like.

Recognizing the flaws in working from self-interest, management needs to focus on how relationships work throughout the supply chain. The base motivations point out root causes of supply chain breakdown and increase risk. People do not want to expand their levels of responsibility even if extra authority comes with it. So management faces a real challenge in changing this cultural stumbling block.

To rectify this self-interest problem and improve supply chain processes, two levels of change are required. The first involves detailed internal controls, checks and balances, and oversight, in which weak links are identified and either eliminated, made less prone to error, or more carefully monitored. This most obvious form of change is dynamic because as one series of defects and weak links is eliminated, new ones continually rise up. The second change to the self-interest problem is cultural. Moving employees from thinking as individuals operating in self-defense to thinking as parts of a larger team effort with an enlightened sense of real job security is a massive task. Initiatives like Six Sigma, a quality control system designed to create effective team approaches to problems, address this issue. Companies employing Six Sigma recognize the dual role, the first process- and quality-driven and the second one cultural. The attitude of top-to-bottom participation in a real sense is one way to change how people perceive their role in the organization, and even come around to redefining what self-interest really means. The revelation may come down to acknowledgment that real self-interest grows from improved supply chain processes and management.

However, self-interest is reality; the action item is to understand the motivations, incentives, and penalties of the individual or function responsible for performing the supply chain risk actions. The need for collaborative tools, rewards, and communications vehicles and an iterative learning process is essential to migrate away from self-interest.

Indirect and Secondary Impacts

Is systemic failure inevitable? Given well-publicized examples of very serious single points of failure (lead paint on toys, melamine in pet food, peanut and heparin infections), you have to ask whether these close calls, these supply chain failures, are just the tip of the iceberg.

There are many troubling signs growing out of internationalized business, outsourcing, and growing dependence on remote supply chains that involve people and organizations outside of centralized control. These are potentially severe, but systematic failure is not inevitable. The solution is to develop an appreciation of the specific laws given in the following chapters, and then apply them to reducing single points of failure in every phase of your supply chain—whether that means a mom-and-pop store or a multinational corporation with thousands of suppliers and vendors.

The basic Laws of the Laws apply to all of the ten specific laws in the following chapters, without exception. All of these laws have to be observed and acknowledged as a matter of survival. But in addition to the immediate and direct impacts you need to plan for, there are numerous indirect impacts as well, which you need to include in a comprehensive supply chain risk management program. These secondary impacts are no less important or critical than the primary ones, but these are not directly related to the supply chain. Outside influences such as these have as much potential impact as the weak link in the immediate supply chain.

These indirect and secondary threats include:

- Legal threats (lawsuits, noncompliance with multiple nations' laws)
- Regulatory repercussions from noncompliance (multinational due diligence, supply chain restrictions)
- IT failures, especially enterprise resource planning, customer and supplier relationship management systems (losses, damage, sabotage, recovery)
- Human resource–based threats (strikes, disputes, inefficiency, apathy)
- Security (internal and external threats, including employee sabotage, industrial espionage and sabotage, piracy)
- Natural disasters (losses from process and transportation problems)
- Health-related (pandemic, chemical, and biological attacks)
- Product flaws (lead and poison in products, dangerous construction)
- Financial and economic (credit issues, embezzlement, recession)
- Environmental (major contamination, pollution, regulatory)
- Energy (supply shortages, expense, alternate fuel costs)

What Can You Conclude?

From this discussion about laws applied to the ten basic laws, you may conclude that:

- Knowing where to start is the key; it invariably demands comprehension of the scope of aggregate risk in the supply chain. It also demands adoption of the enlightened view that we are all part of the supply chain, without exception. You will need to understand uncertainty through the supply chain and your organization's specific (measurable) exposure to uncertainty.

- Your role in the big picture is going to be crucial, especially if you are among the minority of enlightened individuals who know how expansive risk is, and how dangerous single point of failure is to the entire big picture (the head of manufacturing at a consumer products company may be intimately aware of the skills, factory, and machinery needed to support his operation, but only when he looks beyond the four walls of the plant does he see all those he is dependent on—transportation carriers, public infrastructure, numerous tiers of suppliers, raw material providers, port operators—to name a few).
- A risk strategy is not a solution if it is offset by poor decisions, most often made by uninformed management. The appropriate strategy demands creative and out-of-the-box thinking, a creative approach to what otherwise might seem a hopeless dilemma. It requires a thorough understanding of behavioral elements, the absence of which can cause root failure. Too often, management settles for a decision (at times, *any* decision) as a way to address the problem, but this ends up not accomplishing any solution at all.
- "The devil is in the details," as the old saying goes. A risk very seldom materializes as a singular failure in a big way, but more often consists of one or more very small single points of failure, a combination of poor judgment, lack of awareness, and wrong assumptions. Like the television show *Seconds from Disaster*, which analyzes the series of connected events leading up to a catastrophic result, the supply chain is a collective of very connected details. In an anthill, a single ant making a wrong move can destroy the whole colony; and the same is true of the supply chain at every link along the way.
- Everyone operates from their own self-interests. This is a limiting factor in addressing single points of failure, but accepting this as a reality helps you articulate an effective risk strategy. There is no shortcut to justifying risk investment; it requires a thorough and well-articulated understanding of risk, the impacts, and the purpose of mitigation or finance investment required.

One final thought: It's important to recognize that all supply chains are unique and different. Because no two are alike, you cannot adopt a program or internal control system from another situation and apply it to your own. As I stated before, "If you've seen one supply chain, you've seen one supply chain." Those are words worth remembering.

Notes

1. Fabian Cambero and Antonio de la Jara, "Venezuela Bans Coke Zero, Cites 'Danger to Health,' " *Yahoo! News*, June 10, 2009.
2. The original source of "risk" from www.riskglossary.com/, which is from the family of Web sites by Glyn Holton (main Web site: www.contingencyanalysis.com/).
3. Mel Duvall, "What's Driving Toyota?" *Baseline Magazine*, September 5, 2006, at www.baselinemag.com/c/b/Projects-Processes.
4. Aaron Clark, "PG&E Shuts Down Diablo Reactor as Jellyfish Threaten Pumps," Bloomberg.com, October 22, 2008.
5. Supply Chain Resource Cooperative, "A Managerial Framework for Reducing the Impact of Disruptions to the Supply Chain," http://scm.ncsu.edu/public/risk/risk3.html.
6. Garrett Hardin, "The Tragedy of the Commons," *Science*, 162(3859), December 13, 1968, 1243–1248.
7. Thucydides (ca. 460 B.C.–ca. 395 B.C.), History of the Peloponnesian War, Book I, Sec. 141.

One final thought: It is important to recognize that all supply chains are unique and different. Because no two are alike, you cannot adopt a program or that control system from another situation and apply it to your own and stand back. "If you've seen one supply chain, you've seen one supply chain." Those are words worth remembering.

Notes

1. Esteban Cambero and Antonio de la Jara, "Venezuela Buys Coke, Gets Taste [illegible]" [illegible] June [illegible].
2. The [illegible] [illegible]
3. [illegible] "What's [illegible]," [illegible] Magazine, September [illegible], 2006.
4. [illegible]
5. Susan Clark, "[illegible] Shut Down [illegible] Reactor [illegible]," [illegible], October 22, [illegible].
6. [illegible] "A Conceptual Framework for Defining the Impact of Disruptions in the Supply Chain," [illegible]
7. Garrett Hardin, "The Tragedy of the Commons," Science 162 (3859), December 13, 1968, 1243–1248.
8. [illegible] History of the Peloponnesian War, [illegible]

CHAPTER 2

Law #1: If You Don't Manage and Lead Change, You Have to Surrender to It

The inherent preferences of organizations are clarity, certainty, and perfection. The inherent nature of human relationships involves ambiguity, uncertainty, and imperfection. How one honors, balances, and integrates the needs of both is the real trick of management.

—Richard Tanner Pascale and Anthony G. Athos,
The Art of Japanese Management, 1981

A change revolution is under way today, and it is global. In choosing a type of revolution, organizations have a choice: They can take charge and lead change as revolutionaries, or they can climb up the steps and passively place their heads on the guillotine. It is a choice of survival or surrender.

It was July 2008 when the news broke on Australian TV Channel 7. One of the 1,500 contractors that make up Nike's vast global supply network, Hytek, located in Malaysia, was accused of having engaged in unfair labor practices. The report claimed that poverty-stricken people from countries such as Bangladesh, Burma, and Vietnam were being offered employment at Hytek.

These unsuspecting people had to pay an up-front fee to secure an opportunity to work equivalent to one year's worth of wages. Once they arrived, their passport was confiscated and they were forced to sign a three-year contract to pay off the cost of the return passport, in a language they couldn't understand. The news story went on to show that these "trapped" workers were subjected to horrific living conditions. The report claimed that Nike profited from this terrible act even though it was not a Nike-owned facility.[1]

This was not the first time Nike had been accused of labor violations. Once again, Nike's brand and the way it operates its supply chains were under attack. Any negative media coverage, whether accurate or not, had the potential to negatively impact demand, thus disrupting the flow of products and cash. Nike, like most other customer-facing organizations, relies on sophisticated forecasting and a global network of contract manufacturers to produce products—700 finished-goods manufacturers and another 800 or so work-in-progress manufacturers. The challenge to Nike, and other large customer-facing organizations, is that by entrusting others in the supply chain to produce or assemble its products, it is also assuming that they will adequately manage the risk to its brand. In other words, the largest organization, that is, the one farthest downstream or closest to the client, typically has the most to lose. The problem of managing the exposure does not stop there.

Nike is considered to be a global leader in corporate social responsibility practices. But one of its practices, performance of social responsibility audits of its contract manufacturers, became almost irrelevant when a link in the chain had been tarnished (the violation had not been detected) and fully exposed in the media. Management had to act quickly to avert a potential crisis. They had to address the question of whether or not this was a systemic issue and quickly determine whether other contract manufacturers were engaged in practices that violated ethical standards, human rights, or labor practices. Nike's management needed to immediately address the following questions:

- Who should have detected this issue?
- What factors allowed this to go undetected and how did it happen?
- When did the violation occur?

- Why did existing social responsibility practices not anticipate and or detect this violation?
- Where else was there potential for a similar violation? Is this an isolated incident, or are other contract manufacturers also in violation of ethical labor practices?
- How widespread was the exposure?
- What triggers or "early warning" signs indicators could have detected this violation?

Once an event of this nature becomes exposed in the media, the flow of accurate, timely, relevant, and quality information becomes essential to manage the risk and contain the crisis. Key stakeholders, such as investors, board members, nongovernment organizations (special interest groups), and customers, will demand immediate answers and resolution of the issue. As a result, the supply chain can be significantly disrupted as the organization investigates, corrects, and remediates the risk issue. In the worst case, demand is severely reduced because customers lose confidence in the product or brand. The supply chain is then subject to over-capacity, excess inventory, and increased cost. A labor-related event, like the one discussed here, is one of many risk triggers that threaten the operations and viability of global supply chains every day. Other triggers can be related to a tightening of available trade credit, security breaches and violations, environmental noncompliance or unfavorable practices, health incidents, weather-related events, geopolitical changes, terrorism, informational and technological failures, social changes, regulatory change, and quality issues. Exhibit 2.1 represents the universe of other potential risk triggers.

A valuable lesson learned in the Nike case is that when one link in the chain begins to tarnish or, worse yet, breaks, the organization must be prepared to quickly determine if other similar links are tarnished or broken. The organization must be prepared to respond to these questions:

- Is the failure isolated or systemic?
- Is the act intentional or accidental?
- Who is at fault?
- Who else is impacted by the event (360-degree view)?

Economic & Financial

- Economic collapse
- Currency devaluation
- Labor disputes, strikes, or unrest
- Labor shortage
- Major decline in stock price, earnings, or significant volatility
- Major market fluctuations
- Decline in major earnings
- Cash flow/liquidity crunch
- Hostile takeover
- Bankruptcy
- Other financial: derivatives, investment, credit, interest rates, transfer velocity, collateral

Political & Social

- Government policy and/or attitude change
- Confinement or imprisonment of employees/family
- Lawlessness and hostile demonstration
- Regulatory change
- Civil unrest
- Government expropriation or renegotiation of royalty streams
- Government change in tax regime
- Unfavorable dividend and share sale proceed transfer
- Military coup
- Unilateral expropriation
- Nationalization

Brand/Reputation

- Product and service
  - Liability, recall, and failure
  - Obsolescence
  - Counterfeiting
- Organization
  - Government or regulatory investigation
  - Special interest group (NGO) protest or inquiry
  - Community action as a result of organization's product, people, and/or technology
  - Human rights abuses
  - Rumors, gossip, and hoaxes
  - Libel and slander
  - Poor customer satisfaction
  - Marketing blunder

Environmental & Man-Made

- Chemical, biological, radioactive, and/or nuclear
- Fire and/or explosions
- Water/soil contamination
- Public utility failures
- Asbestos and mold
- Emissions levels and waste clean-up
- Noise/dust pollution
- CO_2 and/or other hazardous gas and liquid emissions
- Liquefaction
- Building, mine, facility collapse, or condemned
- Water leaks and/or floods
- Insect infestations

Compliance & Governance

- Noncompliance (labor, environment, security, safety, quality, etc.)
  - Legal
  - Regulatory
  - Statutory
  - Contractual
- Class action or mass tort lawsuits
- Corporate governance issues and whistleblowers
- Executive misdeeds, bribes, offenses, security, and/or code of conduct violations
- Oversight, over-extended authority, accidents, errors, and commissions

Psychopathic, Criminal & Terrorist

- Product tampering
- Terrorist acts
- Arson and explosion
- Industrial/economic espionage
- Sabotage
- Kidnap
- Extortion
- Fraud
- Theft
- Terrorist using product or materials as weapon
- Workplace violence
- Suspicious mail/package
- Counterfeiting

Health

- Epidemic or pandemic (e.g., TB, SARS, Avian Flu)
- Long-term health issues

Labor

- Human resource failures
- Defections and resignations
- Inability to attract/retain talent
- Labor and skills shortage
- Sexual harassment, workplace discrimination, wrongful dismissal

Strategy

- Unanticipated competition
- Product misplacement
- Disintermediation
- Poor marketing strategy
- Poor sales strategy
- Failure to innovate

Operational

- Project management failure
- Out of stock
- Sourcing failure
- Pricing misalignment
- Change control failure
- Transportation/logistics accident
- Walkouts, slowdowns, and strikes
- Disruptions, delays (piracy, seizure)
- Leakage
- Restricted access
- Infrastructure deterioration or obsolescence

Weather

- Hurricane, typhoon, tropical cyclone
- Rising water, wind, projectiles
- Earthquake
- Tornado and waterspouts
- Rising water (flood, tidal wave, tsunamin—onhurricane caused)
- Wildfire
- Mudslides
- Extreme heat
- Extreme cold
- Climate change

Technology

- Technology hardware failure
- Technology software failure (rogue code, viruses, poor quality)
- Capacity issues
- Performance issues
- Other malicious acts
- Technology obsolescence and/or lack of relevance

Informational

- Loss of proprietary and/or confidential data (e.g., privacy, trade secrets)
- Information integrity and quality issues
- Loss of key customer, supplier, marketing, production, and/or financial data
- Privacy, integrity, or security issues

Risk Triggers

Exhibit 2.1 Sample Universe of Events That Trigger the Risk Parasite

While the data collection and investigation are underway, lean operating environments—a supply chain practice where there is little inventory and sole sourced providers, resulting in little tolerance for slippage—could be impacted as key resources are diverted to address and correct other occurrences. The investigation and subsequent inspection process are expensive, disruptive, and distracting. These additional remediation activities are needed at a time when the organization must also mobilize resources to defend the brand—whether they are guilty or not guilty of the violation. However, the investigation of all facilities becomes nonnegotiable to avoid a repeat of the same problem or even systemic failure.

Another valuable lesson learned is that the use of point-in-time or static risk practices, such as periodic third-party audits, is not sufficient by itself to manage risk in a continuously changing business and supply chain environment. A combination of a broader set of *historical, predictive, trigger-based, intelligent,* and *dynamic* risk practices needs to be adopted to close the gap. One method is to focus on any major demand change itself as a trigger (sometimes referred to as signal detection). Abnormal or large-scale changes to the business or supply chain model (demand, operations, or supply shifts) would trigger the need for a greater risk consciousness; that is, need for additional risk identification, evaluation, measurement, and mitigation. For example, a significant shift to demand was expected when it was learned that Nike had won the contract to supply the 2008 Olympics in China. The huge spike in demand was sure to place a burden on the manually intensive production process, thus generating the risk conscious question "Where would the additional labor come from and how will this impact our risk practices?" Of course, I have oversimplified the Nike example (and hindsight is 20/20) but the lesson learned is that the obvious risk question must be posed, flow freely up and down the chain, and always be resolved.

The organization could have leveraged its vast past experience to better understand what risk scenarios were relevant and what lessons had been learned to avoid a repeat of this trend. It's likely that this is not the first time an event like this occurred, nor the risk surfaced. Change is the trigger. Or knowing that additional labor would be needed, management could have analyzed the possible sources of new labor (the ones that were different from the previously audited practices), measured the impact and investment alternative, and then provided additional mitigation practices.

I use the Nike story to demonstrate how just *one* type of change—one of many possible triggers—could unexpectedly occur, how an organization's business and supply chain become immediately at risk, and how supply chain risk practices need to evolve. One small change ripple can create a risk tsunami (exponential repercussions), altering a previously well-managed risk profile. The good news is that Nike is a learning organization, one that continues to lead in its commitment to continuously improve its risk practices and close these types of gaps, as evident in its commitment to corporate responsibility.

Nike has developed a comprehensive, multi-tiered action plan aimed at ensuring corporate responsibility. At the board level, Nike's Vice President of Corporate Responsibility reports directly to the CEO; the Corporate Responsibility Committee of the Board was established in 2001 to review significant policies and activities and make recommendations to the Board of Directors. At the executive level, responsibilities include oversight and review of many levels of accountability; and at the operations level, nearly 120 Nike employees work on corporate responsibility as their primary function or as a major portion of their overall workload. (Note: At the time this book went to print, I was advised that Nike was once again evolving its corporate responsibility and risk practices.)[2]

One final lesson learned is to be prepared and expect problems to occur rather than waiting and then responding. As the title of this chapter states, if you don't manage and lead change, you have to surrender to it. A well-defined, managed, and practiced crisis planning and communication process is needed. This issue is examined further in Chapter 9, which discusses supply chain risk management.

Was the risk-specific issue unique to Nike? Not by any stretch. Over the past decade, business decisions were being made that required organizations to dramatically alter their supply chain strategies in order to achieve greater efficiency, execute with greater velocity, and be more responsive to customer needs. These organizations were driving deeply into the fog at inconceivable speeds. As a result, their strategic supply chain network configuration morphed into one of a modularized design, with distributed processes shifting to others around the globe (outsourcing of manufacturing, assembly, sourcing, and logistics). At the operational level, the resources that are used to support the supply chain—

warehouses, processes, inventory, labor, suppliers, and so on—were being reconfigured and restructured regularly. The critical question is whether organizations have sacrificed prudent supply chain risk management practices in lieu of rapidly executing on the opportunity. And was each instance of risk being realized a symptom or rather an indication of a much greater looming threat?

The problem everyone faces is that even with rapid response to known threats, change occurs not only in technology or with operations but also in the nature of risk itself. The symptoms—representing an evolving risk parasite matching change in the organization—mean that something troubling is occurring: As the organization improves its systems and internal controls, the risk parasite adapts and changes into a different form.

This phenomenon was called the *red queen hypothesis* by famed biologist William Hamilton. He named this tendency after a character in Lewis Carroll's *Through the Looking Glass.* The Red Queen advises Alice that "It takes all the running you can do to keep in the same place." Referring to biology, Hamilton saw something that applies equally to today's organization.

> Hamilton used the idea as an illustration of the evolutionary arms race between an organism and its parasites. You evolve to get rid of your parasites; then they too evolve to use you as a host again.[3]

This provides insight into how your organization evolves and why it can never escape its risk parasite entirely. An organization is very much like a living thing. The path chosen might not be as hazard-free as expected. Assumptions about how others were managing their organization's supply chain risk—quality, continuity, security, privacy, labor practices, IT, and environmental—might be horribly inaccurate or, if accurate today, they might be inaccurate in the extreme within a few months. For example, should a U.S., UK, European, or Australian organization expect a start-up contractor or manufacturer in Asia, one without any risk training or experience, to understand their risk expectations and philosophy?

As supply chains deverticalized in the 1980s and 1990s and ownership for the management of risk grayed, an endless stream of vulnerabilities was created, and began to be realized, across the extended supply chain. This ever-expanding risk parasite is at least as adaptable as the organization, so change mandates that your organization has to do more than simply react to current past environments; it has to anticipate future developments in the nature and attribute of the new risk parasite. An obvious example of this in a broad sense has been witnessed in the development of automated systems for virtually all phases of operations. Speed-of-light processing, storage, and communication is a miracle of efficiency and it reduces costs and promotes convenience at all levels. It also introduces a pervasive and dangerous new army of risk parasites, in the form of internal and external vulnerabilities and the need for a much higher level of diligence. Many of these I wrote about in my previous book, *At Your Own Risk* (John Wiley & Sons, 2008). Everyone is aware of the rapid expansion of IT and associated threats; as time moves forward, this is not going to go away, but it is likely to worsen.

Through all this change, another bad assumption was being permutated—that is, third-party suppliers suddenly were not just responsible for managing the risk; they were now being assumed to be the de facto owner of the risk. Preposterous, but they were guilty by association. These third parties were expected to perform against an undefined expectation at virtually no additional cost to the product they were producing. The result: raw material and production quality issues that led to massive contamination of medicine, food, and beverages; labor violations in factories around the world; the inadequate handling of intellectual property that led to leakage of trade secrets; and the absence of proper security practices that resulted in massive counterfeiting and product shrinkage by theft.

These are all symptoms of a much greater problem: Supply chain risk management practices have not kept pace with the rate of business and operational change. Traditional risk management thinking, what I refer to as historical, static, or point-in-time supply chain risk management practices, are simply not enough to manage this rapidly intensifying problem. The need for more predictive, trigger-based (greater risk consciousness and activities occur when change takes place), dynamic (continuous risk practices that are integrated into the operational flow—threats are immediately detected, analyzed, and activities launched), and risk-conscious practices are now needed to respond to this escalating risk.

As social, economic, and geopolitical factors continue to drive opportunities and spawn the continuous reconfiguration of global supply chains, risks become more pervasive, the parasite more widespread, and potential impacts exponentially greater. Can one of these single points of failure in an organization's global supply chains cause systemic disruption, resulting in irreversible brand (reputational) damage as well as material financial impact? Who will be impacted? Are other organizations and societies at risk as well, since these global supply chains have become so intertwined and interdependent? Is another financial meltdown imminent?

You cannot know the answers to these troubling questions unless you first study the drivers behind the evolving risk parasite. Any innovation made in any level of systems and processes in your organization has an unavoidable set of *new* risks that go along with it. You need to understand what drives these underlying risks if you have any hope of anticipating and preventing them.

The Risk Wake-Up Call—Planned Change, Unplanned Consequences

It was 7 A.M. and I had just arrived at the corporate offices of a major consumer products company. The CEO invited me in to discuss supply chain risk management. This might sound a little stuffy to some, but little did I know that my morning was going to provide me with profound insights about how his decisions were about to create new risk parasites throughout his supply chains.

I had been told that the CEO was well versed on the topic; he had to be, since the viability of his organization depended on the effective management of its supply chain. We began the discussion with the usual friendly small talk, but it didn't take long for the CEO to change the topic. "Gary, as you know, we are in the consumer products business and I think we do a great job at managing risk to our supply chain." I had no reason to believe that this was not the case, since his organization had a stellar history of avoiding big events. "Every day our people are dealing with dozens of weather related events, transportation disruptions, and human mistakes—any of which could cripple our supply lines," he said. "But that's not my primary worry since we know how to fight fires."

I listened attentively, waiting for him to get to his concern about risk. "Today, more than ever, our business, the operating and financial model, are significantly different; the pressures are diverse and the volatility is extreme." He continued: "But that's not my primary concern either; we have great people, processes, and systems for addressing these issues." He leaned forward and in a quiet whisper, similar to that of two friends sharing a closely guarded secret, he said, "Gary, I'm worried about the unknown risks brought about by tomorrow's change—some of which I am about to sanction. The markets, clients, and the geopolitical landscape are changing at unprecedented speeds. We must now respond to change in days, not months—and that time frame continues to shrink. A misstep either in our ability to exploit the opportunity or alter our supply chains to react to the change could cripple us." He then went on to say, "Our supply chains are the throttle; they determine whether or not we can capitalize on the change or how effectively we react to a crisis. Our destiny is in the hands of those that manage our supply chain. But this change creates a new set of parameters. I'm worried about the risk to our supply chains that I don't understand, have not yet experienced, or cannot see. I worry about the risk managed by those I don't know."

He continued: "Gary, I pride myself on being a good leader—one with great instinct." He paused. "My instinct is telling me that I need to be concerned, very concerned." *How refreshing,* I thought. A leader who gets it; he was looking out the windshield to view the road ahead rather than looking at it through the rear-view mirror while driving at 70 mph. More important, he was astutely aware that he was about to be the genesis for a whole new breed of risk parasites. All of this was great conversation, but I needed to get a better perspective: What were the planned changes, how big a change, which stakeholders would be involved or impacted, what was the timing of the change and how fast would it happen? Where would the change most likely take place? These were just a few of the many questions that needed to be addressed as part of the risk understanding and identification process. I began asking the questions: "What are you promising the external stakeholders—customers, analysts, and investors? What are your organizational goals for the coming months or year?"

He responded, "We plan to provide *sustainable, consistent,* and *profitable* growth over the coming year."

The business objectives were clear—sustainable, consistent, and profitable. But how would this affect the supply chain risk profile? I began to visualize what I refer to as the risk overlay.

- *Sustainable.* This sounds as if the firm will be seeking greater opportunities to gain competitive advantage through riskier innovation. It probably also translates into a strong organizational policy to "do no harm to others" (a reference to corporate social responsibility as well as to the environment and the community). Those managing risk will need to pay careful attention to the innovation angle; will they be seeking opportunities in riskier environments, such as sourcing ingredients from unstable locations; or will they exploit new and emerging technologies and processes?

- *Consistent.* Okay, this attribute is straightforward. Managers will have to ensure that the organization can maintain a stable and resilient operational and financial model. This requires a disciplined, measurable, predictable, agile, and responsive operational model. Existing risk management programs should get them part of the way there—business continuity, disaster recovery, crisis management, emergency planning, and so on.
- *Profitable.* Warning! Warning! Warning! Okay, let's not jump to any unsubstantiated conclusions (I already did) but I think the CEO was referring to cutting costs—dramatically cutting costs. And the throttle to do so: the supply chain. It's where the saving traditionally originates. It's where margins are improved by reducing inventory, facility, and labor costs. Oh no, did he mean that they will be creating greater single points of failure, reducing safety stock, consolidating facilities, losing corporate experience and memory? How many and what type of risk parasites will his actions be creating? It was time to probe further. I needed to know more about the change—how much and how fast.

I mentioned previously that the supply chain is the primary cost throttle. The other throttle is time, or rather the speed in which change will take place; it's a great barometer for determining how much effort must occur in what time frame. It's critical when trying to understand the likelihood of success in adequately managing risk (how fast can risk practices be implemented—can they keep pace with change?). Unfortunately, this change was going to be fast and furious. The CEO had set a goal: to achieve approximately $300 million in savings over the next 12 to 18 months. The warning lights began to blink; the CEO's worries were justified! I began to understand more about the root cause of increased risk. The supply chain and the organization were about to be exposed to a new universe of parasites, creating potential vulnerability across multiple processes and resources. The CEO's goal of providing consistent and sustainable growth could be at risk.

Slowly, the pieces were coming together. However, more detail was required; after all, as I explained in Chapter 1, "The Laws of the Laws," it's all in the details! I needed to understand specifically how the organization's strategic supply chain network design would be changed and how the operational activities would be impacted. To understand, evaluate, measure, and treat risk the details are essential. With that in mind, I asked the CEO to describe the specific initiatives and constructs that would be used to achieve the massive savings. He described the expected changes as follows:

- Outsource the majority of manufacturing to overseas, low-cost contractors.
- Consolidate twenty-plus distribution centers down to three.
- Significantly reduce safety stock from 6 months to 1 month.
- Reduce complexity and carrying costs by lowering the number of products (stock keeping units, or SKUs) by 25 percent.
- Achieve greater purchasing leverage by reducing the number of suppliers, centralizing purchasing, and pressure existing suppliers to lower prices by 15 percent over the next two years.
- Fully deploy an integrated enterprise resource planning (ERP) system within the next 12 to 24 months.

Realizing that the organization was going to be running full throttle (change to be implemented quickly), I began to think about historical examples of how others were exposed or failed when making similar change. I again applied the risk overlay: Identify the business initiative, analyze potential risk issues, and apply industry's negative experience with these types of initiatives. Not conducting this step is an example of how the supply chain risk topic gets glossed over when large-scale business change is made. Exhibit 2.2 illustrates the overlay.

The CEO's goal was to capitalize on an opportunity to dramatically reduce operational costs (thus satisfying the analysts and investors) and to improve the organization's capital structure. Beyond the initial concern, the risk conversation was omitted or, at a minimum, being addressed only at a functional level. This is the typical thinking—we stretch capacities and bend standard processes within the supply chains and expect they won't break. If they do, we will just pick up the pieces and move on; we are resilient.

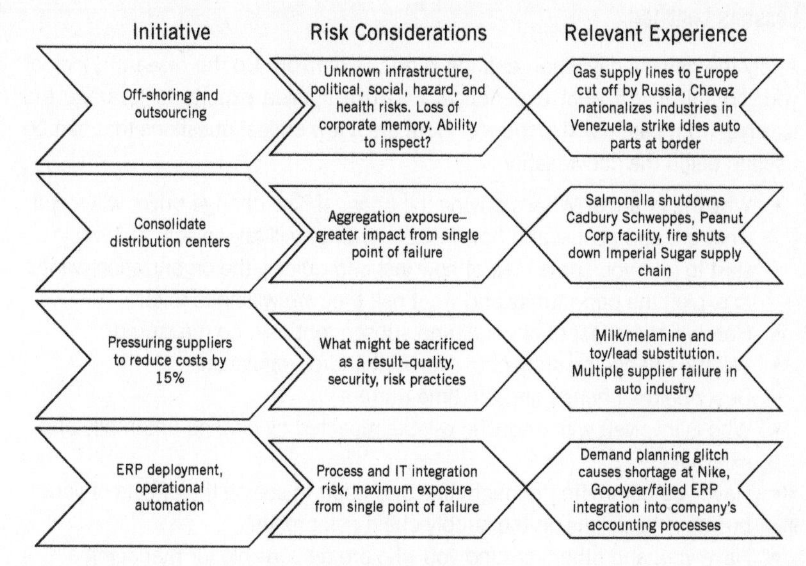

Exhibit 2.2 Risk Overlay

We have insurance and contingency plans so we must be okay, right? Unfortunately, this is simply not the case. Assumptions about excess capacity used to absorb the reduction elsewhere, the facility to rebuild quickly, and the ability to control or limit brand damage are just a few of the many supply chain risk myths.

We Can't Change the Past, but . . . Can We Change the Future?

Is systemic failure of global supply chains inevitable? Are global economies and their organizations once again threatened by a "meltdown" similar to that of the 2008 financial markets? Have years of deploying defensive supply chain strategies and relying on sole sourced providers left organizations vulnerable? These strategies had the singular goal to improve margins, productivity, and customer service in lieu of exercising sound risk management practices, so are we doomed to repeat this mistake? Is our economic and social norm threatened because of the fragility of critical food, health, mining, and energy supply chains? And has globalization created an opportunity for failure by interlinking an

Lessons Learned

Apply the risk overlay when change is on the horizon. Do the research, look at your organization's prior experience, and use outside experts to leverage the learning from past risk experience. Here are a few critical questions that can be used to begin the conversation.

- Why the change? What's driving the change? The change driver will reveal what the end goal is and how fast the change will take place. This will start to give you some idea of how fast and quickly the organization wants to exploit the opportunity and what risk they are willing to take.
- How will the effect of change, and subsequent risk, be measured?
- Will the change be subject to oversight and/or regulation?
- Describe the change and the time frame.
- Who is involved with and who will be impacted by change (internally and externally)?
- Have you committed enough time and effort to seeing the effects of your business decisions on the supply chain risk profile?
- Have you, and others around you who are responsible for managing a piece of the supply chain (remember the Laws of the Laws—we all are part of the supply chain), zoomed out from the day-to-day picture to better understand the aggregate and interdependency risk brought about by change?
- While the decisions have been made and the organization must live with them for the time being, do the stakeholders understand the potential consequences of the design and operating decisions? If you don't know, how can you find out?
- What risk practices—strategy, philosophy, operating principles, communications protocols, technology—have been deployed by your organization to address the continuous change principle?
- Is your supply chain risk philosophy and strategy dynamic, effective, and modern, or is it static, ineffective, and outdated?

infinite number of complex supply chains, across unstable geopolitical infrastructures—in an interdependent and inconspicuous manner?

To understand whether or not systemic risk to global supply chains is possible, we need to understand how performance-driven change to business and supporting supply chains has impacted the risk profile. Just how corroded are these links and the connections between links? Risk management has all too often taken a back seat to the need for greater financial performance in an environment assuming risk as an unchanging and manageable constant, rather than as a rapidly changing and unmanageable variable. It has also been a decade of assumptions such as "I know my risk"—without quantifying the impacts and investment decisions and the view that "it hasn't happened before" without acknowledging that the supply chain network and resource configuration have significantly changed. So I will begin to assess the viability of the question "Is systemic supply chain failure possible?" by revealing an alarming parallel between the root causes of the 2008 systemic financial meltdown and the inherent risk that has been built into today's global supply chain networks. The risk mismanagement similarities are staggering.

- *Lack of visibility and transparency.* One of the key issues leading to the 2008 financial meltdown was the inability of those in the financial markets to identify and understand the risk of complex financial instruments such as collateralized debt obligations (CDOs). Offshoring, outsourcing, and lowest-cost supplier strategies have created a similar problem for those managing the risk of global supply chains. These initiatives modularized portions of the supply chain and redistributed the operations to a broad group of third parties. Visibility into the extended network became obscured by the complexity of many layers, translation issues, cultural differences, diverse time zones, and the absence of accurate data flow. In a 2009 IBM survey of 400 supply chain executives in 25 countries, more than 70 percent of the respondents ranked supply chain visibility as the challenge that impacts their supply chain to a very significant extent.[4] If your organization does not *know* about risks, visible or not, then surprise is inevitable. By strengthening transparency at all levels, you build an effective, proactive supply chain risk management program. Ask your supply chain organization, "Do you have a detailed end-to-end process and resource flow map?"
- *Dispersed and unclear ownership of risk accountability.* A transition from a supply chain that has been under the organization's control to one of being in someone else's control reflects the trend toward giving away responsibility, moving away from years of disciplined risk practices, and relying on inexperienced or untrained others to manage risk creates brittle

links in the entire supply chain. By doing so, you lose control and quality diminishes. Who was responsible for originating million-dollar mortgages for individuals earning $30K annually? Was it the banks or independent, freewheeling mortgage brokers? Or both? The risk qualifications, experience, and corporate memory of the decision makers should always be challenged when turning over the operation of the supply chain to third parties.

- *Mob mentality.* Everyone's doing it, so should we. In the race to deploy supply chain initiatives that improve profitability, few were willing to opt out or say no, even though they were aware that they were exposing their organization to increased risk (the prevailing mentality that we are making so much money that we can manage our way out of any problem). The use of contract manufacturers in third-world countries where poor infrastructure, political instability, and little regulation were all accepted practice actually *invites* problems; a widespread assumption, one that is false, is that second- and third-tier manufacturers somehow magically adhere to mandated risk management practices. The simple truth: They do not. Unfortunately, the mob that charges forward without considering supply chain risks is the same whether organizations are experiencing unpredictable volatility in their supply chain costs or are constantly under attack from the media and nongovernmental organizations (NGOs).
- *Accelerated continuous change.* The repeal of the Glass Steagall Act,[5] new collateralized debt vehicles, and sovereign wealth funds for investors were just a few of the changes that enabled systemic failure in the financial systems. Supply, and now supplier variability, demand uncertainty, consolidation of facilities, layoffs, failed suppliers, new markets, and alternative materials are just a few of the many strategic changes that happen with tactical frequency. There are too many moving parts, each one presenting new and unknown risk. Everything is, indeed, speeding up and this begs the question: Are we really managing risk on a cost-effective basis? Should we shrink the geographic supply chain? Restrict the use of second-tier manufacturers? Enforce rigid control standards?
- *Aggregation exposure.* As the saying goes, don't put all of your eggs in one basket. The financial meltdown also revealed that

putting your eggs in the owners of a few of the biggest baskets is also a recipe for systemic failure. This happened with the underwriting of financial instruments and now it is happening in the supply chain world. Systemic risk is also enabled when multiple industries rely on the same scarce resources; concentrate labor pools (China); physical assets (five major ports); technology platforms (SAP); and relationship resources (sole source supplier). All of these examples create a *single point of failure.* The rise of the cluster concept in supply chain risk management fueled the exposure. Clusters are created when the majority of one product is produced by many in a concentrated geographic region. Clustering is not a new concept; however, concentrating critical supply-side resources in emerging economies creates much greater exposure. These economies typically face runaway inflation, poor infrastructure, and the lack of a regulatory structure. An example of clustering can be found in Shengzhou, China, where fewer than 1,000 factories produce 40 percent of the world's neckties. Furthermore, in China's Guangdong province, 50 percent of the world's microwaves are manufactured.[6] Thus, does it make sense to undiversify your supply chain by clumping your indispensable dependencies with everyone else?

- *Failure of external independent evaluator.* Rating agencies did not adequately rate the financial risk, usually because they could not discern the actual risk through complex, interdependent handoffs and relationships. Therefore, the aggregate or potential systemic risk could not be measured. The overall lack of acceptable industry standards added to the complexity and as a result the role of oversight and audit was undermined. Domestic and international regulatory agencies and external auditors charged with checking internal control systems all were ineffective. In the reality of modern risk, all outside evaluation has been a dismal failure. For example, consider the question: How do you measure the risks associated with collateralized debt obligations, credit ratings, undisclosed or underreported liabilities, and off-balance-sheet obligations? Auditors are not exempt; many lacked a thorough understanding of the potential for systemic failure—the big picture. A thorough multiparty assessment of risk across the supply chain is today's exception.

- *Selling off the risk to unsuspecting third parties* and expecting them to manage and comply (the norm during the bull days of financial markets as well as the supply chain designed). Organizations outsourced everything, not only processes, transportation, and labor, but risk as well. Never assume that third parties are going to take on risk management tasks. If risk management is not done in your direct field of vision, it probably will not be done at all.
- *Creation of new, little understood complex transfer policies and procedures.* The use of inadequate insurance as the whole enchilada of risk management is not only an ineffective solution; it betrays a poor understanding of what kinds of risk transfer is required. Underwriting the risk of creative financial products created huge profits; however, when the risk became clear, the house of cards tumbled. Simply put, the risk was not understood nor priced. Until 2008, the insurance industry was only willing to underwrite a portion of supply chain risk—specifically, property-related events that were triggered by a limited set of perils (fire, rising water, wind). Insurance carriers such as AIG and Zurich added capacity to the market to cover nonproperty-related events, such as supplier breach of legislation, quality of supply, labor strikes, and pandemics. Price risk failure, the inability for experts in the financial community to price the risk of complex instruments (failed debt obligations), fueled the systemic failure. Risk that cannot be measured properly or underwritten, and eventually financed by others, is then retained by the organization, whether it is qualified to do so or not. Risk underwriters typically price only the physical aspects of supply chain risk, such as cargo or a facility. In many situations, they simply do not insure the risk at all. This "price risk failure" is a huge threat if not addressed in a cost-effective, risk-reducing manner.

Can You See the Icebergs Ahead?

Let's begin by looking at how we can address the first symptom—*lack of visibility and transparency*. I will use a story that many of us are familiar with. Was it only the iceberg that caused the *Titanic* to sink? Actually, a variety of small, invisible, and unseen circumstances all added to the disaster. One of these was an important change. The northern split of the Gulf Stream usually extends from Newfoundland eastward. In 1912, an unusual event occurred, with the route dipping much farther south. This allowed colder waters from the west coast of Greenland to extend farther south; and in those waters was the infamous iceberg.

The lesson to be learned is not the southern extension of the iceberg, however, even though this represented an unusual change. The real lesson is that no fewer than five warning messages were sent to the *Titanic* on April 14, but none concerned the captain enough to make him slow down their speed or—as some other ships had done—to stop completely and wait for morning.

Change—that insidious force—causes enough mischief by itself. But being warned of change and taking no action is where the real problems arise. Applied to the supply chain where you need only a single point of failure, you soon realize that the organization's waters, like the Atlantic shipping lanes, are full of unseen icebergs.

What we can learn, a way forward, is that the iceberg is only the most obvious portion of a much larger problem. Uncertainty and exposure to uncertainty lead to a series of failures that, by themselves, would not spell disaster, but when added together become quite large and disastrous outcomes. Remember, your organization, like the *Titanic*, is not unsinkable. No one is too big to fail.

The process of identifying and heading off disaster begins by recognizing the simple reality that products or services of value are at risk. To do that, we need to look at both the threats and vulnerabilities. How are these distinct? What is within the scope of our control and what can we not predict and control? The threat is a potential risk that might occur; it can be mitigated or even prevented as long as you know where your vulnerabilities lie. The problem is twofold in most organizations: The threat is not known (and/or there are just too many potential threats), but equally as serious, the vulnerability itself is not recognized (and/or there are just too many vulnerabilities to manage). You could be at risk for a catastrophic loss that is neither being prevented nor mitigated. Not being aware is perhaps the biggest problem because it is quite difficult to convince management to fund risk programs for something no one else even sees or can measure.

In our analysis, threats represent uncertainty and vulnerabilities represent exposure to uncertainty. We will need to see, hear, and touch to better understand risk and its potential impact. Let's start with the assumption that you can manage risk only when you can see it and understand it. Complexity exists when there are many choices, such as a large number of possible combinations of suppliers, locations, logistics, and options. When supply chains span geographical boundaries, new variables are introduced, such as national customs authorities, port operators, freight forwarders, shippers, or public infrastructure providers. In other words, the complexity of the supply chain creates variability and that translates into much greater risk potential.

This can make the whole issue overwhelming. Where do you start? More to the point, where do you start given the reality that the environment is changing continuously and rapidly? How much complexity is there in your organization's supply chain and what can you do about it? The biggest single point of failure is not considering risk at the beginning of the change process. The first step is to get a visual of the entire supply chain, from source to destination, for a particular product(s) and/or service(s). If you can't see it, you can't manage it, and if you don't look at it in its entirety then you are falling into the trap of arcane practices. Just because the organization has outsourced the management of its supply chain does not mean that the responsibility for risk has been outsourced as well. We witnessed this in our opening case. You need the big picture. Managing the risk to the big picture can be done in smaller segments, but the question of which small segments should be managed leads us to the next point of action. Threats are more relevant and vulnerabilities are more prevalent so the risk management strategy must be engineered for the process of continuous prioritization. The impact of risk realized to the business will need to be continuously monitored and calculated. Prioritization by itself is not enough; simply identifying which risks are most severe is only one of several required steps. However, it does little good to prioritize if you cannot also communicate the urgency up and down the chain to those who have the ability to fix (or the vulnerability to suffer from) the risk itself. This raises another issue: How do your suppliers manage the risks you prioritize and identify?

When you think about expanding the scope of supply chain risk practices, it is helpful to return to your original definition of risk—there must be uncertainty and relevance to uncertainty. In today's world of complex global supply chains, uncertainty itself is certain since there are so many combinations of resources (labor, technology, physical assets, and relationships) that are exposed to a broader scope of threats. It is for this reason that the supply chain must be viewed in its entirety and in a level of detail that has never been analyzed before. New operating assumptions must be applied. The operating assumptions must include:

- *Expect the unexpected now should be considered the norm.* The impact must be better understood, measured, and monitored, as well as viewed in its aggregate.
- The *risk of low-frequency/high-impact events* and high-frequency/previously perceived impact events should not be managed separately; the consequences of both can be one and the same.

Transactional or everyday events typically are managed at the logistics, operations, and sourcing level. The outcome of these events is typically controllable or containable, meaning that the local function can adapt to the disruption for a short duration. The inconvenience to the customer is usually temporary. These events include snowstorms, short labor strikes, failure of noncritical suppliers, equipment outages, and illness. Managing transactional risk is part of the job.

But as I discussed earlier, the fragility of today's interdependent supply chains can initiate a string of adverse outcomes. For example, when the housing market slows, there is a sawdust shortage. Sawdust prices rise in 15 months from $25 a ton to more than $100 a ton. Farms use sawdust as cozy and clean bedding, and particleboard makers use sawdust as a cheap building material. Auto parts manufacturers, wineries, and oil rig operators are also impacted. This example represents a small, overlooked weak link in critical value chains. Losses can be substantial across multiple industries. The failure of a small, remote, inconspicuous resource that typically is easily managed can suddenly trigger a catastrophic unfolding of interdependent events.

It doesn't make sense to map an entire ocean and all its threats without knowing the path of ships and exposure to uncertainty. Continuous prioritization is needed as we move along the process of identifying, anticipating, and preventing. And who makes the call? To avoid a repeat of our second symptom, *dispersed and unclear ownership of risk accountability*, we are telling others to follow a few specific guidelines.

Manage interdependency. This exists in long, geographically distributed supply chains with an increased number of touch points, and it requires the cooperation, collaboration, and synchronization of many partners. All of these partners are dependent of one another. Obstacles to success and synchronization include differing cultures, languages, systems, processes, and working conditions or differences in work schedules. IBM, for example, must ensure that its approximately 30,000 active suppliers can comply with its standards for managing supply chain risk (labor, environmental, quality, security, and so on). Interdependency augments the chances for the whole matter to fall apart, especially if a simple assumption on your part does not pan out in a foreign country a tier removed from direct communication with you. How much new interdependency did your organization's supply chains experience as a result of globalization? A significant point of failure is the false assumption that the custodians of their enterprise and those relying on them were managing their risk. They have come to realize that the scope of their risk programs is limited to:

- Their organization and first-tier suppliers (that is, what they can see)
- What the organization owns and manages
- Physical assets (driven primarily by what is insurable)
- Previously identified risk events such as a hurricane or typhoon
- What is insurable
- What can be qualitatively measured, not what can be quantifiably measured
- Low-probability, high-impact events, not the transactional risks that can add up or be systemic in nature
- Functional owners, rather that process owners

Expand your understanding of broad-scope risk. Besides living with bad assumptions, the leaders of the organization are expected, either overtly or discretely, by their stakeholders to understand and manage risk. The common thread is not that their supply chain risk is not being addressed at all, but rather that current supply chain risk practices are insular; the scope of what is being done must be broadened. For example, supply chain risk practices should incorporate a full life-cycle view of the product, from the materials to the customer. Ownership is now a shared and virtual principle—in fact, ownership is irrelevant in most instances. What matters to the organization is the creation of value; selling, producing, delivering, and servicing product (and getting paid for it). It does not matter if the failure was caused by a provider of materials, a manufacturer of product, or the shipper of goods—the bottom line is that when one stakeholder fails, all stakeholders fail regardless of ownership.

Challenge Old Assumptions; Say No When Something Is Wrong To avoid a repeat of our third symptom, *mob mentality*, the *Titanic* decided to break course without analyzing and monitoring the full set of risks—including those that others were aware of. Knowing when to say no is critical, but in practice, matters are more often the other way around. To resist bad decisions, we need rules, corporate governance, and, most important, clearly defined risk expectations from key stakeholders. Key people need to say no when everything is too good to be true, without having to hesitate and consider whether their very job is at risk for not just going along. And if it seems this way, it probably is. The captain of the *Titanic* went along with the manufacturer's representative who was on board, who ordered him to increase speed to set a new Atlantic crossing speed record. The captain knew better, but instead of following his gut, he acted like a good company man. The result: more than 1,500 dead.

Manage Accelerated and Continuous Change Remember, change is constant. Rapid change, accompanied by competitive demand and supply markets, is constant, persistent, relevant, and dramatic. Ironically, if competitive demand does change, it usually means your organization is dying. Survivors do not learn to escape change but to manage it more effectively. Take the 2008 terrorist attacks in Mumbai as an example. In a matter of seconds, terrorist attacks on the city of Mumbai caused a significant decline in the profitability of the traditional Indian tourist season. Bookings at five-star hotels dropped two-thirds after the attacks. Two of the most profitable hotels saw occupancy rates tumble to 50 percent. In order to manage these large deficits, hotels are informally offering discounts of up to 20 percent to avoid cutting prices up front. These Mumbai hotels are operating in fear that they will have to publicly admit that their rooms are largely empty.[7] *Are you plugged-in and aware of change at all levels of the organization and supply chain?*

What drives business change and how do we begin to monitor this change to understand the potential impact to our supply chain network design or the day-to-day operational processes? Managing supply chain risk would be an easy task if we could control what, when, and how change takes place. Maybe we need a crystal ball to see or anticipate change long before it occurs. But we know this is not reality. The market, clients, regulators, or natural hazards, to name just a few, can initiate change. Demand-driven change is typically initiated by the organization in pursuit of a speculative opportunity, such as selling product into a new market, or it can be triggered by other factors such as a need to fulfill greater customer service expectations. An unexpected trigger, an incident or circumstance that is usually thrust upon the organization without notice, drives change as well, whether you're ready for it or not. Exhibit 2.3 illustrates these two types of business change: demand driven, an action or reaction to the market or client need (i.e., exploiting the opportunity), and event driven, reaction to a threat being realized. The organization needs to be on the lookout for both types of change.

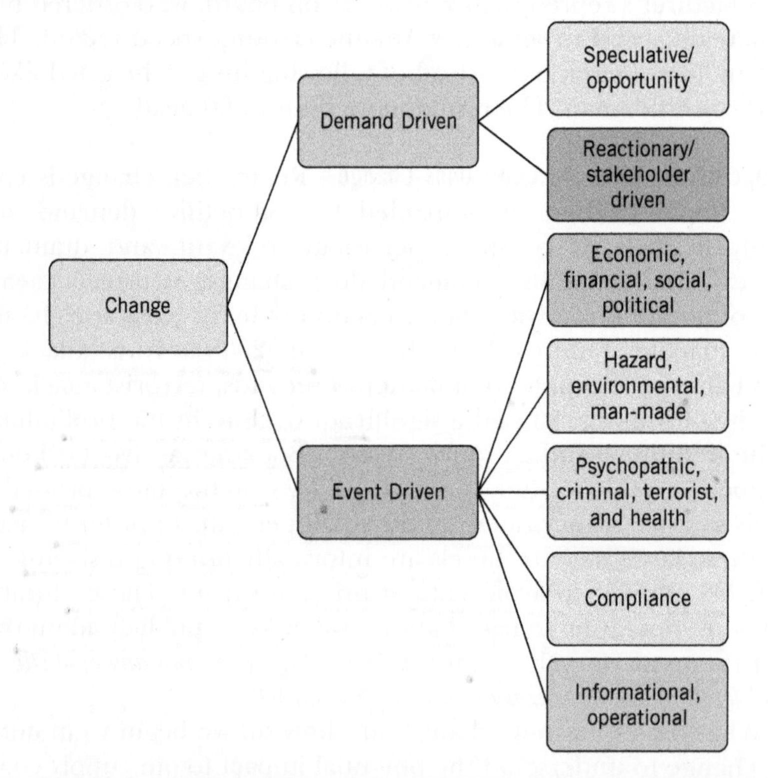

Exhibit 2.3 Change Can Be Driven by Demand (Market and Clients) or an Event

Unfortunately, changes are now coming to organizations at an unrelenting pace and at an accelerating rate. Like ripples in a small pond, this causes more waves across globally distributed interdependent supply chains. New and lower-priced competition, the need to move product into the market in less time, and increasing customer expectations for better service are just a few examples. And these examples just represent demand-driven change. What about event-driven change? This is the change that just happens, at the worst possible time and maybe more than once. This was the case at Mattel prior to the 2007 holiday season, a time when retailers and manufacturers realize the majority of their revenue. Mattel and its subsidiary, Fisher-Price, were forced to declare five recalls of some 20 million toxic and dangerous toys infected with lead paint.[8] This was also the primary concern of a dozen CEOs and business owners when asked the question "Now that your businesses and supply chains have survived such a devastating event, what worries you the most going forward?" Their response: "A repeat event within the next few months."[9]

For an organization to be prepared for the unexpected, it has to identify potential triggers (whether individual events or the aggregate of warning signs), listen to the risk-conscious culture (and move qualified information quickly), rapidly escalate issues to those in authority, and take action. It must also leverage existing risk programs, such as business continuity, crisis management, disaster recovery, and emergency management. In the Mattel case, officials in Asia did not notify Mattel's senior management for nearly one month. Unfortunately, in my experience, this is often the case because local management is trying to figure it out before they report back to the people who are responsible for their jobs. These events force the organization to react, possibly in an unplanned way. The supply chain will temporarily or, most likely, permanently change in these instances—whether it be the loss of a key supplier as in the case of Lee Der and Mattel (approximately $30 million in business); Sanlu Group and Fonterra (melamine baby formula disaster); or Wal-Mart changing its ingredients strategy to cheaper grades of stainless steel for fasteners used in its furniture to ones that contained little or no nickel (this softened the nickel commodity market in 2005, shifted from a five-month rise of 25 percent to a loss in the second half of the year by 30 percent after the Wal-Mart announcement).[10]

Each change, whether by choice or by force, is likely to massively reverberate through the entire supply chain. The effects parallel the "bullwhip effect," a term used in supply chain management to reflect the oscillating effect inaccurate information or improper forecasts (small changes in customer demand) can have on inventory levels and manufacturing by multiple parties across the supply chain. Understanding more about the root cause of change and the downstream effect it will have on the supply chain is one of the most critical steps in supply chain risk management. This is where the supply chain risk management process begins—listening, observing, and collecting data about change. This is sometimes referred to as the discovery phase. Exhibit 2.4 illustrates some of the many catalysts of demand and unplanned business change.

Adding to the already difficult challenge of seeing, feeling, and anticipating change is the task of gauging how frequently change will occur. As we witnessed in 2007 and again in 2008, changes in commodity and energy prices—core materials in most supply chains—were unpredictable and erratic. The market change threw the risk prioritization process into a tailspin. One day the organization was

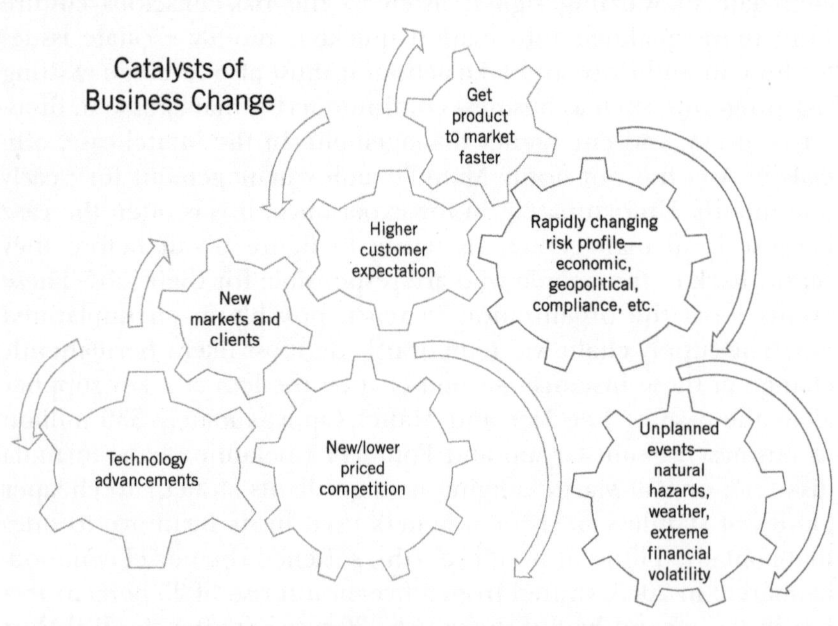

Exhibit 2.4 Linking Business Change to Catalysts

worried about rising shipping costs, fueled by exponentially increasing energy costs, and the next day it was the fluctuating currency prices. Of course, all of the macro-economic forces were intertwined so when fuel prices rose and imports to the United States decreased there were fewer shipping containers stored at ports. The U.S. dollar weakened, making exports more appealing. In 2007, export vessel space was plentiful, according to Scott Szwast, Market Director of United Parcel Service. Vessel operating carriers were absorbing the cost to move empty containers back to Asia in the absence of export cargo. In 2008, Szwast said, "This has completely flipped, due to the relative valuation weakness of the dollar; containers and capacity are in short supply. Export rates increased more than 22 percent and at the time there was the potential for a five-week lead-time secure outbound space. Most did not factor that into their business plans."[11] Another example of continuously shifting risk priorities resulting from economic and business change was evident in a survey conducted by the McKinsey Group in 2007. The risk priorities for an event- or threat-driven risk vary between geographic locations. This means that no single approach is going to work everywhere. One thing is for sure, the list will keep changing (see Exhibit 2.5).

Contrast this to another study of 110 risk managers, conducted by Marsh's Supply Chain Risk Management Group (sorry, free advertisement) in 2008. The risk profile again changed, as shown in Exhibit 2.6.

Aggregation exposure and concentration of critical resources—your risks are not reduced by going into an arrangement with other

Latin America	Mature Countries	Emerging Economies
Fluctuation in foreign exchange	Supply chain availability	Infrastructure
Regulatory concerns	Cost and quality of labor	Access to transportation
Commodity shortages and price fluctuations	Regulatory concerns	Limitations terrain
Supply chain infrastructure	Reliability of suppliers	Weather related and timing

Exhibit 2.5 Diverse Geographical Risk Priorities

1. Pricing risks
2. Risk and delays with our suppliers
3. Risks with our own plants, warehouses, stores
4. Logistics delays and disruptions
5. Natural disasters
6. Customer facing risks (demand volatility)
7. Brand reputation risk (product recalls, fair labor)
8. Intellectual property theft, counterfeiting, gray market

Exhibit 2.6 Diverse Role-Based Risk Priorities

organizations. For example, consolidating warehousing and transportation might seem like a wise idea because it cuts costs; but what new and unanticipated threats could bring the entire thing to a crashing halt? Sharing risks with competitors is a small comfort, but it only increases overall risks. Excessive focus on profitability, ironically, can lead to less profit rather than to more. *How concentrated did your organization's supply chain process and resources become as a result of globalization?*

When it comes to the management of supply chain risk, no matter what anyone says, you're dealing with a moving target; managing supply chain risk is a matter of never-ending vigilance because change is your only constant. The case of my meeting with the CEO of the consumer products company makes the point that true risk management often occurs only when you are confronted with the unexpected. The looming catastrophe sharpens your response time and often, in the direst of circumstances, you perform best. Of course, avoiding catastrophic situations is the real goal, and it is not an easy one considering the nature of change itself.

So what do we do about it? We need to revolutionize our way of thinking at the core. This new thinking is characterized by the concepts of collaboration, visibility, consciousness, measurement (quantification, modeling, prioritizing), diversity, continuous improvement, embedded monitoring, decision modeling, and expedited qualified information flows. With this new and enlightened, holistic approach, risk can become truly manageable. Without it, organizations end up

The Sum of the Parts, the Power of Aggregation

Wal-Mart's corporate objective was to reduce packaging in its supply chain by 5 percent by 2013 (*definition*), a goal articulated by Wal-Mart spokeswoman Shannon Frederick, senior communications manager at corporation headquarters. By February 1, 2008, online scorecards were available to all buyers to use as tools to make more informed purchasing decisions; buyers could show preference to those suppliers, demonstrating a commitment to producing more sustainable packaging (*measurement*). The goal was to be supplied 100 percent via renewable energy, create zero waste, and sell sustainable products (*decision*); this included participation by 8,199 unique vendors and 170,000 individual items. The following nine metrics form the foundation of the scorecard (*systems*):

1. Greenhouse gas emissions created during package production, with a weight of 15 percent
2. The packaging material's sustainability, weighted by 15 percent
3. Average distance the material is transported, 10 percent
4. Package to product ratio, 15 percent
5. Cube utilization, 15 percent
6. Recycled content, 10 percent
7. Recovery value, 10 percent
8. Renewable energy use (%?)
9. Utilizing fewer trucks more efficiently and with better packaging allowed 9 percent more product on a truck. Wal-Mart estimated that replacing the plastic lid and seal on yogurt packaging would eliminate 930 tons of greenhouse gas emissions annually.[12]

applying twentieth-century thinking to twenty-first-century problems. And that will not work.

Francois Nader, President and CEO of NPS Pharmaceutical, who addressed the issues of self-definition at the New Jersey National Association of Corporate Directors meeting in 2008, best summed up the point. He stated, "The premise that we built our organization might not be valid anymore." Dr. Nader highlighted permanent change to an organization's business model, supply chains, and risk management that requires us to think and act differently—and to make this fundamental change *now.*

Nader's message characterized an approach to this problem that makes perfect sense. It was simple and to the point. Change is the constant, and if you're not out front leading change and shaping it, then you will forever be behind trying to catch up.

Notes

1. Australia TV Channel 7 News, www.youtube.com/watch?v=e9ZktmrGGMU.
2. "Nike Responsibility Governance: Nike Was Founded on a Handshake," www.nikebiz.com/responsibility/cr_governance.html.
3. Michael Brooks, *13 Things That Don't Make Sense.* New York: Doubleday, 2008, 141.
4. IBM, "The Smarter Supply Chain of the Future Report," www-935.ibm.com/services/us/gbs/bus/html/gbs-csco-study.html.
5. The repeal enabled commercial lenders such as Citigroup, which was in 1999 the largest U.S. bank by assets, to underwrite and trade instruments such as mortgage-backed securities and collateralized debt obligations and establish so-called structured investment vehicles, or SIVs, that bought those securities. Source: Barth et al. (2000), "Policy Watch: The Repeal of Glass-Steagall and the Advent of Broad Banking," *Journal of Economic Perspectives* 14 (2): 191–204. www.occ.treas.gov/ftp/workpaper/wp2000-5.pdf.
6. Alexandra Harney, *The China Price: The True Cost of Chinese Competitive Advantage.* New York: Penguin Press, 2008.
7. Sumit Sharma, "Mumbai Hotels, in Spotlight After Attacks, Struggle to Recover," www.bloomberg.com/apps/news?pid=20601080&sid=az_PD CcOW Srs&refer=asia.
8. Jerry Oppenheimer, *Toy Monster: The Big, Bad World of Mattel.* Hoboken, NJ: John Wiley & Sons, 2009.
9. Interviews by Gary Lynch of CEOs and business owners in the Cayman Islands, post-Hurricane Ivan, 2004.
10. Charles Fishman, *The Wal-Mart Effect.* New York: Penguin Press, 2006.
11. Scott Szwast, Director of Marketing for International Freight at UPS, "RiskTalk: Supply Chain: Risks and Responsibilities," Marsh, 2008.
12. Kate Bertrand Connolly, "Wal-Mart's Scorecard Drives Sustainable Packaging," from foodprocessing.com/articles/2008/371.html.

CHAPTER 3

Law #2: The Paradigm Should Destroy the Parasite

BEGIN BY DEFINING THE PARADIGM, NOT BY FIGHTING THE PARASITE

If standards are not formulated systematically at the top, they will be formulated haphazardly and impulsively in the field.

—John C. Bigler,
quoted by Robert W. Kent in *Money Talks*, 1985

Floating helplessly 200,000 miles from Earth was a disabled spacecraft, Apollo 13. Aboard, astronauts were desperately trying to understand a barrage of unexpected, potentially catastrophic events. What they had come to know as the norm for their environment was rapidly deteriorating, threatening their mission, health, and safety. One event triggered another event, which then triggered other events. With a gift for understatement, Commander Jim Lovell reported, "Houston we have a problem." Seconds later, he blurted out, "Another master alarm, Houston—multiple cautions and warnings, Houston." Time was running out. The environment continued to change. The crew was losing oxygen, carbon dioxide levels were rising, and the pilot was unable to control the ship. Which risks were the most detrimental? Where should they start? How should the crew and resources from Houston Mission Control go about making informed decisions while so much change was taking place?

Organized chaos ensued as everyone yelled out what they were experiencing based on rapid-fire changes. But priorities could not be established and action could not be taken until correct, accurate, timely, and, most important, relevant information about the event could be presented. The first step in risk management, risk identification, and analysis finally began when Commander Lovell reported, "Houston, we are venting something out into space. I can see it outside of window one right now. It's definitely a gas of some sort." Lovell then clarified: "It's got to be the oxygen." Houston replied, "Roger Odyssey, we copy—you're venting." At that moment, the priority became clear. Mission Control and the astronauts of Apollo 13 had accurate, timely, and reliable information that could be used to establish priorities and make informed decisions.

In the previous Law, I introduced the risk parasite, an insidious force embedded in all processes and resources, disguised as a vulnerability waiting to replicate. But with so many parasites entrenched in your supply chains, how do you begin to think about managing that risk? If you are like most organizations, your supply chain risk management practices are fragmented across organizational functions and defined internally by a variety of functional or departmental managers. However, the reality of managing supply chain risk in today's constantly changing, complex global environment is that there is simply too much to manage and not enough resources to do it with—a single point of failure. Additionally, the absence of industry and organizational policies, processes, and protocols for prioritizing supply chain risk represents yet another significant single point of failure. Faced with this challenge, how can the organization apply the basic principles of economics to get the greatest return from the least investment?

The process begins by establishing priorities. Who drives the prioritization? Today, supply chain risk activities are typically driven by, first, functional risk groups (security, environmental, health and safety, continuity) within an organization, working with business or operational stakeholders (security group and the head of distribution work together on managing a security risk such as product shrinkage or theft); and second, executive management via an executive mandate, normally defined at the top and communicated down through the organization by a senior executive such as the Chief Executive Officer (CEO) or Chief Financial Officer (CFO).

While both are important, there is yet another often-overlooked source for prioritizing the organization's supply chain risk. It is the owners of the risk, more commonly referred to as the external stakeholders. These owners represent customers, investors, regulators, underwriters, rating agencies, and, in some instances, the government. They have the most to lose; they are responsible for setting the risk priorities or what I refer to as the *risk paradigm.* The external stakeholders *define* the risk expectations that the organization must *execute.* This is a subtle but critical distinction that, if not conformed with, can lead to significant operational inefficiency or, worse yet, to a *single point of failure.*

A risk paradigm set by the stakeholders rather than the organization yields more aligned, efficient, and resilient supply chain risk management.

The risk paradigm is non-negotiable and represents a contract between the owners and the custodians (those who will execute). When managing supply chain risk, the organization has little say in setting risk thresholds and priorities.

For example, when the Food and Drug Administration in the United States introduced a Compliance Policy Guide for the Prescription Drug Marketing Act [drug pedigree[1]] that required compliance with new traceability documentation standards, drug manufacturers suddenly had a new paradigm.[2] The operational supply chain activities suddenly changed and so did the risk priorities. As a result, on January 5, 2007, an international standard was ratified that specifies an XML (extensible markup language) description of the life history of a product across an arbitrarily complex supply chain. The documentation and collection process advanced from spreadsheets and PDFs to a new electronic standard for exchange of data. These new requirements represented a new paradigm by bumping supply chain risk compliance activities to the top of the organization's risk agenda (e.g., risk register).

For many internal executives, the reality that the supply chain risk paradigm is established externally is a profound and surprising one, since they typically believe that the organization and its department heads are in control of setting the risk paradigm. It's important to say again: *The internal priorities are established once the external stakeholders set their risk expectations.* Here are a few questions to consider when addressing the risk paradigm:

- Does the organization know the externally defined paradigm and has it been evaluated to determine supply chain risk expectations? (Does Houston know that there is a problem and what that problem is?)
- Once understood, have the stakeholders' expectations been defined and articulated to the organization? (Are you venting oxygen, or something else?)
- Has your organization taken the time, and does it have ongoing process and protocols, to collect, analyze, filter, and then clearly understand the risk expectations and act on them? (Do you know how to get your astronauts back to Earth?)
- Once known and acknowledged, has the organization declared these expectations as its priorities and communicated this throughout its internal and external supply chain risk management stakeholders? (Is Mission Control in control, or are they just sitting around waiting for someone else to act? Do you even have a Mission Control?)
- Have the expectations been reflected in the organization's governance framework, its public statements (in the United States, the 10-K), risk committee, risk register, and operational risk practices? (Do you have a procedure for repair and survival or will you die in outer space?)

Why is it important to set a risk paradigm? These external risk expectations truly serve as the priority set and will be measured. Engineering efficiency into the supply chain is mandatory and so is the effective and efficient allocation of risk resources. The identified risk paradigm will receive the investment benefit of resources, capital, management attention, and time. All of this might appear to be a no-brainer, since most assume that is what is currently being done to address the *why* and *what* questions of supply chain risk management. Are you right in this assumption?

My day job takes me to all parts of the world and gives me the opportunity to speak with business executives in many different industries, all with diverse interests and points of view. While traveling,

I asked more than four dozen executives, "How do you define your supply chain risk priorities?" The good news is that almost all responded by saying that they were setting priorities as result of external forces. Unfortunately, they went on to say that they were basing the expectations on only one source—the media. Although the media is considered an important external source, it is far from the primary source. Many of the executives I interviewed confessed that they were listening to the media and the masses to define their risk priorities. Others inferred by their actions that they were being driven by media events. Either way, supply chain risk priorities were being driven by the latest event. Depending on the time and place, this included doing business in China and India, pandemics, cyclones and hurricanes, product quality, rising energy costs, earthquakes, and, most recently, third-party supplier viability (the closest I came to hearing the slightest mention of an external stakeholder was from a pharmaceutical executive who referred to the need to manage supply chain risk in compliance with regulatory standards). Of all the executives interviewed, not one suggested that they collected the demands or expectations of the external stakeholders and used them to set priorities.

Although they affirmed that it was an excellent idea that needed to be considered, most confessed that it was not practiced. In fact, further conversation confirmed my original belief that supply chain risk management priorities were being set internally—mostly at the functional level. Ironically, nearly all were frustrated with their current practice of constantly chasing whatever became the next big event. "This approach is horribly inefficient, there has to be a better way," stated one CFO. Following a reactive approach costs the organization time and money because it is unable to identify, prioritize, and deploy risk mitigation and financing solutions before the next risk issue arises. This trend of not keeping pace is illustrated in Exhibit 3.1.

The practice of chasing wild and abrupt change has impacted risk priorities, but not as much as it has impacted an organization's ability to implement supply chain risk solutions. In some instances, it has caused false starts, and in others delayed or completely derailed the execution of risk management initiatives. The organization begins to deploy a risk mitigation strategy to address the latest supply chain initiative, only to find out that another is already on its way. Unfortunately, the resources, time, management

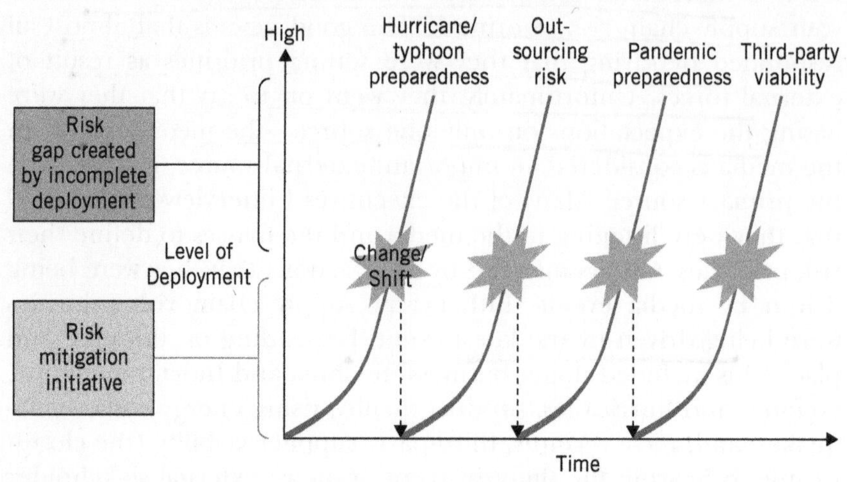

Exhibit 3.1 Media-Driven Change and the Risk Execution Gap

attention, and funding shifts create a gap and increase risk rather than decrease it. The parasite morphs and the exposure to uncertainty increases, thereby creating more risk.

So what should organizations do to address this repeating pattern? Does your supply chain risk philosophy and strategy assume the certainty of change? Is it designed for a changing environment versus one that is static? Can it be deployed quickly or does it take years? One practice to consider is to base supply chain risk strategies on the assumption that resources and capital will be limited, the timeline will be finite, and the risk activities have to be designed for maximum impact. This requires alignment of risk activities with value, a constant prioritization driven by the stakeholders' paradigm.

Exhibits 3.2 and 3.3 illustrate how you might quickly assess whether or not your organization has aligned its paradigm with the business, operations, and supply chain risk programs. Misaligned stakeholder, business, supply chain (operational), and risk priorities are shown in Exhibit 3.2 versus aligned in Exhibit 3.3.

The Paradigm in Action

It was a blustery winter night in Frederick, Maryland. I was looking forward to my dinner meeting with Gary Mucha, Senior VP of Business Integration and Performance Excellence, BAE Systems North America.

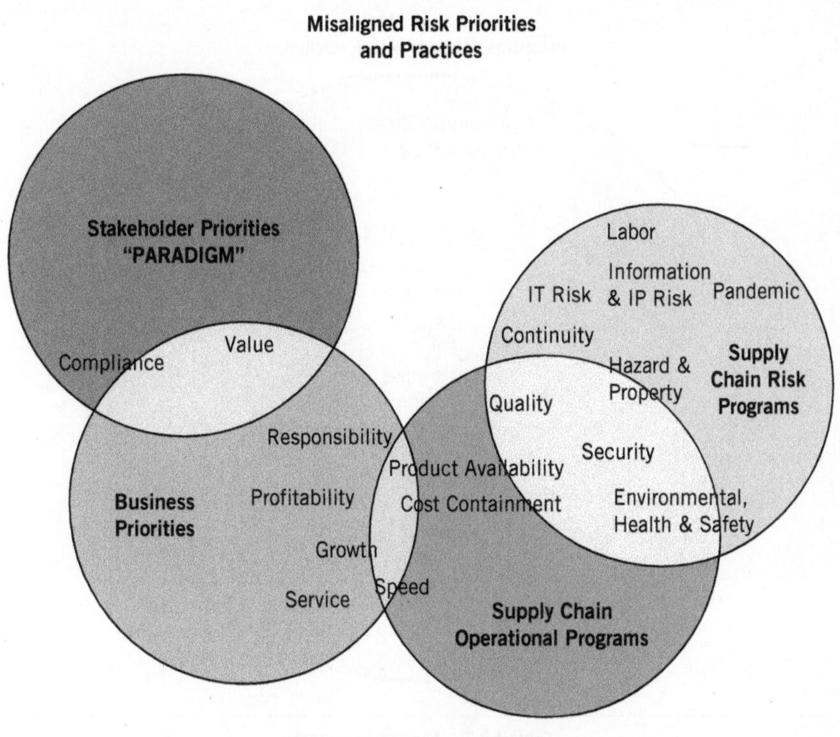

Exhibit 3.2 Misaligned Risk Priorities

As a 40-year industry veteran, his business and operations experience is extensive, having been involved with numerous acquisitions, divestures, factory closures, crises, and massive growth. BAE Systems Inc. is the U.S. subsidiary of BAE Systems plc, an international company engaged in the development, delivery, and support of advanced defense and aerospace systems in the air, land, sea, and space. Headquartered in Rockville, Maryland, BAE has more than 100,000 employees in the United States, United Kingdom, Sweden, Israel, and South Africa, generating annual sales of over $30 billion.[3] BAE operates hundreds of supply chains to support its diverse business projects.

My conversation with Gary began the same way it ended a year before, with an in-depth discussion about the importance of the external stakeholders setting, and the organization knowing the risk paradigm. Gary reverted to our original conversation about the importance of this risk paradigm. He was quick to point out that

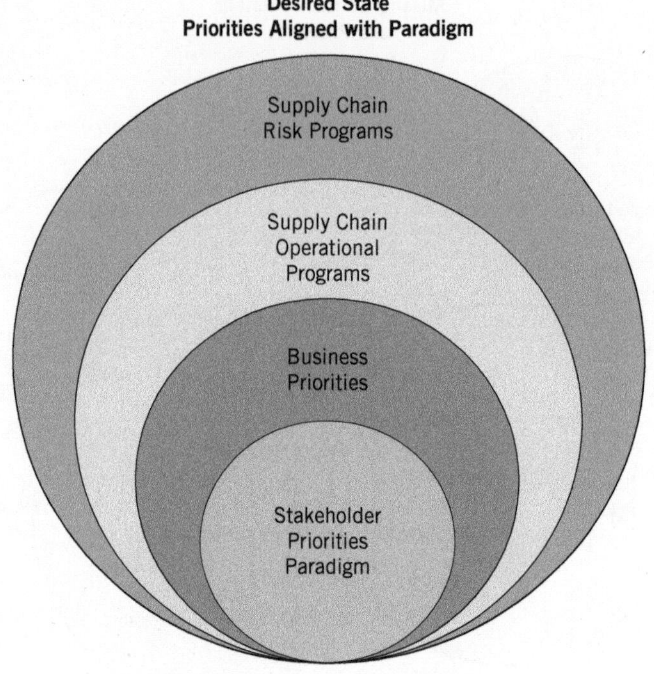

Exhibit 3.3 Aligned Paradigm

those who did not know their organization's risk paradigm, or align their risk initiatives against it, would fail to gain management support and investment resources. As someone who has managed businesses for more than three decades, Gary also added, "Their personal careers would also be at risk."

We discussed the evolution of quality management practices, for example, Six Sigma.[4] The lesson learned is that all of these practices begin by collecting, interpreting, and identifying the stakeholder, with customer expectations as a key element. By definition, if these expectations are not met, there is little likelihood that the organization's products will be successful over time; it's that simple. The same is true with supply chain risk management. Internally, the organization might believe that it is executing the top supply chain risk priority of the external stakeholders, such as health and safety, security, environmental, continuity, IT risk, succession and emergency, quality; however, this might be far from reality. If the organization does not satisfy the external stakeholders' risk requirements, the consequences could be devastating, including brand damage in the media, financial penalties or censorship for noncompliance, or, in the worst case, individual liability or penalty. This was the case when China executed its former top food and drug regulator for taking bribes to approve untested medicine, as the Beijing leadership scrambled to show that it was serious about improving the safety of Chinese products. The Beijing No. 1 Intermediate People's Court carried out the death sentence against 62-year-old, former head of the State Food and Drug Administration, Zheng Xiaoyu, shortly after the country's Supreme Court rejected his final appeal.[5] The execution card was played again when two men were sent to death for their role in the production and sale of melamine-tainted milk that killed at least six children and caused nearly 300,000 to fall ill.[6] Of course, this is an example of negligence, but regardless, it still reflects an extreme penalty for noncompliance with what the external stakeholders have defined as the expected standard.

With all of the risk activity the organization is managing, how do you know which is most important, and which is worthy of maximum risk investment? Mucha explained that "In our case, the external stakeholders, the Secretary of Defense and the Department of Defense, set the paradigm. It's very clear. Our Board knows and acknowledges these macro-level priorities. Last year, our industry was facing a daunting cyber and information exposure, and it still is. We defined IT risk and security as our 2008 risk paradigm. That's where we made substantial investment, focused resources, monitored and measured progress, continuously validated our practices, and reported the results to the Board, who in turn reported them to our external stakeholders. Prior to the external paradigm there was little room for the cyber discussion in the Board Room and little real resource allocation toward a potential resolution. When the customer thought it was important it became important. It immediately moved up the priority list and became linked into strategy.

"Of course, the organization was deeply engaged in other risk management activity but it was not the risk paradigm—the one set by the external priorities. Although these other supply chain risk initiatives received attention and funding, they did not receive the majority of our senior level risk attention or investment. The scope of our work included the information and systems used to support our business, and manage our supply chains—or the DOD's supply chains—whether they were internally or externally owned. There were no physical or organizational borders, nor was it a static one-time effort. It's now integrated living and breathing, as part of the operational processes. More importantly, our IT risk practices have been designed to adjust, adapt, and grow with change." Gary then added that in 2009, one of their major risk paradigms was "to ensure that what we produce is not used by the wrong people for the wrong purpose." Our discussion reinforced a key characteristic of the risk paradigm:

> Risk expectations are set downstream in the supply chain (demand side) and typically outside the organization, and are communicated upstream.

Exhibit 3.4 is an illustration of this concept.

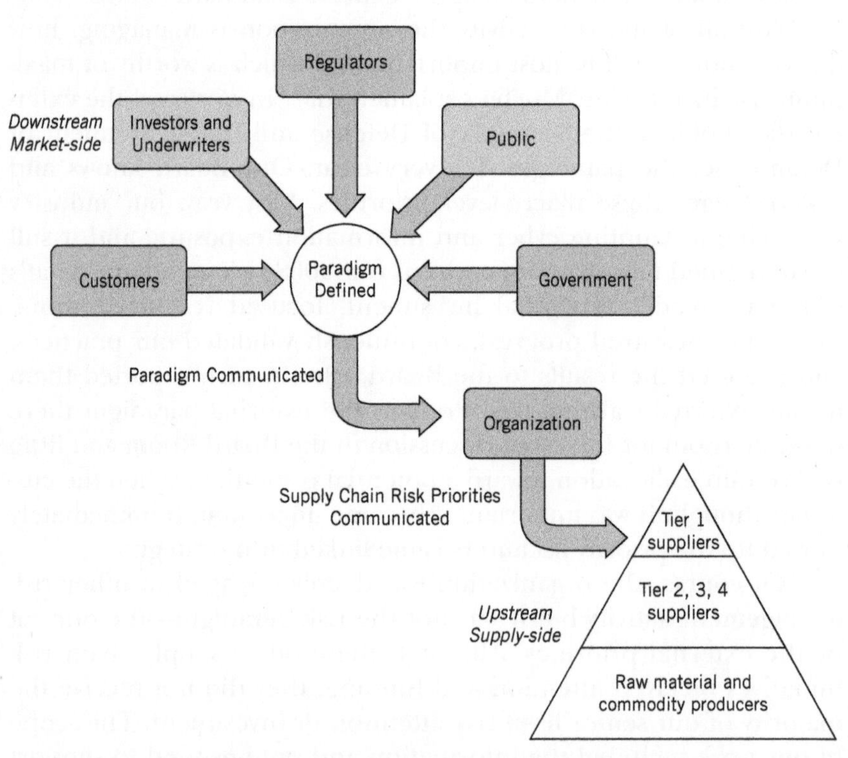

Exhibit 3.4 Defining and Communicating the Paradigm

So where have the supply risk priorities and risk paradigm been established? In my experience, the most common practice is for the priorities to be set within the organization at a functional level, even if it conflicts with another group's priorities. However, this overlap leads to widespread internal inefficiencies, misalignment of resources, and political infighting (or as I call them, "holy organizational wars"). The dilemma of choosing what to do, in what order, and at what cost often paralyzes decisions and prevents action. The inability to act ends the entire exercise, and sadly, this is where the majority of organizations end up. This also leads to an insular view of risk prioritization; we can only see what we can see or imagine.

Why Does the Organization Need to Identify a Supply Chain Risk Paradigm?

Just acknowledging that external stakeholders set the risk paradigm, regardless of internal efforts, is not enough to address the issue. That is only the first step toward discovering how to manage the risk paradigm. It is popular practice among organizational management to assume that "we decide not only what is important, but also how to address it." Realistically, a change in culture is demanded by modern organizations. One valuable lesson learned over the past decade is that the more effective, responsive, and profitable supply chain management system is the one where all parties, up- and downstream, collaborate and contribute. Many of today's most critical supply chain management initiatives have evolved from this inclusive practice, such as Vendor Managed Inventory (VMI) and Collaborative Planning, Forecasting & Replenishment (CPFR).

Setting the risk paradigm is out of your hands; however, it is critical for organizations to identify the relevant risk paradigm and determine how best to function within it. It is like playing a game of chess. If you think your purpose is to capture your opponent's queen, you lack a comprehensive strategy. The astute opponent will offer a queen sacrifice and you will immediately hear the word "checkmate." In other words, if you do not understand your game, then your outcome is going to be all wrong.

The reasons you need to set the risk paradigm are:

- *To establish a clear business case to effectively and efficiently manage your organization's supply chain risk mitigation and finance activities and investments.* Your available funding, resources, time, and management attention to address supply chain risk are finite needs that should be measured and monitored. What is important? Obtaining external stakeholder buy-in validates the business activities and investment and defuses the internal organizational battles about what is important. This might sound trivial, but if you ask most risk professionals what their greatest barrier to implementation is they will respond, "Not having clear priorities and subsequent organizational conflicts due to lack of clarity." When it comes to contending with financial resistance, the unfortunate truth is that risk management, as most often perceived by nonrisk background management, adds nothing to the top line and, from their perspective, nothing to the bottom line either. Any form of discretionary expenditure is tough to move up in the agenda. Your task should be based on (1) identifying the stakeholders setting the risk paradigm; (2) demonstrably identifying profit or loss consequences of not responding; and (3) ultimately, quantifying the cost/benefit relationship. Your challenge is to demonstrate, perhaps to management with a purely internal accounting or marketing background, that the *uncertainty cost* of the risk paradigm is not affordable. Your ability to rapidly see and measure becomes more important when you are looking at outcomes, causes, and allocation of resources.

- *To justify (quantify and qualify) the business case for supply chain risk mitigation and financing investments.* Once the paradigm is defined and understood, don't assume that the capital and resources needed to support the risk investment will be available. If the paradigm is known, then the organization will be better positioned to define the assumptions and scope of risk activities associated with addressing that paradigm. For example, a multibillion-dollar U.S. manufacturer that I was doing work for decided to establish a new paradigm after Hurricanes Katrina and Wilma. Their primary stakeholders required the organization to clearly demonstrate that they understood and could manage the risk to their Americas-based supply chains. Corporate management acknowledged the paradigm by mandating that the operating companies assess and report on their level of risk preparedness. Numerous vulnerabilities were identified with their current approach to managing the risk of rising water and winds in excess of 74 mph (hurricane force). However, the cost of mitigating and eliminating all supply chain risk was prohibitive. By quantifying the revenue streams and the supporting supply chains, as well as identifying and quantifying risk mitigation alternatives associated with the paradigm, the organization was able to quickly address the single points of failure that would result in the greatest impact. One note here: What was determined to reflect the greatest exposure at the operating level was not by default the most significant at the organizational level. When the measured results were aggregated at the corporate level it became clear which initiatives should be addressed first.

- *To align supply chain risk activities.* Every organization consists of multiple constituencies and is organizationally fragmented. This may seem like an oxymoron but it is true. Today's multinational, multidivisional organization is made up of many parts, some of which may never meet to talk with one another. This reality makes response to stakeholders very challenging, but it is a reality. In such an organization, the only portion that gets addressed is the one that management is aware of; so the big challenge in responding to the risk paradigm is to bring all of these interests together or, in some cases, to recognize that your organization may be required to serve several risk paradigms. You need to not only set proprieties for the best-known risk paradigm, but also ensure that all risk paradigms (set by all stakeholders) are addressed in the same set of priorities. Exhibit 3.5 illustrates this point of view by identifying risk mitigation activities that are associated with each resources class.

It is an interesting challenge, but one that many organizations face. Different segments of the organizations operating in geographically diverse areas, selling different products, and working in relatively isolated risk paradigms cannot be brought under a single umbrella. You may need to confront another reality: You deal with multiple stakeholder sets in different dimensions, and you need more than one response methodology. Making risk response efficient demands initiatives that are all worthwhile in the view of many; in fact, the syndrome recognizes that it *might* be possible to maximize

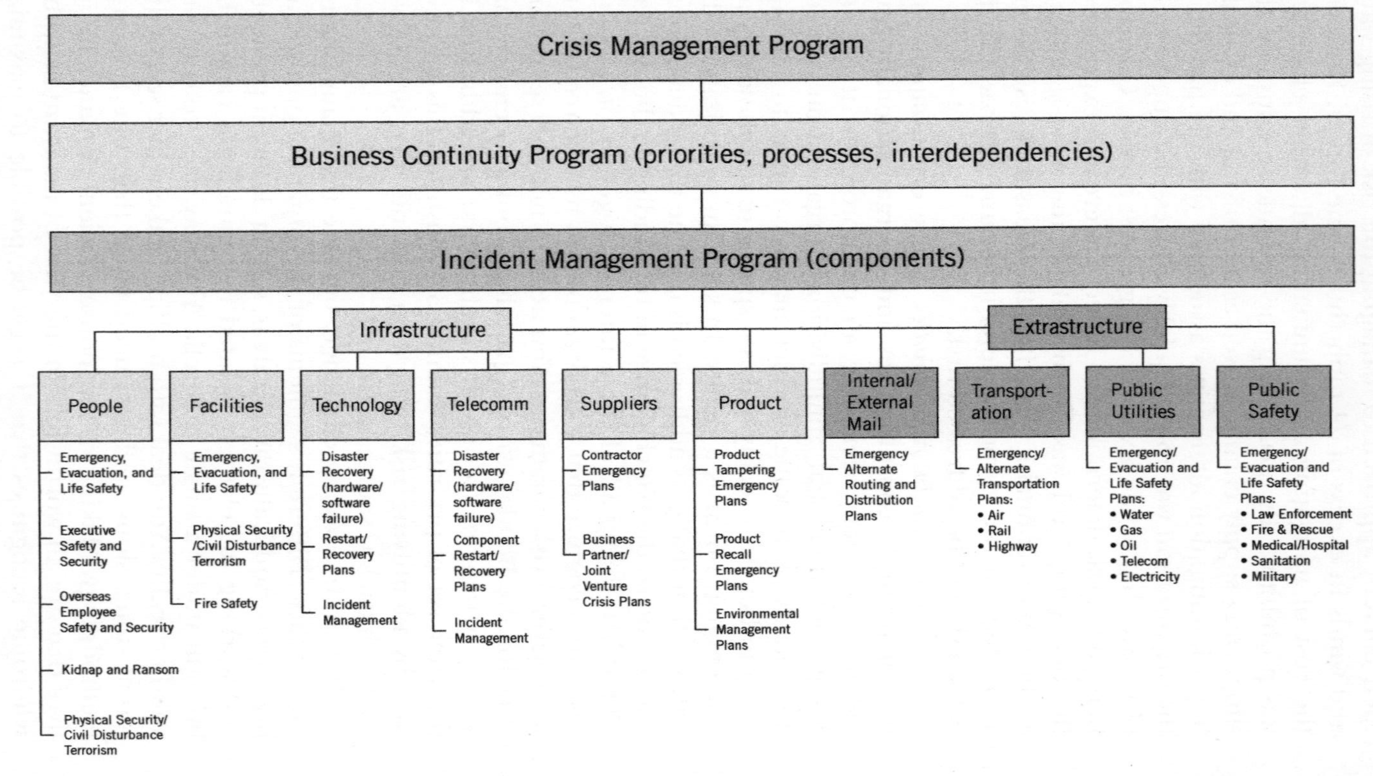

Exhibit 3.5 Sample Risk Mitigation Activities

efficiencies of risk and operational management processes while achieving the greatest balance. But think about this for a moment. What does it really mean? In fact, you can use the initiative approach to make your case, to prove to management that it is smart to pick and choose among many possible initiatives. So your strategic argument could be, "Our risk paradigm is set outside of our control," but you probably won't convince everyone because, more often, the unasked questions are related to what something is going to cost or what profits it will produce. Instead, your argument should be, "Which initiative is going to be most effective in responding to the risk paradigm set by our stakeholders?"

- *Communicate to others, such as rating agencies, regulators, and underwriters, that supply chain risks are being prudently managed by the organization.* The insurance value point of view tells the traditional executive that if it's not measured, then it's not managed. This is true in some identifiable risks, but the risk paradigm is far more encompassing than a traditional risk mitigation approach. The risk paradigm has to merge the many potential methodologies of response as part of the priority-setting phase. Financing and insuring to mitigate risk is one of many potential responses, but it is not a yes-or-no decision. It has to be folded into a larger program and used in conjunction with many other approaches.

The preceding points address some of the organizational methods for approaching and dealing with the risk paradigm. This assumes an orderly dialogue in an environment that remains the same, at least long enough for the discussion to take place and an action plan developed. Unfortunately, like so many management decisions, such as budgeting and forecasting, marketing plans, and financing, an unchanging environment is rare.

Beware! The Paradigm Can Shift without Notice

Even when your organization has defined its risk paradigm and been executing well against it, continuously measuring progress and closing the gaps, nothing is permanent or fixed. What happens, for example, if your organization is confronted by a wide-scale outbreak of Avian flu (or Swine flu, H1N1)? The region where you

Lessons Learned

Anticipating change is a fairly safe bet because change always occurs. So even in addressing the externally set paradigm, keep these additional steps in mind:

1. The clear business case that you make cannot be set in stone, but rather has to provide guidelines based on today's structure but flexible enough to change as the entire situation evolves. This also relates to financing activities and investments; base the strategy on what you know today but provide flexibility and adaptability.
2. You can best justify your business case by emphasizing its flexibility. Even those who resist creating a supply chain risk management program recognize its ever-changing nature, and the most effective methodology has to remain fluid.
3. You cannot align the current supply chain risk activities for tomorrow's environment because it will be completely changed. Rather, your alignment has to be based on the strategic response rather than on the specific risk paradigm you face today.
4. The best communication should not be limited to the program, but to the strategy. Unlike the fixed-in-time corporate report so favored by traditional executives, your risk paradigm is a growing and changing aspect of the supply chain. The measurement of your effectiveness is continual and changing.

sell and source your goods is now at risk and so are your supply chains. Faced with the critical risk decision, does your organization forgo the current paradigm in lieu of a new one? Your decision will depend on how exposed you are to this uncertainty. Is the clock ticking slowly or is it rapidly advancing? What is the degree of urgency? And finally the most critical question: What level of importance or concern do your stakeholders place on this issue? Will organizations have to respond by dramatically improving their personnel and physical security practices, as was the case after 9/11?

This scenario is real. In 2005, the media raised awareness of a huge spike in human H5N1 cases. This newfound parasite created the need for a new paradigm. Key stakeholders began to question whether the organization was exposed to the new parasite. Public health organizations, federal/state/local governments, regulators, investors, and underwriters began to ask questions such as:

- What experience does the organization have managing the supply chain risk of a pandemic, that is, people/skills/labor-based related failures?
- How is the organization's supply chain exposed, directly or indirectly, to the uncertainty presented by a pandemic? Specifically (remember, it's all in the details), how will the organization's supply chain processes (sourcing, production, logistics) and resources (labor, technology, physical assets) be affected?
- What will be the financial, brand, regulatory, strategic, and liquidity impact if the risk is realized?
- What will be the consequential damage if the organization's interdependent third parties are impacted? Are the organization and its supply chains facing isolated, widespread but containable, or systemic risk?
- Does the organization have governance structure, policy, process, and protocols to manage the supply chain risk?

If your stakeholders are asking these questions, a new paradigm is more than likely on the way. This was the case in 2005 through 2007. Although the first case of H5N1 was reported in Hong Kong in 2003, spread of the virus did not accelerate until 2005. Within months, the virus spread to eight countries and in December the first human case was reported in Vietnam. The virus expanded geographically to parts of Central Asia, Europe, Africa, and the Middle East by 2005. There were 113 deaths and 205 confirmed human cases in nine countries by April of 2006. Between December 1, 2003, and April 30, 2006, infected birds were found in 50 countries, including the United Kingdom and Germany, and most of the largest exporting countries had at least one case.[7] It was at this point that organizations began to embrace the new paradigm and communicate it as a priority. Armed with the external stakeholders' questions, the CEOs, CFOs, heads of global supply chains, and other senior executives began to assess the degree of preparedness. Other questions that they posed to their organizations were:

- How does threat of a pandemic differ from other catastrophic events? What will be the effect on our supply chain, specifically our ability to source materials and products;

move product, transportation systems and infrastructure (including port operations); store and distribute products; warehouse, IT systems, and distribution centers; and understand and forecast demand?
- Are our supply chains insured? Do business interruption, contingent business interruption, and other insurance policies cover a disruption triggered by a pandemic?
- What is the estimated overall cost to the organization? How long will the cost last and how does that impact our financial strength, long-term profitability, and competitive position?

According to a Bloomberg report on October 17, 2008, the World Bank estimated that an influenza pandemic could cost the global economy more than $3 trillion and could result in the deaths of 71 million people worldwide. In June 2006, the World Bank estimated that in a pandemic the global gross domestic product (GDP) would drop by 3.1 percent, or around $2 trillion. However, this more recent estimate by the World Bank indicates that a pandemic could cause the global GDP to drop by 4.8 percent. A decrease in tourism, retail sales, and transportation, as well as an increase in employee absenteeism would contribute to the drop in GDP. However, the World Bank estimates that "measures to avoid infection," including vaccine development and poultry slaughter, would account for most of the costs in a pandemic. World Bank economists stated that because a global pandemic would spread very quickly, adequate preparation on a global level is necessary.[8]

In this example, a paradigm shift occurred without any warning. At the time this book went to print, a new pandemic threat, the H1N1 virus, began to reset the organizational paradigm again. The scary fact about a pandemic scenario is that unlike a natural hazard that strikes once, a health event can manifest as multiple, simultaneous, reoccurring, and geographically distributed events. It is important to quickly identify which supply chain resources will be impacted when a paradigm shift occurs. Avoid falling into the trap of thinking about resources only in a physical asset context. Technology, information, relationships, and processes are examples of nonphysical resources and all have the potential to be a single point of failure. A pandemic event would cause a significant loss of people—employees, customers, investors, and those individuals that support the public infrastructure. In addressing all of these complex problems, it is the range of planning considerations that define the effectiveness of response. The scope and assumptions that apply to a pandemic paradigm and are used to conduct supply chain risk management activities should be expanded to include:

- Loss of critical infrastructure such as transportation, energy, communications, and public health/safety.
- Cooperative preparedness activities throughout the extended supply, service, and innovation chains.
- Consideration of socially disruptive events such as quarantine, isolation, social distancing, and civil unrest at any point in the chain.
- Three orders of succession and delegation.
- Community survival activities (first-responder mentality) for at least the first 72 hours after an outbreak—activities that require cooperation between local public and private sector entities. Behavioral challenges—people will become incoherent, irrational, difficult to motivate, isolated, and defensive.
- Limited medical supplies and trained personnel.

A further example of how the people resource might be affected at a utility provider is illustrated in Exhibit 3.6. The impact from a loss of this type will most likely far exceed any physical asset failure. Global Tamiflu Product Manager James Irwin from Roche summed it up the best when he stated, "To make supply chain happen you have to have your people driving trucks, doing the finance, sourcing the goods. You can have all the plans in the world but if you don't have your people supply chains won't function. It's as simple as that."

The management of supply chain risk is not limited to just the organization's supply chain and neither is the risk paradigm. The organization is part of one continuous and many contiguous supply chains, all of which are constantly changing. In other words, your organization's supply chains represent one link in the boundless number of globally interconnected and interdependent chains. This is similar to the small-world phenomenon of the six degrees of separation set in the movie about Hollywood actor Kevin Bacon. The theory is that everyone can be linked in no more than six layers of separation. I haven't done the math, but I believe it's true

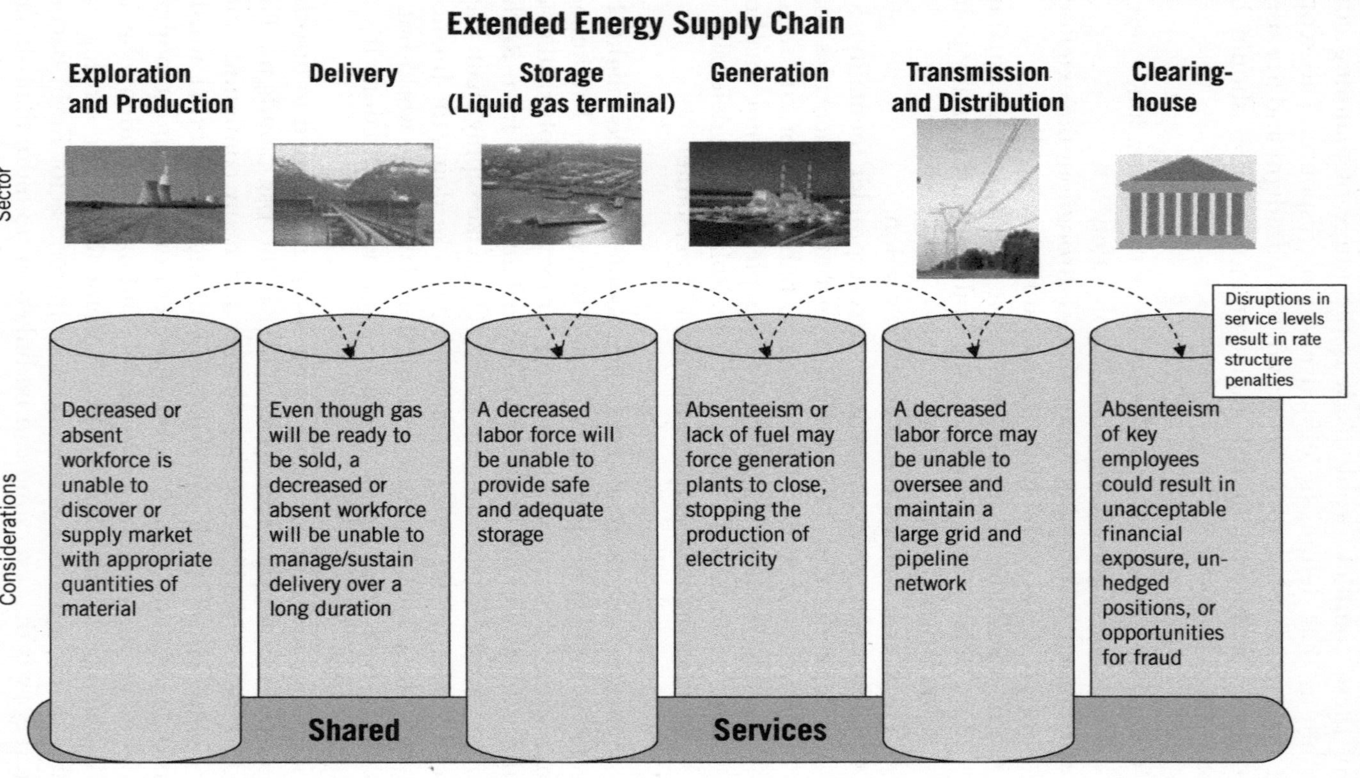

Exhibit 3.6 How Might a Utility Company's Resources Be Affected by a Pandemic?

Source: Marsh, *Supply Chain Risk Practice*

in our world of interwoven supply chains. This makes the ultimate point: No one is able to operate in isolation, and no supply chain is self-contained. We are all interdependent and we all rely on one another. This simple reality tells the whole story of the risk paradigm. The one set by your external stakeholders affects many other risk paradigms in a continuum of priorities set by a universal range of stakeholders. We need to work together or the risk parasite finally will consume the entire organization. The solution is in recognizing this as a fact of life.

For example, if you are in the health care business, let's say in a hospital, you are part of the agriculture and food, medical devices, pharmaceutical, transportation, textile, energy, technology, real estate, financial services, and other supply chains. From your vantage point, it may appear that your chain is at the center and all others connect to it, but that is only because you've decided to crop your picture around your world. For this reason, gaining transparency up and down the chain is one of the most critical challenges of supply chain risk management. The process of establishing the risk paradigm requires a collective process, one where each organization in the supply chain evaluates how much it can influence and alter the paradigm. Upstream suppliers of dominant customer-facing organizations, such as Target, Toyota, or Procter & Gamble, are at the mercy of their risk paradigm. They must acknowledge and comply with this externally set paradigm or face the risk of losing their primary source of revenue. Is your organization in a similar situation—is the majority of your business derived from any one distributor, retailer, or buyer on the demand side of the equation? Are you aware and do you comply with their risk paradigm?

A lesson learned: Define and acknowledge expectations before risk resources are allocated. For example, if the risk analysis has been completed and you are not sure how much spend is necessary, then revisit your stakeholder assumptions and expectations—that is where you will usually find the risk tolerance defined.

If the Shoe Fits

What and who create the risk paradigm? Remember, it is *not* the organization. Various stakeholders and even outside forces have much more to do with an organization's risk paradigm than management.

So management's task is to increase its own awareness of the aggregate paradigm and then remove, transfer, or mitigate it to avoid single points of failure. Without any doubt, the Secret Service had reviewed all kinds of scenarios to protect President Bush on a visit to Iraq near the end of his presidency. A room full of press had been searched and scanned for explosives and weapons and, nothing obviously threatening having been found, Bush was allowed to stand directly in front of the audience, all of whom were wearing shoes. So when two shoes went flying, a single point of failure became evident, but too late. (This appeared to be a trend; it happened again in March 2009, when three Canadians were arrested and others threw shoes in protest against George W. Bush when he gave his first post-presidential speech in western Canada's oil fields.)

So what is the solution? Should journalists be required to remove their shoes just like air travelers? Should the Secret Service erect a Plexiglas barricade in front of the president? Should all future press conferences be canceled? The real issue here is not how future shoe attacks can be prevented, but rather why all of the security precautions in the world did not prevent a simplistic and ineffective attack from occurring. If it is the Secret Service's job to prevent *all* attacks, then they failed. If their job is to prevent *deadly* attacks, they managed to keep the president alive for the entire eight years of his administration.

The shoe incident points out how a paradigm actually works. The characteristics of the risk paradigm tell the whole story.

- It is set externally—this does not mean that you have no control over the risk paradigm. It does mean, however, that organizational efforts are best focused on anticipation and a risk strategy in *response* to the externally set paradigm. Many organizations believe, contrary to reality, that risk management is defined as setting the paradigm
- Uncertainty is real and so is an organization's exposure to uncertainty. Your organization can digest only one, maybe two uncertainties at a time. But realistically, it is uncertainty itself that defines not only the problem but also the appropriate response. Many organizations make the effort to identify actual risks and then prevent or transfer them. This procedure ignores the obvious problem: You cannot anticipate the next serious risk.

- The risk paradigm represents a significant threat to brand, financials (materials, cash flow, credit), and customer requirements. Your organization's exposure to uncertainty cannot be resolved with initiatives that anticipate a repeat of past single points of failure, because they are never the same; new and unexpected risks are certain to arise. Thus, the effective risk management program has to address the impact issue, and not just try to prevent past failures from occurring again. Will a president ever have a shoe thrown at him again? Perhaps, but this does not mean the Secret Service should ignore all other possible threats. Working on response, awareness, and diligence is the key to continuing the protective functions they hold, and the same approach works in your organization as well.
- Risk has to be acknowledged and monitored, and practices have to be validated against risk, not against a specific event. Expectations are often clear but so are actions (for example, at Target its about relentless protection of the brand).
- Risk awareness forces accountability, measurement, actions/solutions, and validation. Without awareness, none of the preventive and protective measures can be created or put into action. If your organization spends its efforts anticipating the next shoe-throwing incident, rather than acknowledging that the next threat might be far more serious, then it cannot expect to measure its response program. Realistically, a response program does not exist if it is based on past single points of failure. Remember, the risk parasite grows and evolves with the organization. If you have had any degree of change in the past year, then so has your risk parasite. It is a different animal.
- Risk cannot be managed by ignoring it. Another common and dangerous problem is the tendency among management to just ignore new or unknown risks, on the philosophy that if you don't see it, then it doesn't exist. This point of view often comes from those with strictly financial backgrounds. These types like to measure everything in tangible terms: profit or loss, positive or negative, all binary outcomes. They resist more than most others any suggestion that funds should be placed in the budget to create a response to an *unknown* risk, based on a paradigm set outside of the organization, that

> might or might not happen. This is a tough sell. Financial executives are gifted individuals, but they also have a blind spot. Sometimes they cannot see the shoe flying directly at them.

Remember: We can do it all but we cannot do everything all at once.

Sponsorship issues also determine how you respond to or even create an alignment between stakeholder priorities and actions. Understanding risk expectations and tolerances, in other words accepting and managing the links, will vary by stakeholders. Risk activities are laser focused and continuously prioritized. But management of your organization's response has to be viewed as a completely different strategic approach to the issue. The paradigm is set externally and your task is to decide how to respond, set priorities, and pick the best initiatives.

So the issue has to be based on methods you need to control, mitigate, and eventually destroy the risk parasite. This requires a six-step approach.

The first step is to figure out the paradigm you face and, if dealing with a complex multinational organization concerned with numerous operating segments, this process may have to be multidimensional. Stop, sense, listen to all stakeholders, collect, analyze, filter, acknowledge, communicate, and communicate again.

Second, you need to develop process, protocols, and systems to monitor and continuously validate the paradigm. If you don't monitor it, the system simply will not work, primarily because the paradigm is shifting and evolving and so must your risk management processes and systems. Endlessly monitor stakeholder and industry trends.

Third, instead of viewing risk management as a transactional, reactive, and insular process, use it and the paradigm to drive and align the organization's supply chain risk priorities. Measure twice, mitigate once. This makes the process dynamic, efficient, proactive and—to satisfy your financial decision makers—a profit center as well (or at the very least a "reduced loss" center).

Fourth, determine the action plan when a paradigm shift occurs. This is not contingency planning; it is going to occur. So you need to develop a methodical response methodology and ensure that well-defined impact and response procedures are known throughout your supply chain.

Fifth, define methods by which you can destroy the parasite. You know the risk parasite is insidious and evolves. Worse yet, the parasite you destroy today may have already hatched eggs throughout your organizational body, so the focused destruction of this parasite is essential. Divide and conquer is a recipe for failure. Use the paradigm to concentrate your risk response and resources against the threats and vulnerabilities that are most relevant and will cause the most harm. This step turns risk management from a preventive system into an aggressive, specific, and effective means for shoring up the weak links in your supply chain and eliminating as many single points of failure as possible.

Sixth, in order to ensure that your executive decision makers are on board, communicate the cost of inaction (quantitative and qualitative). Just as the budgeting and forecasting process has to follow the markets your organization serves, your supply chain risk management program has to follow the paradigm as it is set by outside stakeholders. This communication effort is essential to preventing reevaluation by financial executives who are forever seeking ways to cut back on the budget. Programs considered as soft and intangible are the first to go, so you need to revolutionize the way risk management is viewed. The cost of inaction is too high to ignore and, just as profit centers generate improved earnings, risk management reduces costs; the net outcome—an improved bottom line—is the same. This is the essential argument you need to convince your organization's top leadership that the consequence of inaction is too high.

These six steps help you to formulate a program for addressing the paradigm. Awareness of the risk parasite and its relentless assault on the organization's body is a graphic but essential message, a recurring theme your management needs to hear. It is most effective when communicated and expressed in the terms every executive understands well. Managing the risk paradigm is probably the most critical form of corporate governance. If it is ignored, it impacts negatively on stock prices, employee procedures, investor attitudes, brand value, competitiveness, and all other aspects of the organization. To truly manage the risk paradigm, it must serve as the core driving force of your organization's identity and culture. Failing to respond to the paradigm translates to a slow deterioration of the organization's health. Responding effectively in today's dynamic environment ensures that the organization will be one of the survivors in the global and ever-changing paradigm.

Notes

1. A drug pedigree is a statement of origin that identifies each prior sale, purchase, or trade of a drug, including the date of those transactions and the names and addresses of all parties to them. "FDA 2006 Compliance Policy Guide for the Prescription Drug Marketing Act."
2. *Ibid.*
3. BAE Systems's About page, www.na.baesystems.com/overview.cfm.
4. Six Sigma seeks to improve quality of process outputs by identifying and removing the causes of defects (errors) and variation in manufacturing and business processes. It uses a set of quality management methods, including statistical methods, and creates a special infrastructure of people within the organization ("Black Belts" and so on) who are experts in these methods. Each Six Sigma project carried out within an organization follows a defined sequence of steps and has quantified financial targets (cost reduction or profit increase). Source: Jiju Antony. "Pros and cons of Six Sigma: an academic perspective," www.onesixsigma.com/node/7630. Retrieved on May 1, 2008; and www.isixsigma.com/sixsigma/six_sigma.asp.
5. "China Quick to Execute Drug Official," *New York Times*, Joseph Kahn, July 11, 2007.
6. "2 face execution over China poison milk scandal." MSNBC, www.msnbc.msn.com/id/28787126.
7. Weekly Epidemiology Record, #26, June 3, 2006.
8. Gale, J., "Flu Pandemic May Cost World Economy up to $3 Trillion," Bloomberg, October 17, 2008, www.bloomberg.com/apps/news?pid=20601202&sid=ashmCPWATNwU&refer=healthcare.

CHAPTER 4

Law #3: Manage Your Business DNA in a Petri Dish of Evolving Risk

A scorpion approached a frog with a request: "Carry me on your back and help me cross the river." The frog refused at first, fearing the scorpion would sting him. But the scorpion reminded him, "If I sting you, we will both drown." This made sense. So the frog invited the scorpion to hop on and they began crossing the river. Halfway across, the scorpion stung the frog. As they began to sink, the frog asked the scorpion, "Why did you do that?" and the scorpion answered, "I couldn't help myself. It's in my nature."

—Fable, unknown author, story cited by Orson Wells in the 1955 movie *Confidential Report*

The scorpion could not help his behavior even though it was self-destructive, because it was in his nature to sting the frog. You might say it was a matter of DNA. We all have certain behaviors that cause us to repeat self-destructive actions. One of those behaviors is found in supply chain risk management. The failure to understand, measure, manage, and monitor threats and vulnerabilities (in lieu of pursuing profits or personal incentives) is a self-destructive tendency that can be overcome and that needs to be changed if you hope to reduce your problems.

The scorpion and the frog story is instructive in many respects. In an organization's supply chain, the microscopic DNA fragments that create many of your problems really add up to what has to be treated as the big picture. Just as billions of human DNA collectively create a living being, the big picture for the organization relies on infinite supply chain configuration possibilities. The scorpion lacked the big picture because his entire universe consisted of the irresistible impulse to sting the frog, even though the frog was essential to the scorpion's survival. Because the scorpion's universe was so limited, even self-destructive behavior could not be avoided. Sadly, the same situation is going to be found in many supply chains. In order for your organization to ensure that it operates not like the scorpion but in a more frog-centric way, you must realize the critical importance of understanding your own organization's DNA.

To map supply chain DNA and to truly understand behaviors that form the basis of how risk is being managed throughout your supply chain requires an understanding of the beginning and the end. Markets and customers aside for a moment, for Wal-Mart and Darden Restaurant's shrimp supply chain, it begins in the fishing villages of Chanthaburi Province in Thailand and continues through to the customer purchase. But it doesn't end there, since returns or dissatisfaction must travel through their service and/or reverse logistics chains. The behaviors, actions, and risk consciousness of the participants along their supply chains define the exposure to Wal-Mart and its customers. These include Rubicon Resources LLC, a U.S. supplier of farmed shrimp, several hundred Thai shrimp farmers, dozens of transportation companies, manufacturers of cold storage equipment, U.S. Customs, and the Thai Department of Fisheries.[1] However, few organizations map the full life cycle of the many supply chains that they depend on to deliver value. The lack of visibility, or what many refer to as transparency, into the extended chain continues to be seen by senior executives as a top supply chain risk management issue. An organization tends to have a clear line of sight to its first- and maybe second-tier suppliers, but beyond that the view is obstructed or the organization chooses blindness over sight. Raw material providers, job shops, contract manufacturers, and the infrastructure providers critical to completing the chain are often omitted. Of course, there are exceptions, such as Harley-Davidson, Tiffany's, Tesco, Target, and Cisco. However, this is simply not the case in two of the most regulated industries: pharmaceuticals and food. The peanut butter and blood thinner contamination of 2007 and 2008 initiated action to improve transparency and safety, but these were voluntary and in the early stages (more about that in the Law about suppliers).

So why is it difficult to understand the DNA of an organization's supply chains? Why do so many lack transparency or visibility—a clear line of sight—up- and downstream? The challenge begins with a question: "Where does my supply chain start and stop and what do I influence control?" If you are Wal-Mart, it begins with the customer (and the market), but if you are an electronics manufacturer, there might be a middleman or client, such as a distributor, in between you and your end customers. To be able to succinctly respond to this question is an enormous accomplishment when managing supply chain risk. Understanding the organization's demarcation points is no small task. Exhibit 4.1 illustrates the complexity and, more important, the

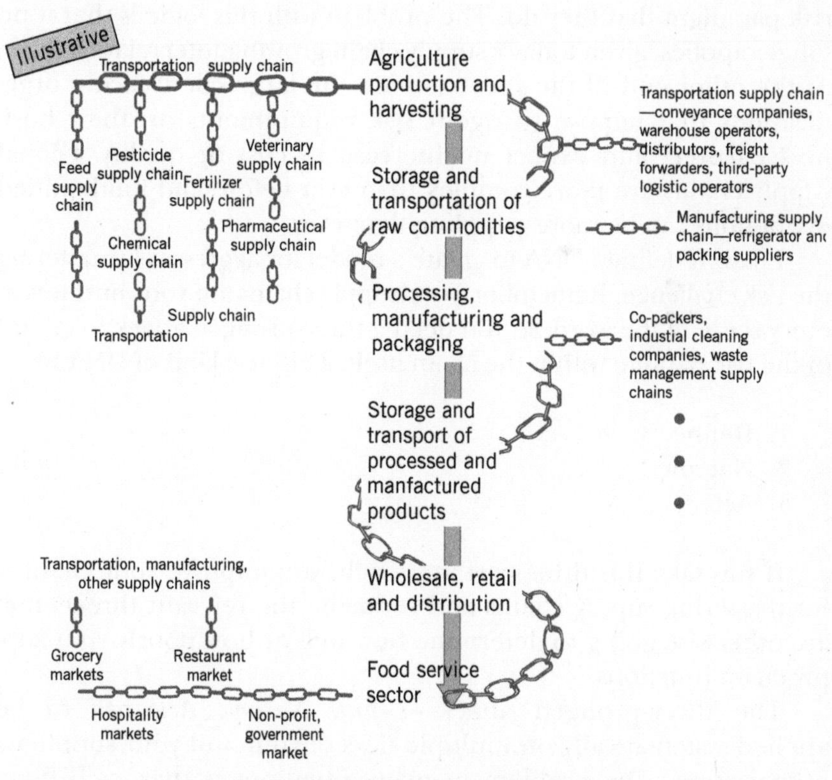

Exhibit 4.1 Illustrative Example of a Food Supply Chain

continuous nature of a supply chain. There's usually no beginning or end, so you have to jump in and decide which contributors are critical to your chain. This knowledge then defines your DNA.

There is another practical reason for organizational blindness. It is the significant day-to-day pressures placed upon global supply chains. The identification, quantification, and mitigation of risks is a detailed, tedious, and unrewarded exercise. If the risks never present themselves, some people will view this as a non-value-added or discretionary activity. It is too easy for a supply chain manager to say, "We will deal with that disruption, if and when it happens." Pressured to resolve today's issues to meet customer satisfaction metrics, many managers feel that since a company cannot prepare for all supply chain risks, and there are not visible rewards for a risk management plan, it is a better use of resources just to fix or respond to risk issues as they occur. These individuals and thus their companies hope that their first- and second-tier suppliers have the same risk paradigm that they do. The problem with this logic is that it no longer applies, given today's supply chain growing interrelationships. At the other end of the spectrum are the large client-facing organizations that impose stringent risk requirements on their business partners and expect no increase in cost or quality. Global supply chains are more complex than ever before and unidentified disruptions can be more crippling than ever.

I have redefined DNA to create a model for aggressively mastering the risk challenge. Remember, your supply chains are your business in every sense of the word, so you need a three-pronged attack to get rid of the risk parasite within the chain itself. This new kind of DNA is:

1. **D**efine
2. **N**arrow
3. **A**ct

If you take this three-part approach, you improve your chances for mastering supply chains and reducing the relevant threats that are otherwise going to determine how well or how poorly your supply chain functions.

The three-pronged attack—*Define, Narrow, Act*—has to be applied systematically on multiple tiers of your and your supplier's organization. The problem in many situations is that each function, department, segment, company, and even individual operates within their own defined universe. The solution to supply chain risk management is to be able to view the entire organizational chromosome and to then understand how your own universe fits into the larger picture.

The *Define, Narrow, Act* approach thus encompasses not only the immediate responsibilities and routines, but it is holistic and inclusive of every piece of the supply chain from end to end. The supply chain is everything in this regard, because it is the route along which everything—product, information, cash, and the risk parasite—travels. But while the supply chain is everything, it can also be nothing without a dynamic, effective, and insightful series of initiatives.

Everyone managing supply chain risk needs to develop an appreciation for the larger organizational universe. Once that is understood, then the collective priorities—*Narrow*—can be pursued. It is a form of multidimensional thinking. For example:

- Your personal dimension involves your self-interest and the priority of keeping a job, gaining career satisfaction, and keeping safe. Your personal dimension is based on judgments balancing requirements placed upon you with survival (in the job sense, for example). The question you ask in this universe is, "What do I have to do to keep my job?"
- Your functional dimension may involve as small a unit as a department or working team, or as large a unit as an operating segment. Your concerns here are with successful execution of functions and satisfactory completion of required tasks, given quality requirements, deadlines, and resources. This dimension views its piece of the supply chain in very primitive but necessary terms: "What comes in, what do we do with it, and what goes out?"
- Your universal dimension encompasses the smaller personal and functional dimensions but sees the entire organization and supply chain as a single organism with many different parts, one of which is the more limited view of those dimensions. However, an essential point to remember is that you need the universal dimension in order to develop a supply chain risk management program. Any program put into place without awareness of the universal dimension is going to be ineffective.

The majority of employees and suppliers operate in either the personal or functional dimension. This is only human nature; few people are able to adopt a universal dimension point of view without training and guidance and new metrics. The key point here is that:

> As long as your supply chain operators (employees, suppliers, subcontractors) have not adopted a universal dimension as their standard operating starting point, you cannot expect to manage, mitigate, and remove supply chain risk.

The irony is that a required point of view—an enlightened, expanded, holistic level of awareness—is counterintuitive. You will recall that one of the Laws of the Laws is that everyone operates in their own self-interest. Is it a contradiction to ask people to abandon self-interest and adopt a broader risk awareness?

In fact, adopting a universal appreciation of risk and its ramifications for everyone in the supply chain is the best way for each individual to protect his or her self-interest. If employees and suppliers do not adopt this higher level of risk awareness, their own jobs are threatened, perhaps directly.

Expanding the Risk Awareness Universe

The universal dimension is not simply made up of an organizational chart as well as customers on one side and vendors on the other. While the structural considerations exist and are important in any organizational initiative, the actual universal dimension has more overlay and less of the traditional hierarchy you associate with management science. The universal dimension is hierarchal in the sense that each step is mandatory or those following will fall apart. But this dimension does not contain individual ranks or reporting status. The hierarchy includes the following parts, with the first being required in order for the second to succeed, and onward down the line, as shown in Exhibit 4.2.

This structure has significant meaning within your organization. Any alteration in the first phase affects every phase that follows. So any realized risk or adjustment to your internal processes has consequences throughout the supply chain. It also helps explain why a supply chain risk strategy that manages risk only at a functional or resource level might be ineffective or inefficient. The following sections are an

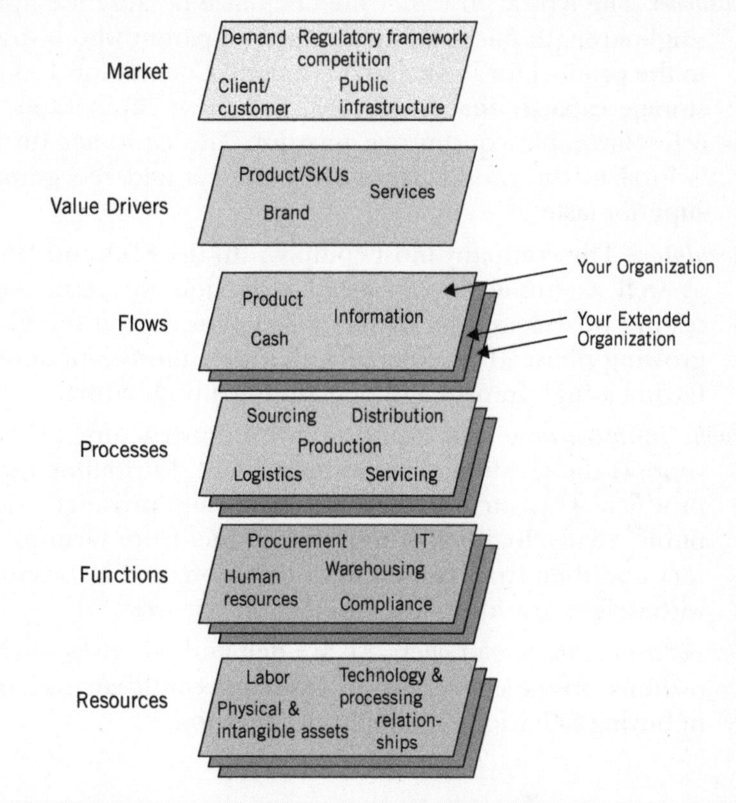

Exhibit 4.2 The Universal Dimension

example, based on the experiences of a real (unnamed) company and using a fictitious product name, to demonstrate this point.

"Joocie's Grape Juice" is a product that relies on raw materials from many different sources and is produced in several varieties. Its best-selling product is its 64-ounce purple grape juice. An analysis of its production process demonstrates how interrelated each of the supply chain elements has to be.

Market

Demand. How big is the market opportunity and what is Joocie's share of the market? The company sells $200 million worth of juice per year.

Customer. The typical customer prefers Joocie because it employs single-strength juice. This customer is a parent who is drawn to the product for its vitamin C content. Competitors lack the storage capacity that Joocie has, and these competitors use a less-favorable concentrate mixture. The customer further is loyal to the product due to its distinct and recognizably superior taste.

Regulators. The company must comply with the FDA and USDA as well as numerous localized irrigation interests, sugar testing processes, and quality inspection during the grape growing phase. The company identifies these functions as having a high impact and demanding a high effort.

Public infrastructure. A safe and secure infrastructure exists to support the creation, transportation, and distribution of the product. This includes the use of locally provided water, public roads, logistics of moving product from farm to factory and then from factory to distribution, and involvement with weighing scales within the delivery process.

Sample risks at the market phase. All are demand-side risks, such as product obsolescence, loss of customer confidence, change in buying behavior, or competitive position.

Value Drivers

Product/SKUs. The product is unique in the market. This is based on the use of a special fruit variety, which produces a distinct taste; the use of single-strength juice instead of concentrate; and the perceived health benefits of nonconcentrate.

Brand. The Joocie brand recognition is a primary benefit, but its vulnerability rests on continued access to this special fruit. Geographical diversification of the harvest is a good method for avoiding weather-related disasters or crop failure. However, a loss of even a portion of the total annual harvest would impact the primary distinction of the product, that of taste.

Sample risks at the value phase. One risk inherent in the method of production is the relationship between the company and its primary stockholder, the co-op that grows the special fruit. If this relationship were to fail or deteriorate, it could destroy the brand reputation in the market. This risk is mitigated because the co-op is a majority owner of the company's stock. Another risk is a pricing strategy change that results in a decrease in demand.

Flows

Product. This includes the flow of final product as well as the resources such crops, grapes, and packaging materials. It also includes the flow of equipment and supplies that support the creation, production, distribution, and retailing of the product. The special fruit is the key ingredient used by Joocie. It costs $100 per ton to grow, and between 5 and 15 tons are generated per acre. Harvest time is between August and September, averaging 30 days and using mechanical harvesting equipment. The harvesting cost is $50 per acre.

Cash. This is the flow of cash from the retailers and consumers, financial partners, retailers, and the organization. North American–harvested crops are sent to one of five U.S. plants, where they are inspected and weighed and then processed. The cost is $10,000 per day/plant during harvesting season, for a total of $1 million in all three plants.

Information. This is the flow of orders, inventories, shipment times, and all other relevant data that supports the creation and delivery of value in the market place. The company relies on the complete process of harvesting, processing, and distribution before Joocie arrives at its market. Along the way, numerous supply chain risks inherent in any agriculturally based product are present. For Joocie, this includes potential crop failure or damage, supply disruption, processing supply chain breakdowns or failures, logistics delays (due to labor disputes, failed inspections, or equipment failure), and emergence of new competitors). The company currently dominates the nonconcentrate market for this juice, notably with its 64-ounce size, which represents half of total revenue. Management has made the effort to identify supply chain vulnerabilities, to diversify its risks, and to focus on areas it considers have the highest impact and pose the greatest threats.

Sample risks at this phase. Disruption to any or all of the flow categories described above. Also includes inefficient or corrupted (for criminal purposes) flows.

Processes

Processes represent a further breakdown of the flows and include all activities that are executed upon to create and deliver value to the market and customers.

Sourcing. Crops received in each of the processing plants are stemmed, washed, and crushed, then put through a heat exchange process and finally filtered.

Production. This involves pressing the crop, adding pressing aids, and pressing once again. Output takes two forms: single strength and concentrate. Juice in both forms is piped to storage tanks until ready for mixing. The mixing process begins when juice is piped from storage. Citric acid, ascorbic acid, and water are added and the mixture is sent to the filler/capper equipment. Bottling begins with heating the mixture to 190 degrees. Two hundred eighty bottles per minute are filled and capped, and contents then cooled. Labels are applied, cases packed, and pallets are then ready for shipment.

Logistics. One of the most serious potential threats in the supply chain involves movement of product from warehouse to retail outlet. Disruption may come from a direct cause, such as a labor strike, or from an indirect cause, such as disruption to public infrastructure such as roadways.

Distribution. Joocie's distribution relies on a consistent provision of product year-round, even though the initial production step, grape harvest, occurs over a 30-day period once per year. Any disruption or delay in this short harvest window would disrupt revenue throughout the remaining 335 days per year. Thus, distribution relies on an orderly and smooth harvest and initial processing of the grape crop.

Servicing. Joocie relies on many sources, including farmers in ten states, expert factory employees during the initial and final processing and bottling of the product, and provision of raw materials. The most vulnerable of the raw materials is the special fruit varieties themselves, which have to be harvested in a once-yearly late-summer window and could be partially lost due to unusual weather or disease. In addition, ascorbic acid comes primarily from suppliers in China. If this supply was cut off or any kind of contamination occurred, the entire Joocie product line could not be marketed. Ascorbic acid enables the product to reach vitamin C levels desired by the customer and required by the government. Chinese companies ship to a Long Beach, California, warehouse. Any disruption in the shipment logistics, in quality control of the ascorbic acid, or in physical environment of the Long Beach container yard or warehouse would prevent Joocie from meeting its full market demand.

Sample risks at this phase. Inefficient or mismanaged processes leading to delays or disruption and eventual brand and/or financial loss.

Functions

The function phase represents the organizational hierarchy that is used to support the creation and delivery of value to the market.

Procurement. Joocie involves several raw materials, which have to be procured from many sources. These materials include the special fruit variety (500,000 tons per year); 64-ounce bottles (provided by one supplier); bottle caps (from three suppliers); ascorbic acid (95 percent of the world supply comes from China); labels (at least three sources); citric acid; water; corrugated cardboard; and shrink wrap (all of the last four raw materials are readily available). Grapes are grown in three locations (Washington, Michigan, and New York), diversifying the risk of natural hazards and crop failure.

IT. The company relies on its ability to control processing from farm to factory by carefully monitoring volume of crop, heating and cooling, and bottling. This all relies on internally designed supply tracking as well as logistics support and tracking of inventory up to and including retail outlets.

Warehousing. Joocie and its raw materials rely on adequate supplies of difficult to find ingredients, notably the two most vulnerable: the special fruit variety and ascorbic acid. This is a particularly sensitive risk vulnerability, especially for the time that raw materials are warehoused before being added to the final mix, because ascorbic acid relies on a regular supply and logistics chain from China to Long Beach, then to warehouse, then to Joocie's plant.

Human resources. Joocie must maintain relationships with its shift employees and their unions; include ongoing safety and quality assurance training programs; and ensure adequate human resources to continue the high production volume of 10,000 cases per shift (80,000 bottles).

Compliance. The company deals with numerous regulatory agencies, including local irrigation districts, USDA and FDA federally, inspections of plant processes, and highway weighing stations. These are considered high-importance and high-effort aspects of the Joocie supply chain.

Sample risks at this phase. Loss of critical functions causing delays or disruptions to the critical supply chain processes, flows, and value.

Resources

Labor. Joocie requires two shifts per day, each eight hours. 10,000 cases are produced per shift.

Technology and processing. Joocie relies on continuing to apply both technology and processing, the most notable being its exceptional storage capacity for single-source juice products. This provides Joocie with much of its competitive edge, so it is essential to maintaining its supply chain. Its enterprise resource planning system supports the material sourcing, production, and inventory management process by providing the smooth flow and integration of critical data to all participants within the supply chain.

Physical and intangible assets. Among the most important are the storage tanks and heating/cooling equipment, harvesting machinery, and bottling plant capability. The most significant intangible asset is the brand and reputation; Joocie dominates the market due to its single-strength product (competitors use concentrate), long-standing reputation for superior and unique taste, and lack of product failure in its history.

Relationships. The co-op that grows the special variety fruit is the majority stockholder in the company and thus represents a key relationship at every phase of the supply chain. Other key relationships include those with employee labor unions, retail outlets, and providers of ascorbic acid.

Sample risks at this phase. This phase, by far, is where the greatest number of vulnerabilities reside. Samples of vulnerabilities at this phase include labor strike, part shortage, transportation disruption, theft of materials, technology failure, deterioration of quality, or environmental hazard.

This detailed analysis of one hypothetical product demonstrates that *all* phases of the organizational universe contain risks and, more to the point, all of those supply chain risks affect the entire process. If the grape harvest fails, nothing else can occur. If the supply of ascorbic acid is cut off, the product cannot be marketed to its primary consumer (parents). If the processing plant equipment fails and juice can no longer be heated and cooled, then it cannot be safely bottled, distributed, and sold. If an FDA inspector determines that plant conditions pose a safety threat, the whole process shuts down. If a labor strike prevents moving product from plant to store, no revenue can be generated. In other words, by performing a detailed analysis of the supply change, it is easy to see that any single point of failure has the potential to bring the entire process to a grinding halt. For this reason, you need to analyze in detail the full scope of your supply chain and all of its components, from farm to factory to store. This means you need to identify *all* of your supply chain surroundings if you expect to know your business—beginning with the first phase of the universal dimension: the market and clients.

Know Your Business—Know Your Surroundings

Remember the advice from "The Laws of the Laws"—the lumberjack at ground level sees only a grouping of trees. But up in a helicopter, his world view is greatly expanded. This is what you need to do in order to comprehend the full world of supply chain risk; you need to see the big picture. So moving from the personal and functional universes up to the universal dimension is part of expanding your own knowledge. The existence of the smaller universe type is not a flaw, it is a reality. But by keeping these in perspective, you free yourself to move to the higher awareness level.

Effective supply chain risk management requires not that you focus only on the functional stages of the supply chain, but that you also understand the threats and vulnerabilities relevant to your extended supply chain—the market, value drivers, flows, processes, functions, and resources that make up your organization.

Supply chain managers typically focus on the when and where: Who does what, when, who checks for quality, how does material or information get passed along, what are the deadlines, and how much does it cost? This functional view is widespread, as explained in the previous section. But it is not exclusively a problem within the rank and file. Management's traditional measure of success in the supply chain involves a very narrow view as well. If you get it done cheaply and with relatively low defects, you succeed. If you can achieve a record number of days without an accident, you get a framed certificate. If your shift is faster than the other shifts, you get a free lunch.

Applying this mentality to supply chains in most organizations, the same mentality rules. Even in the information or service business, the supply chain involves movement of data rather than of raw material through to finished product. The data starts out raw; it is managed and sorted; and a final (perhaps more useful) summary is produced at the end. The supply chain, whether involving physical material, data, or other forms of information, is always going to be subject to the same kinds of risk parasites. Some supply chains are more vulnerable than others, but no two are ever going to be the same.

So the important aspect of changing a management style and mentality is to *define* the business value footprint and relevant threat triggers, such as natural hazards, and threat agents, such as people and their motivations. This may involve internal sabotage by a disgruntled employee, theft, infiltration and sabotage by an aggressive competitor, or simple negligence. Next, the change is subject to the process of *narrow* or communication of priorities. It includes detailed, action-oriented messaging to everyone involved in the supply chain. This includes the markets you serve, sources you depend on, and the operations that create value (this may involve anything from packaging of a final product to design of an information output). While you cannot control many threats that can disrupt your operation (e.g., hurricanes, earthquakes, political instability, pandemics, or terrorism), you can set risk priorities. You can *act* to identify and measure relevant threats and vulnerabilities. Those that can be prevented require a specific series of controls and process-specific changes to mitigate or eliminate the most relevant single points of failure most likely to occur. Those you cannot control are subjected to a different series of actions. These can include diversification of plant, process, and management in safer areas. Why hold your most essential supply link in hurricane-prone regions of the Gulf Coast? Why not move at least a portion of that operation north to safer territory?

The essential change that you need to enact to protect your supply chain develops from a progressive and comprehensive understanding of the range of threats, relevance and impact of the exposure, and creation of risk priorities. This must extend beyond the immediate environment and include the extended supply chain. Today, virtually everyone relies on multigeographic supply chains, often international in character. At one time, DNA was simple because you had a less-complex and volatile limited market and operational environment. Today, international supply chains make DNA far more complex, so risk priorities have to be expanded to address the realities of a global economy and organizational operating environment, market, and risk paradigm.

The extended supply chain includes market dynamics (opportunity), sales drivers (demand environment), product creation (innovation environment), building and assembly (production environment), materials and products (suppliers), and customers (service environment). In the case of Joocie, these three areas are easily defined:

- The demand environment relies on unique taste, nonconcentrate product and health benefits.

- The innovative environment is unique in Joocie's case, because the company has exceptional storage capacity and it can produce single-source juice; competitors all use concentrate because their innovative environment prevents them from competing in the same venue.
- The supply environment relies on many products that are widely available. Its two most important dependencies are on the Concord grape harvest and ascorbic acid.

The customer environment is primarily that of parents who want to provide products to their families with acceptable vitamin C levels, exceptional taste, and brand recognition.

The Keys to Your Risk Kingdom

The key questions to be addressed in identifying the DNA of your risk paradigm are:

- •Knowing that there are an overwhelming number of threats, how should you and your organization determine which threats are most relevant to your supply chains and, if realized, would result in the greatest impact?
- How do you and your organization better understand, monitor, and manage the risk from these threats to their supply chains?
- More to the point, how do you define those threats and vulnerabilities to the universal dimension of the organization and address issues beyond the functional universe?

These are profound questions because they are the key to effectiveness in supply chain risk management. A point to realize and remember: The vast majority of supply chain risk management programs, whether initiated from management or elsewhere, address only the known functional issues and do not address the larger universal issues such as interdependency risk. In practice, few people are even aware of the universal dimension, so how can they be expected to design a program that takes the entire organization into account?

Just as you need a super microscope to have any hope of ever viewing human DNA, your supply chain risk (and its reliance on the process of *Define, Narrow, Act*) has to be viewed, and continuously re-reviewed, through a macro-threat lens. In other words, it is not going to be effective to broad-stroke risk as a single issue to be addressed. The historical and static approach (insure against specific risks, delegate and transfer to suppliers, vendors, employees or even customers, or simply pretend they don't even exist) is not going to work. You need to pick apart the entire DNA of the risk parasite and destroy its effectiveness, remove it, or neutralize its destructive force in minute detail.

So, while you need an expanded view of the level of threats, you also need a very detailed strategy to attack risk, weaken or destroy the parasite, and fix flaws in the DNA. The paradox of supply chain risk management, as I said earlier, is everything but it is nothing. Now we can expand this to observe that solutions are big, but they are also small. In the context of how problems have to be addressed and fixed, the paradox has very real meaning, and observing these seemingly contradictory attributes can be instructive once you appreciate the need for the two parts: universal appreciation of the problem, coupled with the microscopic solution base from which you begin. Where you locate your suppliers, production facilities, and distribution centers directly affects the degree of threats and vulnerabilities at the process, functional, and resource phase.

The issues are addressed with recognition of several limiting factors. These include at the very least:

- There are simply too many risks to name, and you can't see them all or even know about them all. The tendency is to try and categorize the infinite number of risks only to realize that the cause, effect, and relevance to an organization are unique.
- Some events cannot typically be controlled through risk management and the opportunity is too great to pass up. In these instances, you can only take steps to minimize the danger through comprehensive disaster recovery, internal mitigation, diversification, and expediting the recovery, resumption, and restoration efforts.
- You may be able to model risk, but do you have the data to estimate probability? If reputable historical or actuarial data are not available, are you able to calculate maximum or estimated foreseeable loss?

- Have you set up a risk-conscious culture (RCC)? For example, Joocie analyzed its entire supply chain and identified primary vulnerabilities. Sensors and education were implemented along the way. Have you addressed the three critical e's—empower, enable, and educate?
- Systems for threat monitoring can do a lot to reduce or even eliminate a finite number of risks in the risk universe. But it is cost and time prohibitive to address them all (and does this information get fed into the supply chain reconfiguration process); you can only prioritize your preventive, responsive, and mitigating steps through the process of DNA (*Define, Narrow, Act*).
- Your *functional* universe (operating environment) needs to be reviewed afresh as it is relevant to where you innovate, design, source, manufacture, distribute, and service.
- Your understanding of risk has to be expanded to include threats (adverse activities), threat agents (people) within multiple environments, impacts (big versus little and systemic versus isolated), interdependencies, and options (it is always nice to have all of your data but in the end you need to make decisions—sometimes with limited data, short time frames, or crisis distractions).

Here are some short examples of how these criteria are applied:

- A review is going to bring you to a stark realization concerning supply chain risk. Like Rip Van Winkle, we have all been asleep for the many years. Thomas Friedman described this dilemma in his book *The World Is Flat: A Brief History of the 21st Century*. Before the expansion of the global economy, credit meltdown, terrorism and piracy threats, and greater likelihood of pandemics, we survived in a cozy little world with limited boundaries, competition, and social interaction (beyond our own borders). This is not a new phenomenon. In the United States in 1900, over 90 percent of all citizens lived in small towns or on farms and had never traveled more than 20 miles from their birthplace. So before airplanes and automobiles, the country was a vastly different place and so were the supply chains that supported everyday life. These chains were vertically integrated where one manufacturing company was responsible for all aspects of sourcing, production, logistics, and service. This also meant that the risk universe was equally small. With expanded access and urbanization, a multitude of new and unexpected threats slowly moved into the scene.

- The same thing has happened again 100 years later, coincidentally starting at the turn of the new century. Global competition added more choice; more suppliers, logistics and configuration options, customers, and volatility. Expanded threats, which deploy with lightening speed, globalization of virtually everything, and political unrest in many places at the same time all threaten the supply chain of every organization. As part of this new paradigm, which, not unexpectedly, is very much like the degree of change from 1900 to 1950, is the increased rapidity of change. Consider, for example, that the majority of once domestically dominated manufacturing has moved offshore. Very little in the realm of textiles and even food production occurs in the United States any more. In fact, the entire U.S. economy has transformed and is currently made up of primary services (79.2 percent), followed by industrial (19.6 percent) and then agricultural (1.2 percent). Contrast that to manufacturing-oriented nations such as China and Russia where 49.2 percent and 41.1 percent, respectively, of their economy is industrial.[2] Virtually complete dependence on overseas supply chains means that old thinking about how to manage risk has to be abandoned entirely. The corner store no longer exists and, consequently, locally provided goods have also disappeared and are now replaced with a complex of internally sourced goods of all kinds and services as well.

Your Operation's Complete Footprint

Before you can put the DNA approach into action, you need to map out the *organizational genome.* This is the complete footprint of your operation.

Today, this has changed just like everything else. If you are like most organizations your business footprint is distributed across multiple geographies, time zones, and cultures. The markets you serve may be in South America and Australia, you might innovate in the United States, and source heavy machinery from Germany and raw materials from South Africa. Your suppliers might source from China and Vietnam. Your distribution centers may be in Latin America and Singapore and you might service customers out of India. In other words, your organization has most likely evolved into a far more complex ecosystem than it and its competitors were a half-century ago, or even a decade ago.

Is evolution a good thing? In the sense of how operations have expanded their competitive stance, profitability, and technology, of course it is. But along with that, the genome has also evolved, meaning today's organization is more fragmented and has more vulnerabilities than in the past. Your supply chain is unlikely to consist of a straight line from demand through operations and delivery systems. Today, supply chains involve a complex of many concurrently operating lines that cross over one another, present infinite weak links, and present opportunities for single points of failure in many points along the supply chain. The expansion of your organizational genome with all of its positive attributes has made you far more vulnerable and, at the same time, has complicated the process of supply chain management in every aspect.

At some point, someone made a conscious decision—we hope—to select the multitude of locations where business is conducted, not only in terms of markets but also in terms of manufacturing, vendors, and transportation. The selections made in the past, once discovered to be aggravating supply chain risk or not solving existing problems, must be changed. Upon discovery of existing risk, the obvious solution is to undo the poor decision and replace it with one that solves the problem. This can be as simple as relocating sensitive facilities to safer neighborhoods, or reducing the very size of the supply chain to avoid and eliminate specific threats. We'd all like to believe that marketing, sales, operations, procurement, human resources, IT, and other functions collectively designed the supply chain. However, if you are like most of us, this is simply not the case. The decisions that were made to move warehousing to a high-crime district might have been driven by some individual incentives, probably related to reducing overhead. The decision to relocate a distribution facility from New York to hurricane-prone Florida probably had more to do with state tax incentives than with strategic location ideals. And locating a customer service center in India was a response to competitive ratings more than it was to a perceived desirability of making this service remote in and of itself. In other words:

> The complexity of your organizational genome is directly related to and caused by the geographic and geopolitical environment in which the new creature has to survive.

Do you know what threats are most relevant to the remote resources engaged in your supply chain processes? More important, do you know what the impact and consequences will be if you experience a break in your chain at these various points? This is a profound question because of its implication. I am confident that a majority of management today have not only failed to consider this question, but also do not know the answer. The following are some aspects to consider in designing and researching an intelligent answer:

- *What markets do you serve, and where are your customers?* Where do you innovate, source, manufacture, distribute, and service customers? Where do *they* source? What and whom do you rely on to create value in each of these processes? Is it local or on the other side of the world (in other words, is your supply chain complex or simple and what do you own or not own)? Do you know what risks are relevant to each of these major processes and functions that you depend on to create value? The trend to source locally and sell locally is gaining support in order to reduce the organization's exposure to energy, commodity, foreign exchange, and regulatory volatility. The flows of information, cash, and product are dependent on everything about your business environment. It is safe to assume that the driving force behind the existing complex supply chain was profit. So remember as you analyze this issue: Short-term gain is long-term pain.
- *Operational and logistics risk.* A matter as simple as scheduling for transportation and delivery can actually become quite complex when you consider the start and stop lead time demanded by the market. So just as identification of your markets is essential before you can even begin to understand the risks you live with, tracking your operational risks is also going to involve questions of location, sourcing, and control.

Supply risk is an example of specific risk at the resource dimension in this supply chain risk universe. The once simple process of purchasing materials, finding a vendor, and service sourcing has to be expanded to acknowledge the very real risk-prone nature of the international and multilayered supply chain.

Your Action Plan

In order to control supply chain risk, you need to map the business genome and apply the concept of DNA (*Define, Narrow, Act*). Change can occur at any time, with or without notice, impacting the supply chain at multiple levels.

- The markets served, product mix, and business flows of products, information, and cash
- The strategic supply chain network design (the long-term view, including optimal placement of distribution centers to customers, and manufacturing to suppliers)
- Master supply chain planning (the shorter-term view, usually seasonally or trend-driven)
- Operational supply chain planning (daily logistics, manufacturing, inventory view)
- Supply chain support systems (enterprise resource planning and customer or supplier relationship management)

For example, the strategic supply chain network design can quickly be interrupted by an unexpected event. This was the case when a fire and explosion in 2009 destroyed PCS Nitrogen's complex at Point Lisas, Trinidad.[3] As a result, the organization's strategic design of the supply chain network had to be reconfigured (expected long-term outage) to operate without this critical facility. Other sources had to be identified and the trade-offs (proximity of facility to customers, storage facilities, logistics cost/alternatives) that occur at the strategic network design level had to be reevaluated and reestablished.

These strategic considerations have to be analyzed with the entire supply chain in mind. As shown in the extended Joocie example earlier in this chapter, each and every portion of the network is interconnected; risks created or ignored in one section have direct and potentially serious consequences in the rest. At the strategic network design dimension the flows and processes are at the greatest risk. The Point Lisas fire and explosion created many understandable priorities for individuals, including whether family members were safe, whether workers still had jobs, and other personal but narrow issues. In the planning functions at an executive level, supply chain managers need to create strategic initiatives that take in the entire organization, the complete supply chain and its components, and in every respect, a focus on the collective priorities of the organization.

These collective priorities are set by the customer in the same way that the supply chain itself generates from the demand view. In addition to the immediate concerns for safety and reduction of further damage, organizational management needs to consider the disruption of the supply chain after a large-scale disaster; how its recovery program remains responsive to ever-emerging and new risk environments; and how stakeholders (including employees) can be brought into the risk-conscious culture in a very real way. This has to include at the very least the strategic action plans required in response to disasters (as well as to smaller, localized threats). So to integrate the entire organization into the risk-conscious culture and to develop concrete response plans and preventive systems, the internal educational effort should be aimed at demonstrating layers of the supply chain. Thus, a box packager on an assembly line needs to understand how improper packaging or incomplete product arrangement can lead to contamination up the supply chain, and how that threat impacts the whole organization. Someone taking shortcuts in processes, for example, has to be enlightened. The sentiment that "If I get caught I could lose my job, so I have to be careful" has to be replaced with "All of the risks in the supply chain threaten everyone from customers on through to the factory floor, including my job, so I cannot afford to take shortcuts." This reeducation, or the comprehensive strategic configuration, affects all phases of the supply chain.

Besides the management of supply chain risk at the strategic network configuration level, such as supplier proximity to manufacturing plants and distribution centers to customers, the seasonal or short-term needs can also dramatically change the risk profile. This includes holiday peak periods for retailers and cyclical demand for the energy industry. For example, in November 2008, U.S. soybean exports rapidly increased because of plunging shipping costs, forcing a modification to the supply chain master schedule planning. Risk may also come in the form of temporary extended disruptions, such as when Venezuelan President Hugo Chavez ordered the government to take control of all rice processing plants in the country, including those being operated by U.S.-owned Cargill. Nationalization in 2007 also resulted in the seizure of plants and offices belonging to Mexican cement giant Cemex.[4] At the seasonal level, the process dimension is at greatest risk. And at the tactical day-to-day level, the DNA and risk profile are constantly changing. In most instances, these are manageable everyday disruptions that require tradeoffs and quick decisions. However, these types of events once isolated to the local process or function now can potentially have massive repercussions up and down the supply chain. The delays or disruptions can quickly evolve from hours to weeks. In February 2007, Ford Motor Company's operational planning had to be revised when workers at a Ford assembly plant were sent home because of a parts shortage resulting from a railway workers strike. At the tactical level, the process dimension is at greatest risk.

The single point of failure was different in all these examples, and so were the impact and the response. And that's just the point. The impact is not derived from known sources or by definition; the sources of those impacts must be unknown and unplanned.

How do you change the supply chain network? The solution is by optimizing cost, speed, convenience, service, and sometimes quality. Risk will likely become more controllable as a result. Exhibit 4.3 is a sample of the initiatives and construct that have arisen, as a result of business change, over the past decade.

The supply chain risk management journey begins by understanding the root cause of risk parasites and their creation, methods of infection, and likely progression. To battle the risk parasite, contain it, and minimize the impact, you and your fellow stakeholders must better understand:

- What drives change to the business model and the supply chains that support the execution (provides better lead time, enabling you to better anticipate change, react, and respond to new risks).
- What initiatives and constructs are created as a result of the need for change (to better understand how the strategic design of the supply chain network might be impacted).
- How change gets implemented and the impact to the supply chain master plan, operational plan, and systems critical to the support of the supply chain (e.g., supplier management, customer management, enterprise resource planning).

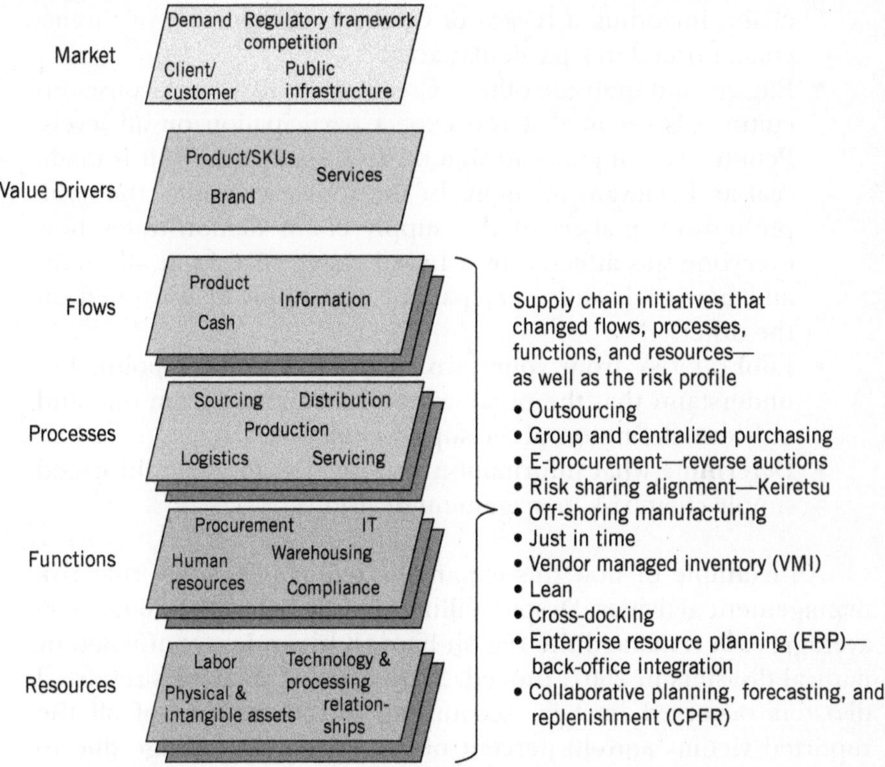

Exhibit 4.3 Recent Supply Chain Initiatives That Dramatically Changed the Universe and Risk Profile

Your action plan has to include these action steps:

- Create a supply chain risk strategy, including risk identification, measurement, mitigation, financing, monitoring, and continuous assessment and improvement.
- Avoid "boiling the ocean" by clearly defining boundaries, meaning the need to prioritize supply chain risk activities according to clearly *defined*, *narrowed*, and *acted* (DNA'ed) risk paradigms.
- Understand the DNA of the supply chain before you try to manage risk. Do the forensics. Measure the impacts before you set the priorities.

- Conduct a profile of relevant risks to the extended supply chain, including a review of the aggregate impact of threats concentrated in a particular area.
- Engage and motivate others. Creating the RCC (risk-conscious culture) is essential if you expect participation on all levels. People are not going to sign on to a concept until it is made real and relevant to them. In the Joocie example, the comprehensive analysis of the supply chain demonstrates how everyone was affected by a broad range of risks at all levels, and how each and every part of the supply chain relied on the other.
- Look at risk from your own functional vantage point, but understand that the organization can operate from one and only one definition of the supply chain.
- Determine what information you needed to make informed supply chain risk management decisions.

An example of how this expanded action plan must rule risk management activities: Despite falling slightly below the 2000–2006 average, Asia remained the region hardest hit and most affected by natural disasters in 2007. Indeed, 37 percent of the year's reported disasters occurred in Asia, accounting for 90 percent of all the reported victims and 46 percent of the economic damage due to natural disasters in the world.[5] Data from the Centre for Research on the Epidemiology of Disasters showed that, in 2008 alone, more than 230,000 people were killed and more than 47 million were affected by two major disasters in Asia—the earthquake in China and Cyclone Nargis in Myanmar.

This situation points out the complexity of supply chain risk today. It's easy to become overwhelmed with the complexity and magnitude of managing supply chain risk—yours and that of everyone you depend on. But the horses have left the barn; the global interconnected and interdependent market arrived and change is now more frequent and constant than ever before. But how has the organization's supply chain risk management framework (policies, organizational structure, processes, technology, tools, procedures, education, and training programs) adapted to this change? From my vantage point, the management of global supply chain risk has not kept pace with this change and, consequently, supply chain risk management is woefully behind the times. We all have to take a deep breath and begin the endless journey.

Notes

1. Kris Hudson and Wilawan Watcharasakwet, "The New Wal-Mart Effect: Cleaner Thai Shrimp Farms," *Wall Street Journal*, July 2007.
2. CIA Factbook, 2008 estimates.
3. "PCS Nitrogen Blast May Cost $Millions," Carolyn Kissoon, South Bureau, *Trinidad & Tobago Express*, March 14, 2009.
4. "Chavez Sends Army to Rice Plants," *BBC News*, March 2009.
5. Centre for Research on the Epidemiology of Disasters (CRED).

CHAPTER 5

Law #4: In Supply Chain Risk Management, Demand Trumps Supply

Human history becomes more and more a race between education and catastrophe.

—H. G. Wells,
The Outline of History, 1920

From Avian (H5N1) to Influenza A (H1N1), Roche's Supply Chain Is Exposed to the Flu

In 2005, a new risk paradigm emerged—the threat of a global pandemic. Unlike prior catastrophes, such as hurricanes, cyclones, tsunamis, and earthquakes, this threat was capable of causing multiple, simultaneous events and impacting everyone around the globe. National governments' and the World Health Organization's (WHO) concern rapidly increased as the number of cases rose by nearly 29-fold in the three-year period from 2003 to 2005. Of greater worry, this strain of influenza (Avian Flu H5N1) infected those between 10 and 29 years of age, averaged a median death rate from onset to death of eight days, and caused death in more than 40 percent of those infected.

As a result, governments such as the United States decided to stockpile masks, sanitizers, and Roche's Tamiflu anti-viral drug. Overnight, the capacity and throughput of critical suppliers' supply chains were seriously challenged; in

(continued)

the case of Roche, demand outstripped supply by approximately four- to sevenfold (Roche's production capacity was being ramped up from 27 to 55 million). Initially, the U.S. government requested 200 million courses of treatment, or 2 billion Tamiflu capsules, however, they were not the only organization seeking to increase inventory. Anticipating even greater demand, Roche's management decided to aggressively increase its global production capacity from 55 to 400 million courses of treatment per year.

Demand would redefine Roche's strategic supply chain network design, especially since the United States demanded its need be filled domestically since the likelihood of a border shutdown in a pandemic was inevitable. James Irwin, Roche product manager, stated, "We have to provide adequate supply if a pandemic were to occur. We realize that global supply chains would become inoperable without the people." He added, "Our management did not hesitate—everyone agreed, capacity and throughput were nonnegotiable." In addition to the need for governments and public health organization stockpiling, Roche believed that demand would increase further as commercial organizations sought to establish their own stocks of critical supplies. After all, the government and WHO deployment strategy was to blanket the infected cluster where the outbreak occurred, not to provide treatment for the entire population or most private organizations.

Critical infrastructure providers, health-care workers, and first responders were included in the initial deployment, but the stockpile was designed to treat only 25 percent of the U.S. population (versus France's strategy of 70 to 75 percent). We all believed that most would see the need: airlines, private transportation companies, mining, metal, and energy organizations, financial institutions, and a host of other commercial organizations. However, this was not the case and the impact to Roche exceeded production capacity and inventory. It appeared that one of the golden rules of the supply chain applied to this scenario as well—do not carry excess inventory. By 2008, three years after the initial concern, less than 4 percent in the financial services industry and 1 percent of overall industry had decided to stockpile the drug. Demand again trumped supply and, to make matters worse, pandemic fatigue began to set in. Again, Roche was faced with a significant shift in demand and the difficult decision to reduce production capacity was made. However, in April 2009 as production was being ramped down, a global outbreak of Influenza H1N1 (commonly referred to as

Swine Flu) occurred and demand rocketed; however, few were prepared. Inventories of essential medical supplies such as masks were depleted and supplies of Tamiflu rapidly decreased as the U.S. government and WHO partially distributed the drug. Market demand again drove supply and rapid replenishment again would be needed. Volatile demand challenged supply chains around the world. The lesson to be learned from this story is that supply chains are extremely vulnerable and volatile, because demand is ultra-sensitive to both perceived and real threats. As a rule,

- Supply chains are a slave to demand.
- Extreme volatility in demand over short time intervals will have magnified effects not just to supply, but to the strategic design of existing supply chain configuration.

Supply chains are a slave to demand. Exhibit 5.1 shows that as demand unexpectedly increases, as in the Tamiflu example, supply is depleted. In response to the shortage of demand, the organization will seek other means to fulfill and move supply and, as in this case, the network design of the supply chain will be permanently altered. Roche had to identify suppliers from around the globe to fill the stockpiling need, especially since several nations insisted on local production.

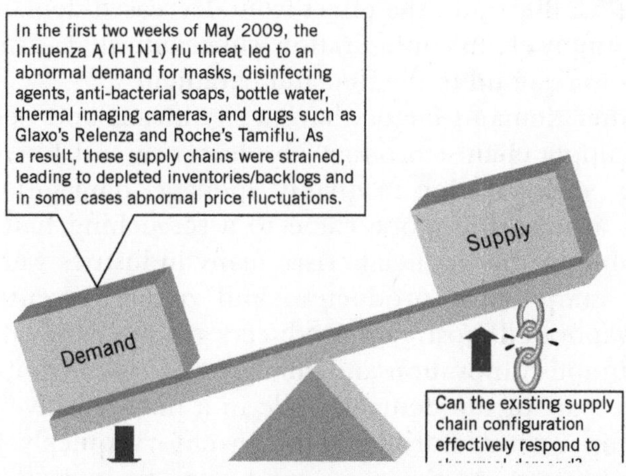

Exhibit 5.1 Increasing Demand Drives Supply Shortages and the Need for Increased Production Capacity

Extreme volatility in demand over short time intervals will have magnified effects not just to supply but to the strategic design of existing supply chain configuration such as the location of key suppliers and warehouses. On the other side of the equation—if the threat is there and the market and/or customers lose confidence, then demand evaporates. Industries subjected to discretionary spending, such as hospitality, food services, and travel, are usually the first to suffer (along with the supply chains that support these industries). May 2009 was the height of the spring tourism season for Mexico, where an estimated $13.3 billion of foreign currency is injected into the economy each year (the third-largest source behind oil exports and migrant worker remittances).[1] However, demand evaporated faster than anyone could have imagined. Mexico's finance secretary estimated that the initial flu outbreak cost the Mexican economy at least $2.2 billion.[2]

Cisco also learned this lesson in the first quarter of 2001 when it was forced to write down $2.25 billion in inventory. The abnormal growth came as a result of the Internet hype and as a result Cisco placed big orders for communications chips, optical lasers, and subassembly boards from its suppliers. Deteriorating economic conditions and the dot-com implosion caught Cisco by surprise and demand fell off the charts.[3] This was the case for many suppliers during the global economic slowdown of 2008 and 2009. But as we will see in a moment, it's not just about the supply of materials. Exhibit 5.2 illustrates the effect from decreased demand. Once again, the supply chain configuration will be adjusted—usually permanently—to respond to the demand paradigm.

Two other demand factors have a significant and permanent effect on supply chains: product obsolescence and loss of confidence (e.g., deterioration in quality, spoilage, damage). As most economies around the globe came to a screeching halt in 2008 and 2009 due to the financial crisis, many industries were forced to rapidly ramp down production and reduce inventories. As demand evaporated, upstream producers got stuck with the inventory. Continuous innovation and changing consumer buying preferences are part of the demand cycle in a time-sensitive business such as chip manufacturing. Static inventory quickly becomes obsolete inventory. As the economy begins to recover and customers return to buying product again, much of the inventory in the warehouses will be considered obsolete because of changing

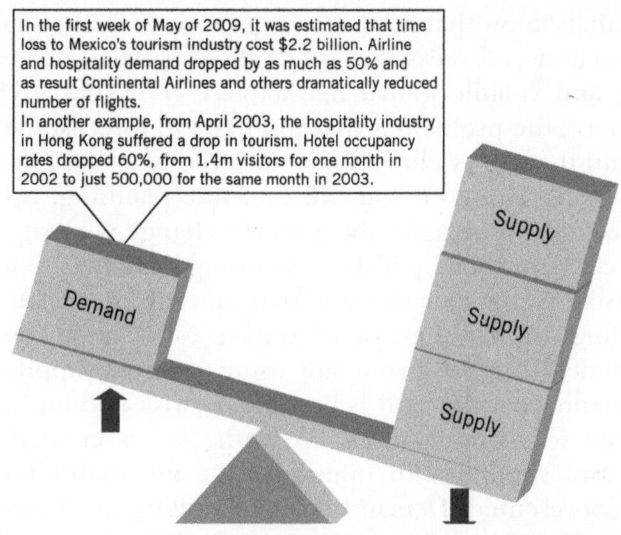

Exhibit 5.2 Decreasing Demand Drives Excess Supply and the Need for Decreased Production Capacity

customer buying preferences (who wants an old version of the iPod?). The demand for innovation does not slow with a slowing economy.

How could organizations better manage supply chain risk by beginning with a demand view? What is needed to provide this demand view? As we suggested, organizations will need to establish greater visibility and transparency into the supply side of the chain. Just as critical, organizations need to begin the demand view by establishing visibility downstream—into the demand side. Specifically, the organization should establish a clear line of sight and better understanding of:

- Customer and demand
- Market trends (local and global) and competition
- Distribution and sales channels (ability to get the product to the market)
- The external environment and the macro economic, cultural, and geopolitical factors that impact it, such as a financial downturn, protectionism/trade restrictions, and geopolitical instability

Of course, some events cannot be planned for. Even professional analysts know that it is becoming more difficult, if not impossible, to accurately forecast market or client patterns in a constantly changing and volatile global marketplace. For supply chain risk management, the problem is that you need to forecast the demand cycle within the supply chain, but you cannot forecast how risks will affect demand. However, you can do some planning, by diversifying supply, remaining agile (be ready to change your supply chain network configuration quickly), providing trusted suppliers with greater visibility into your demand data and inventory patterns, and by spreading risk. (In the case of tourism for a single country, this is not practical, but for a company using multiple supply chains to meet demand, that demand is best met by risk pooling[4] and planning ahead for contingencies.) A push/pull is created between demand and supply (with operations in the middle) whenever a threat is presented. Demand rules by pulling on the operations and supply. The demand-based question is "What is the effect of an event on demand/forecasting? What are the organization's upper and lower thresholds before the stress forces reconfiguration of the upstream? What customers and relationships are most important? What consumer regions, facilities, and raw materials are affected?" On the supply side, the question is quite different: "What is the effect of an event on inventory/supply?" (See Exhibit 5.3.)

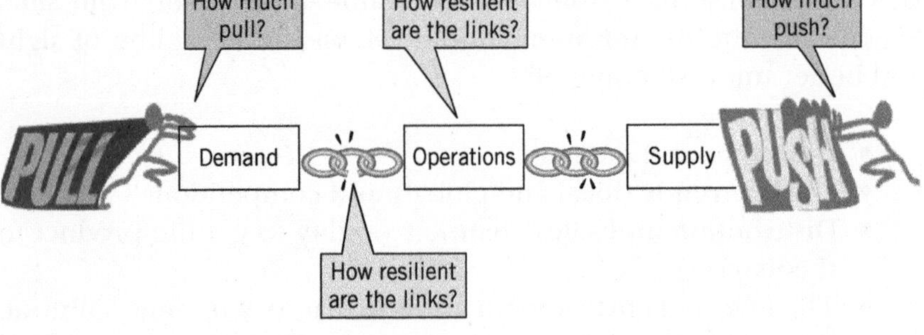

Exhibit 5.3 Demand Pull and Supply Push

While the Mexican government could do little to mitigate its risks for the tourism business (decreasing demand pull), some future steps can be taken, including heightened preparedness and improved public information and communications (supply push). How would the government instill confidence again in the market? Who are the most critical customers and what are the most important products—the ones that define success? What incentives would be needed to accelerate demand? Are supply chains nimble enough to respond and adjust to a geographical shift in demand, let's say if a particular state in Mexico were to recover faster than others. In another example, in November 2008, terrorists attacked Mumbai, India's major business and tourism center, focusing on a train station, Jewish center, and luxury hotels where foreign visitors stayed. The death toll was 195, with another 300 injured. Many local business owners began feeling the effects immediately and estimates were that tourism levels would not return for at least a full year.[5] Lessons can be learned from this example as well as others on how to best restore confidence and expedite the return to normalcy.

Business and government learned this valuable lesson after Hurricane Ivan devastated the Caymans in 2004 and Katrina hit New Orleans and surrounding communities in 2005. Tremendous public and private sector efforts and expense went into restoring confidence and reestablishing brand. The battered supply chains were reconfigured and, in some instances, new players emerged. Of course, the platinum standard case is the way in which Johnson & Johnson was able to reestablish its position as market leader by effectively managing the 1982 Tylenol contamination. Its supply chain configuration changed as packaging requirements became more stringent and the need for reverse logistics to support a recall had to be more efficient. Once again, demand drove supply. In all instances, to more effectively and efficiently manage supply chain risk, the organization had to gain better insight into the markets and customers they serve, as well as the geopolitical environment.

The point of view about the origins of business activity affects how you define and design a supply chain. This inevitably also affects how you address supply chain risks, if at all. Mandyam M. Srinivasan best summed up the role of the supply chain in relation to demand in his book *Streamlined* (South-Western Educational, 2004):[6]

> The role of the operations strategy is to give the enterprise the ability to cope with changing customer preferences. [Supply chain] products and process should be designed to promote strategic flexibility

The relationship of demand in the food chain to operations and supply exists in the context of the supply chain universe, as described in Chapter 4. The illustration has been modified slightly in Exhibit 5.4 to show the relationship between the layers in the universe and demand, operations, and supply. Contrary to popular practice, the process of managing supply chain risk begins at the top, not the bottom. Alignment is necessary to ensure efficient and effective allocation of critical and scarce supply chain management resources.

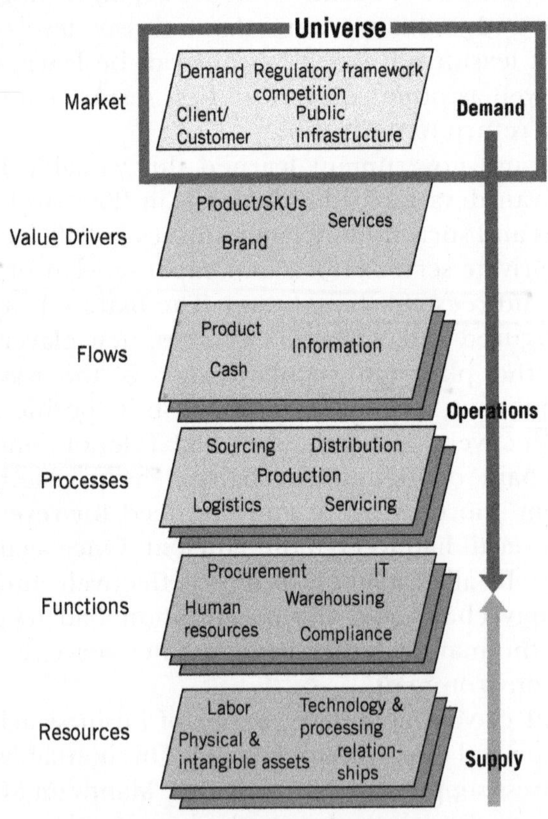

Exhibit 5.4 Supply Chain Universe

For example, a salesman who spends 100 percent of his effort and time placing orders and meeting with customers will believe the organization is in the business of selling product (flow layer). A clerk in the mail room might make a convincing argument that the organization is in the business of receiving, distributing, packaging, and sending mail (process layer). And an accountant will surely view the organization as existing to pay bills, make payroll, prepare financial statements, and document transactions (function layer). In other words, all the workers have their own organizational view, and none is entirely accurate.

This makes the demand side of the supply chain exceptionally vulnerable. For example, when Microsoft issued the new Xbox on Black Friday after Thanksgiving, known as the biggest sales day of the year, several disasters occurred all at once. First of all, Wal-Mart's Web site went down and spokeswoman Amy Colella blamed a "higher than anticipated traffic surge." This led to an operational or supply-side failure, depending on your point of view (which led to the shortage, production, or sourcing issues?). Given that this was such a large shopping day, it seems obvious that just such a surge should have been expected and steps taken to manage it. The Wal-Mart site gets about 22.8 million hits per month, so the November volume growth would be expected. Another problem grew from the fact that demand far outpaced supply. On Amazon.com, the limited Xbox supply sold out in 29 seconds. It seems that Microsoft underestimated the demand, and its retail partners only made matters worse.

The design of an effective risk management system requires that the supply chain be completely understood, from source to final destination. This of course must start with an understanding of demand. This requires that everyone in your organization:

- Questions their own basic assumptions about the business
- Broadens their organizational view (scope) to include not only the immediate environment but also the remote environment of suppliers, vendors, and even customers
- Evolves this level of comprehension to understand where demand comes from
- Engages all parties, upstream and downstream, to collectively manage risk

Everyone's Customer

How can you understand your supply chain if you don't know the origins of demand? Yes, this is a rhetorical question, but what is the answer? You cannot, of course. Just as various people in your organization have different opinions about why the organization exists, everyone has an equally limited view of the *customer* and how a customer base generates a specific task or routine, and how that customer creates the origins of demand itself. This is especially true when analyzing customer and market segmentation.

So where does one turn to better understand the demand side of the equation? You must seek input from the experts—internal and external marketing, branding, business development, the sales force, industry analysts, and the distribution channel. Soliciting their input provides greater visibility into the market, clients, or macro-geopolitical issues; this is key and one could never have too many sources of data. A company comes into existence because someone recognized a demand that was either not being addressed or that they could better address. Ask the question to these experts: What's the value proposition that distinguishes the organization and its products from the competition? What's the unique value that the organization provides? As a result, an organization can grow and add the pieces that make up the entire structure. Like an ant hill, an organization is extremely busy and complex; every segment has its own series of tasks. Few of the ants understand how the entire hive operates, and the same can be said of a large, complex, multinational company.

But it is not enough to simply know about the problems on the demand side. The effective supply chain risk manager also needs to define tolerances and deploy risk policy, protocols, and techniques, such as demand monitoring, simulation, situational analysis, stress testing, and trigger-based risk assessment. Controls need to be put into effect to prevent disasters due to simple mistakes. For example, in April 2009 a misprint on a cereal box led customers not to the Golden Temple of Oregon, which markets 13 varieties of cereal, but to a phone sex line. The problem affects demand directly as customers associate poor controls over the boxing and proofreading of text with questions about the contents as well.[7]

In response to the corporate decision not to stockpile Tamiflu, Roche decided to design a new service whereby it would be responsible for managing the product inventory and absorbing the expense. This created new supply chain capabilities and products when it was acknowledged that organizations would not stockpile drugs. Roche then created a custodian service that allowed it to sell futures of the Tamiflu product.

Remember that the customer, whom a majority of employees never meet and whom few even understand, is the original driver of the entire supply chain; and all of the risks that your organization faces as part of that supply chain are traced directly back to the customer. A simple typo on a cereal box raises doubts and affects a company's reputation; a country's entire tourism industry is decimated by a senseless act lasting only a few days. So many influences, internal and external, help the risk parasite to strengthen its hold on the host supply chain; and with a devious twist, the parasite disguises itself so that few of the individuals who operate the supply chain are aware that the risk parasite is at work. It is as though the risk parasite has deadened its host's nerve endings so that it is not aware of the damage being done.

The customer, however, is the guiding force behind the supply chain. Although the customer is the end receiver of the supply chain's output, that does not occur in isolation. In a study by AMR Research Inc., 100 companies were asked to identify their greatest supply chain risk. Much to everyone's surprise, the supply-side disruption was not the number-one concern. Demand-side risk dominated the list of concerns specifically in the area of increasing demand errors. Demand volatility was cited as the greatest challenge (second was logistics and materials, followed by supplier relationship concerns). Many organizational theories about supply chain appear to view the customer almost as an afterthought, a final stage in a *supply-driven* force. In other words, if this were true, the genesis of the entire supply chain effort would exist on the sourcing of materials and creation and manufacturing side, and the customer is simply the individual buyer or user. When confronted with this suggestion, most businesspeople will naturally dispute the claim. However, they may continue to act as though this were the case. But consider the case of Saks Fifth Avenue, whose supply consists of designer clothes and higher-end luxury items. You would think that the Saks customer base would be insulated from a recessionary trend, but the company discovered that demand continues to rule. After revenues were feared to slow down during the 2008 holiday season, Saks cut prices as much as 70 percent and the customers responded, flocking to pick up bargains. This strategy was by no means supply driven. It all had to do with identifying what the customer (demand side) would respond to.[8]

Any management that continues to believe it controls demand by how it manages supply is living in a dream world (remember the VCR, typewriter, and tube-based TV?). Just ask anyone at the top of Kodak if you think supply is where the paradigm begins. It is a flaw for anyone to believe that demand can be controlled or changed, or that it can be directed by supply. This is true, at the very least, in a healthy economy. In cold war–era Russia, the complete disintegration of the economy included the complete lack of ability on the part of the customer to create demand. When President Richard Nixon visited Moscow, he saw a long line of people waiting patiently, so long that he could not even see where the line led. Through an interpreter, he asked a woman at the back of the line what they were waiting for. She replied, "I don't know, but whatever it is, I hope they don't run out before I get to the front."

In the case of Communist-run Moscow, there was no demand and almost no supply. This also led to a complete breakdown of the economy, to the extent that the ruble lost much of its value and the state began paying workers in bricks. This led to a comment by one worker: "They pretend to pay us and we pretend to work."

Sad Russian examples aside, the point remains that believing an organization can create or control demand is flawed thinking and so is setting contingency levels on a guess or hunch and not by collecting customer expectations. Recognizing this flaw also addresses many of the supply chain threats that every organization faces. If you do not understand how your organization operates, you cannot understand the risk parasite, and you cannot neutralize or remove it. So many of the more serious supply chain risks are unavoidably related to whether or not the customer will buy your product or the product of a competitor and what will cause abnormal shifts (and how quickly you can recover). This core reality has to be taken down the line all the way to the supplier. This is true not only to the edges of your warehouse's loading dock or the container at the closest port. It must go all the way to the location where raw materials are brought into the process and first put together. This is why an enlightened supply chain risk management initiative (which *begins* with the customer definition/paradigm) has to *extend* to the remote plant, the early stop in the supply chain. If that step creates or builds a risk into the process, the threat is carried all the way through. So a decision maker who has never visited that remote factory or farm is not going to ever understand how the risk parasite enters the host and grows. The CEO may be perplexed upon realizing that the risk parasite exists, but without having any idea about how to remove it. So the internal education process has to begin with a definition of the origins of demand, and an expansion of knowledge all the way to your boardroom.

Building Your Demand-Based Strategy

As you forecast where your organization is going in the coming fiscal years, you have to be concerned about the financials: revenues and earnings as well as maintenance of cash flow and availability of financing. These are big issues, but you also have to worry about the less-obvious but equally important issues of risk. Specifically, risks that threaten the customer perception of your company and its presence in the market are risks you cannot afford to suffer. It is becoming obvious to anyone in an organization with a complex and multi-track supply chain that the organization cannot do it all. So how do you even begin to think about understanding and managing the complex issues of supply chain risk management? Here are some recommendations based on the priority of the demand view:

- *Always begin by gaining insight into the customers, distribution, market, and external environment; then prioritize.* The first step in risk management is always to identify, then prioritize (and measure). This applies in all situations. In your organization, priorities in risk management identify the highest priority first and go from there. For example, demand may quickly shift the source of supply if the sentiment in the local geography leans toward protectionism or turning inward. When 10 percent or greater of your working population is dependent on a domestic-based industry, as was the case in France according to Francois Roudier, the director of communications for the French Carmakers Trade Association (CCFA), the likelihood of abnormal demand shifts became quite real. Your organization's products and services must be rationalized and prioritized as well.

- *Look for ways to effectively partner with suppliers to focus better on the demand end of the chain.* Begin managing supply chain risk by immediately developing effective initiatives to partner with suppliers. Define the demand element and then adjust the supply side to make it a better fit. This partnership should include understanding customer and market expectations of quality; development of specific and strict quality standards; methods for monitoring production to ensure that the standards are met; funding by your organization to help suppliers comply with these new requirements; and finally, reaction standards in case of noncompliance. Given the fact that you are addressing a range of risks that are virtually life-threatening to your organization, the reaction to noncompliance—especially if your organization has funded change—is to immediately cut off a supplier and find one that will work with you. The customer expects that these steps are taken to prevent such basic problems as product contamination; realistically, though, the essential and basic steps are not taken.
- *If you decide to transfer or assign risk to a third party, you have to include an overlay of direct oversight of the demand risks that are most important.* If you do not, then you cannot provide assurances to your customers that all is well. Many responses to the introduction of high-priority risk involve simplistic solutions. For example, why not simply transfer or assign the risk to your suppliers? In other words, just tell your suppliers that they have to shore up their own supply chain. Even if you fund an improvement in the supply chain, however, it is not going to work unless you also impose direct oversight. In this regard, you are responding to the demand element by making sure that quality control moves all the way to the far end of the supply chain. You cannot trust anyone else to care for product quality as much as you, and the real stakeholder in your company must protect these interests even if that means putting inspectors and quality control monitors in the suppliers' factories. The demand expectations are not limited to just quality. Your customers, and/or the market, could place greater emphasis on the environment (green), security, speed of innovation, or performance. Understanding the organization's unique value proposition in the context of the market or client is critical.

- *Remember that geographic proximity affects your organization's effectiveness.* In small business, it is fairly easy to operate a single retail store, but owners realize upon opening a second or third outlet that the more remote the location, the greater the complexity and thus the risk management problems. Consequently, the growing remoteness of the supply chain also adversely affects the customer, too. Employees don't open up the doors, thefts occur, merchandising is not done to your specifications, and overall revenues and profits never match the first store where you have your finger on everything. The same is true for multinational major corporations doing business on several continents. The farther away your supplier and manufacturer, the more problems you are going to have. This is one example of how your organization does not create or manage demand; rather, demand manages and directs your supply chain. If demand expectations are not met, customers are going to go elsewhere.

  This brings up a serious question concerning high-priority risks like product contamination: If you cannot afford to have the risk carry through to the customer, can you afford to rely on suppliers that are so remote? The trend today is beginning to reverse from the past two decades and shift to source and sell locally. In this recent past, a frenzy of offshoring was touted as promising cheap labor and higher profit margins. But the reality has been quite different. The costs of labor, transportation, warehousing, insurance, and lean everything have grown to levels not imagined when the simple cheap labor motive first arose. But all of these costs are only the obvious ones. A far greater cost occurs in the risk arena. That risk parasite has grown as a geometric progression along with the supply chain. In the old days, when you had a single supply chain and it was easily understood, the risk parasite was an infant. Today, it is engorged and huge and is expanding at least as rapidly as your supply chain itself. The point of crossover has already begun. Organizations are looking at the equation once again, and questioning whether the totality of costs and risks is really economical when the supplier and manufacturer facilities are so far away. This requires a revisit to the question of whether to "reverticalize" and "deglobalize" your supply chain.

These trend reversals could end up revolutionizing your supply chain and, essentially, eliminating the more serious supply chain risks altogether.

Try this: Go to your next meeting with the decision makers in your company and make the statement, "I think we have to consider moving our supply chain closer to home, and perhaps even negotiating alternative agreements with factories closer to home." Of course, do your homework first, evaluate the impact of foreign exchange, labor, trade credit, and energy volatility. The reaction of surprise and denial should be expected, but once you make your case, the concept will begin to make sense. Crunch the numbers and attempt to quantify your logistics risk exposure in specific terms, such as:

- The time element required for assembly, warehousing, shipping, transfer, storage, and assembly.
- Shipping costs when relying on other-side-of-the-world suppliers.
- Maritime insurance, including business interruption (be sure to specify the differences between insured losses, uninsurable loss exposure, and copay/deductible limits, in addition to the premium costs).
- Potential cost from piracy, terrorism, and losses at sea, expressed as an actuarially calculated uninsured loss versus likelihood of the occurrence.
- Efficiency savings through local control, elimination of second-tier manufacturing risks and logistics, faster access, eliminated transportation costs, and improved just-in-time delivery and control (remember the Best Buy example).

- The risk of organizational identity loss may be one you cannot afford to take. In this case, you have to consider shrinking your supply chain. Your ultimate argument for bringing your supply chain closer to home—in fact, shrinking it geographically—has to be based on the very real threat that your product identity will be damaged, possibly forever, due to a single point of failure in a remote factory. This may occur in a second-tier manufacturing plant in a country removed from your first-tier supplier. The consequential damage to the organizations's brand caused by third parties extends far beyond the local audience (remember the opening story in Law #1). Negative news travels fast in today's Internet-enabled society: Web sites, social networking, blogs, e-mail, and instant messaging. The problem may arise at the farm or plant level where the individuals responsible have no concept about how their cost-cutting decisions will affect your end-user, and they might not care, especially if they are impoverished and struggling to make minimum margins to put food on the tables of their own families. The fact is, the more remote your supply chain, the greater the threat of catastrophic reputation loss and resulting product distrust.

- Shrinking your supply chain does not solve the problem by itself. But the proximity of the supplier to your central headquarters is a crucial determining factor in how well you are able to partner with companies, develop and install improved standards, and monitor processing. It is also more likely when factories are close to home that the necessities of product excellence will be appreciated by employees on the factory floor.
- *Develop relationships only with first-tier suppliers; ban second-tier manufacturing to offset the threats.* Demand to know, to see upstream. Empower the trusted suppliers and provide them greater visibility into your forecasted demand. The threat of product quality decline is greatly reduced when you prevent second-tier agreements. You may impose very strict requirements on your supplier, only to discover that the supplier is acting as a middleman for the manufacturing being performed in yet another country—a great opportunity to delay. In this case, you have no direct control over quality and you place yourself at great risk.
- *The solution is to impose a new rule on all of your suppliers.* They must manufacture your product on-site and under your supervision and quality control standards, subject to frequent audits. Using multiple-tier manufacturing in even more remote countries only exposes you to far greater risks. The highest priority has to be getting control of the first stage in your supply chain, improving direct supervision, and, for many organizations, shrinking the geographic area of the entire supply chain itself. Develop migration plans for sole-source or long-lead suppliers.

- *For example, Coca-Cola—with its sterling name identity and reputation worldwide—discovered in 2007 that two-thirds of its suppliers in China failed audits.* The failures related to nonproduct issues such as workers' rights and the environment, but also involved problems with packaging and ingredients. These failures included 255 out of 371 suppliers. Of these, 48 were "significantly" out of compliance and presented "a critical risk to operations." Another 144 were moderately out of compliance, and only 63 were reported as guilty of minor issues.[9]

This report did not specify how many of those high-risk audit failures included potential ingredient and packaging dangers, but it makes the point that imposition of strict quality control standards and follow-up audits is essential to protect both the supply chain as a whole and to curtail logistics-based risks. With corporate responsibility reporting on the rise, there will be more negative reports like this.

Volatility in the Demand Cycle

The Mumbai tragedy makes the case that you do not control demand. The loss of life augmented by the loss of the tourism revenue flow makes this an expensive lesson in the nature of demand. When you think about demand, you are likely to make the same mistake that virtually everyone makes, *assuming* that demand is the constant and everything else is the variable. In fact, volatility in the demand cycle causes chaos in your supply chain because demand is where everything begins. Demand is both volatile and brittle. For example, the instantaneous evaporation of Mexico's tourism industry in the first week of May 2009 demonstrates how delicate and vulnerable demand can be. Another example: Eastman Kodak made a huge mistake in the 1990s by assuming that old-style film, a product the company had always dominated, would continue to be its main revenue source. The company was so committed to what it supplied that it failed to notice that demand was shifting toward the digital camera market. Kodak entered the market far too late and has not caught up, even 10 years later.

In a sense, Kodak was applying a defensive strategy based on dominating the supply side. Unfortunately, it is easy to become smug when you are the leading supplier of a product no one wants any more. The blinders an organization decides to wear make it easy to go on the defense, assuming that the primary job is to make sure no one else gets a piece of your market. What these organizations miss is that, in fact, it is not the supply side where the threat exists; it is a shrinking or disappearing market that poses the problem.

Supply chain practices have dramatically evolved over the past decade from what I refer to as "defensive" to "offensive" practices. Kodak, for example, focused on maintaining a high-quality product and did not recognize the causes of its competition actually moving into new markets. These competitors went on the offense by recognizing that demand was shifting rapidly, was highly volatile, and was likely to respond to an aggressive marketing of new products. Meanwhile, Kodak remained on defense, smugly dominating its film market while the market itself shrank every year.

The problem with a defensive strategy is largely based on changes in demand. However, defensive moves often are counterproductive throughout the supply chain, especially when management imposes a traditional profit-based rule: "Lower your costs, and deliver more profits." While on defense, supply chain managers were asked to do "whatever it takes" to increase the velocity of information, cash, product, and, of course, profits. Because they were also expected to significantly reduce costs year over year, take out excess inventory, labor, facilities, and other significant overhead, and the whole issue of supply chain risk management was a distant priority or was forgotten entirely. When you are on defense, you cannot forecast future threats or their solutions.

There is a solution to the problem, in which profits can be grown while supply chain risk management is actually improved. UPS (United Parcel Service) presents a good example of this worthwhile goal, and the key is to focus not on supply but on demand. Over the past two decades business has achieved a 34 percent reduction in the ratio of inventory to sales—an estimated reduction of more than $4.6 trillion, according to Scott Szwast, Director of Marketing for International Freight for UPS. Scott also commented that "while accomplishing such an incredible achievement, this so-called 'leaning' of the supply chain has pretty much removed the margin for error. When you are in such a lean supply chain, changes in transportation capacity or any of the other supply chain flows can have immediate detrimental effect on your business"[10] By the very nature of this definition, it was difficult to advance any proposal to increase the supply chain risk investment. As these changes were taking place, the seeds of offensive supply chain practices were planted. The offensive strategy shifted the focus from the supply side of the chain to the demand side. UPS designed its products and deployed the technology to meet the diverse demands of the global marketplace. For many organizations, the new era has already begun and as a result they are using the supply chain as the differentiator. The scope of supply chain practices has moved upstream to demand-side marketing, innovation, and, most important, customer linkages. The efficient and integrated flow of information, product, and cash from the demand side, as illustrated in Exhibit 5.5, is what drives change.

This shift in strategy recognized the volatility of the demand cycle and took an offensive approach to fixing a company's revenue-to-earnings ratio, while continuing to aggressively attack risk in the leaner supply chain.

The shift is often counterintuitive, because so many managers have come up through a management philosophy preaching that demand is fixed and the real key to control is to improve supply. But in what can be called the *innovation chain*, companies have begun to realize that demand is anything but fixed and the need to work more closely with the marketing group is essential in defining

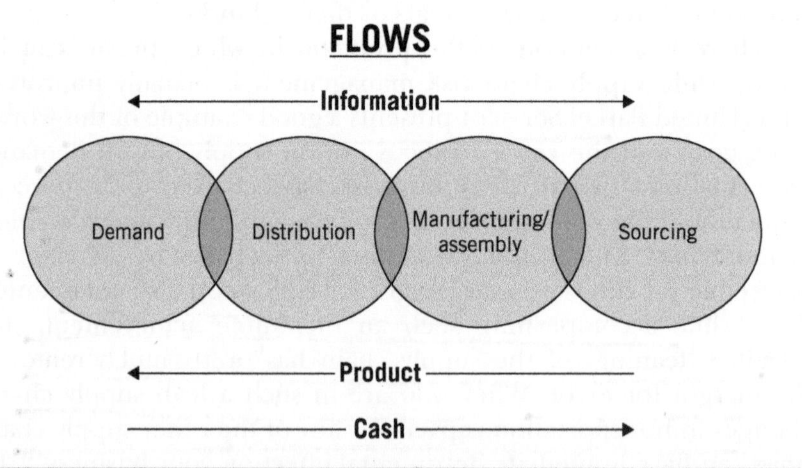

Exhibit 5.5 Supply Chain Flows

and communicating risk expectations. The demand is volatile, fragile, and changeable. It can also change instantaneously.

Technology-based organizations such as Cisco, Microsoft, Nokia, and Apple have embedded the innovation chain into the natural flow of supply chain practices, processes, and design. As they capture market and client knowledge, the product design is tweaked and the supply chain modified; this is the epitome of an offensive strategy focused on demand. Retail giants like Wal-Mart, Neiman Marcus, and Tesco, and consumer product companies like Nike, have evolved their business strategy from partitioned, functional silos to dynamic strategies that are invariably customer driven. The offensive supply chain optimizes the financial model, is driven by innovation, and radically improves customer intimacy. This entire trend is not only part of evolving in terms of organizational points of view in a changed world, but also is part of a generational shift that is social, cultural, philosophical, and financial, to name only a few of its aspects. The new world in which we are functioning has been variously described as "post-9/11," "new century," and "global." It doesn't matter how this is characterized; the point is that organizations are slowly realizing that the new approach is dynamic, strategic, and advanced. As always, change brings along new risks and makes old risks more complex. The protocols for all risk are impacted in so many ways, many of which remain invisible; and that is the crux of the problem.

So the question remains: Do offensive supply chain practices include a comprehensive risk construct and well-defined protocols? Are these market and client-driven chains risk-aware, agile, resilient, sustainable, and intelligent? Unfortunately, the defensive supply chain rarely includes these risk attributes, and it is even questionable that the appropriate practices are included in the offensive strategy. In other words, the defensive supply chains were strung together with many brittle links, leaving both the link and the connection between links vulnerable. Too many of the leaders in organizations today are like those twentieth-century French generals trying to fight World War II with World War I tactics; it took the Germans only six weeks to defeat France.

Market and Client Factors to Consider

Within the broad range of processes of the complete supply chain, your task is to identify the relevant threats and priorities. Thus, you do not have to be overwhelmed by a vast threat universe; it can be quantified and defined in terms of likely risks, cost factors, and internal priorities. The prioritized threats can be effectively managed by the following five initiatives.

Exposure Diversification Some threats can be so severe that they could bring an entire organization to its knees. This is especially true if you rely on a single source for essential supply chain processes. This means solitary vendors, transportation routes, warehousing, or delivery/storage facilities. Again, looking at the issue from the demand lens, the severity of some threats takes the issue to the top of the priority list.

To offset this threat, diversification of the supply chain itself protects your organization against the most likely, but impossible to control, range of threats. For example, poison seeping into raw materials used in manufacture in a single plant effectively shuts down the entire product line. A port strike or sinking of a large container ship in the *only* narrow channel port you rely on prevents goods from reaching your market, perhaps indefinitely. A warehouse hit by a hurricane, tornado, or earthquake may demand not only days but weeks or months to get back to full operations. All of these serious threats can be mitigated by development of two or more alternate supply chain routing systems. This may cost more, but compare that to the cost of living with the threat; also consider the cost you incur when the disaster occurs. Your organization cannot rely on a single source for essential deliveries, diversifying the supply chain among multiple vendors, transportation routes, warehousing, and delivery/storage facilities eliminates the threat of a total disruption.

An example of where lack of diversification affected an outcome was on 9/11, when World Trade Center building #7 collapsed. While building #7 was not hit by the planes that struck buildings #1 and #2, the fire that broke out led, seven hours later, to that building's collapse as well. A change in the original design of the building shifted loads so that the overall load was tied together through a series of columns. So when one column failed after several hours of exposure to fire, a vertical progression of failure moved from the seventh floor up to the penthouse. After this, the weakness spread horizontally and, finally, the entire building collapsed. Conspiracy theories aside, the combination of a multi-hours fire, limited resources to fight the fire, and structural flaws in the building's design resulted in its collapse. In a symbolic sense, the collapse of WTC #7 accurately described how many supply chains are constructed and where the flaws come from—most notably by failing to diversify exposure.

Transfer and Sharing Plans Many risks can be transferred to vendors or suppliers, and for many this represents the ultimate solution. But what happens if the transferred threat is realized on the other end. Remember, supply chains do not start and stop in your immediate organizational universe but extend from the farm to the store. So you cannot transfer 100 percent of any risk to a vendor overseas. Remember the case of milk tainted with melamine? From the demand perspective, this was a true disaster. But how did it occur and why? The risk of narrowing profits was transferred to the dairy farmers, but they solved the problem by artificially boosting the nutrient reading by adding poison. In this case, the transferred risk created a *larger* and more deadly risk. When you take the demand perspective, the supply-based threats move into focus and solutions are more easily identified.

This reality leads to the sensible solution: sharing risks. You can ensure greater overall supply chain threat reduction by a series of steps in a shared-risk program. These include development of minimum quality standards, education, internal audit and enforcement, and fast reaction to lapses in the process. If your organization relies on products manufactured overseas, your supply chain risk is gigantic and your risk parasite has a ravenous appetite. That parasite is slowly eroding your organizational insides and you are not even aware of it—until you take firm and proactive steps to share the supply chain risks, from top to bottom and all along the supply chain.

In preparation for the 2008 Beijing Olympic Games, the Chinese government acknowledged the concerns among many visitors concerning food safety, along with other environmental, human rights, and terrorism-related risks. Rather than attempting to fix all of the food-related problems and address the risks with a single initiative, the Beijing Organizing Committee announced an initiative and a diverse committee to share response to both perceived and real threats. This committee included seven bureaus (notably the Bureaus of Health and Agriculture) and 15 members from the Centre for Control and Prevention, Association of

Food and eight foreign agency experts. This committee analyzed the supply chain of food and identified emergency response and prevention measures it needed to take to mitigate and transfer the risks.[11]

Extensive and Far-Reaching Audits and Enforcement of Standards Under the old-style traditional approach to risk management, an organization established rules for quality levels and expected suppliers to conform. It was only when a vendor violated one of those standards that any action would be taken; replacing a supplier would be an extreme step under this reactive form of management. Indeed, given the cost benefits of picking the most economical of arrangements, many risk managers in the past were either unwilling to enforce requirements or were not allowed to because of a solitary fiscal emphasis.

Today, it is no longer sensible to operate solely on the basis of working with the most cost-effective supplier. Your organization needs to set strict quality and performance standards and enforce them, or the entire supply chain is at risk of collapse. Given the probability that a once-domestic organization operates today in many international arenas, perhaps dozens of countries and depending on thousands of suppliers, your company can no longer simply assume compliance; it needs to become a threat reduction enforcement concern as well as a marketing concern. It is not a choice between economics of raw materials or customer service. The two are actually one and the same.

The previously cited Beijing Games preparedness plan included an extensive program for enforcement of standards. Issues addressed in the plan included food safety and security, delivery and vending inside and outside the park area, specific deliberate threats to food, and methods for dealing with foodborne illnesses.

Internal Education and Expanded Knowledge Base Chances are that many of your fellow organization leaders come from an old school of thought. In other words, they tend to view risk management as an intrusion into an otherwise smooth-running operation. They see the supply chain as something that probably works if you just leave it alone. Your task is to overcome this shortsighted organizational view and to move into a more enlightened arena of management.

This requires serious internal education, if only to get managers to begin thinking beyond the world that is merely visible. Those invisible worlds overseas and in small factories in third-world countries are just as important a part of the supply chain as the shipping and receiving department, customer service, or skilled sales force. The degree of expanded and enlightened organizational view that your organization instills throughout is going to determine how effectively you anticipate, define, manage, control, mitigate, and prevent risk. This is why the analogy of the risk parasite is so crucial in your efforts to spread the word about the range and types of threats you face. It is sad but true that many of today's best-educated managers (educated in the sense of book learning, anyhow) are like rural lads who have never been to the big city. They are quite sophisticated in terms of crop management, livestock feed formulas, and marketing of crops, but they have never been on a subway or in a taxi, so they really don't understand the big city and its risks or dangers. (And like the boy in the musical *Oklahoma!* they have probably never been in a building seven stories high or gone to a "burly-que" show.) So even the most sophisticated accounts manager, sales professional, human resources manager, or accountant may be quite skilled and sophisticated in the small world of their expertise. But they know nothing about the squalor, pollution, and power shortages of industrial China, the poverty of farmers in India, or the working conditions in Mexican factories. How, then, can they define and enact an effective risk management program? They cannot, and to overcome this short-sightedness, even the most educated executive needs to go through a reeducation process in which the real world is brought to that shiny mahogany table on the fifty-third floor.

Does this mean that the educated manager of today is ineffective? No, it does not. It does mean, however, that the knowledge base has to be expanded beyond the comfort zone most managers enjoy and opened up to the entire supply chain and not just the one existing in headquarters or even in a branch office.

Development of Disaster Recovery Plans The most effective risk management plan does need to consider the entire supply chain. Just as a general maps out strategy and tactics days before the battle and focuses on the importance of artillery and protecting flanks, lines of supply, and intelligence about the enemy, today's supply chain risk manager has to think like a general, anticipate the worst, and prepare today to win the battle tomorrow, to minimize casualties, and to use recon teams to find out what is lurking over the next hill. Think of internal initiatives (transfer, insurance, internal audit) as your risk management artillery, the force that *prevents* the risk from being realized at the beginning of the battle. Your flanks—those sides of your lines where you are the most vulnerable—are the unknown risks; and to the degree that you protect those vulnerabilities, you are far better prepared than you have ever been before. Your lines of supply (militarily speaking) are resources and the participation of your suppliers, vendors, and other stakeholders. And your education and knowledge base (not to mention the steps you take to improve and expand this base) are your organizational recon.

Military analogies aside, the point I am trying to make is that you need to develop a worst-case preparedness plan. This means anticipating the worst supply chain disaster and taking steps today to prevent it through supply chain diversification; deal with it through an extensive disaster recovery plan; and work from the worst-case scenario downward and outward. This means that by preparing for the worst you can imagine, you can then develop secondary preventive and responsive plans for additional risk scenarios. The worst case does not always occur, but a series of nearly-as-bad-case outcomes can just as effectively stop your supply chain in its tracks.

Positive and Negative Factors Impacting the Supply Chain

Every organization exists to create value, which should be the number-one priority and the reason for being in business. But is it? For some managers, value is just a marketing concept, an illusion to get customers in the door, a teaser without any substance. Inevitably, this cynical view leads to loss of customers and market share, so value creation in a real sense becomes essential for survival of the organization and for ensuring quality within all phases of the supply chain.

Applying the quality ideals of Six Sigma to the concept of value creation is a natural and sensible mix. This is one of the reasons that Six Sigma has been so popular and has been adopted by so many big companies and government agencies. Its benefits are apparent and its approach to problems (such as supply chain risk) is effective.

Acknowledge the first objective—create value and seize opportunities (otherwise your organization cannot continue to compete). Believe me, your competitors are eventually going to realize that creating value *is* seizing the opportunity. Your organization must remain competitive on all fronts—cost control, product quality, and service quality. The supply chain becomes the tool to accomplish these. Note that the descriptors in these (quality and control) are the essential purposes and attributes in supply chain risk management. Many think of quality control as a variation to cost reduction initiatives or internal controls meant to reduce defects. While these are essential elements, they are only the most obvious in a range of important risk-reduction requirements.

You can already see evidence of the evolving new attitude toward supply chain risk management, which has become the enlightened approach on many fronts. Reduction in total inventory levels, reduction in employee salary and benefits through outsourcing, and improved customer service levels have all been made possible by effective and efficient supply chain management. However, with each change comes risk, most often a multitude of different risks and not all visible. This is the reality of the new, leaner, just-in-time organizational model. You can reduce this year's overhead through outsourcing, but you have to be prepared to ensure that you're getting exactly what you expect from a cheaper source. And you can reduce inventory levels as long as you apply the science of improved supply and warehousing tiers to make sure the goods get to the shelves before the customer gets there. You can operate on a thinner internal staff, but you have to make sure that your control systems address likely threats within the supply chain.

Notes

1. "Peso Tumble, Swine Flu May Prompt Mexico to Tap IMF." Bloomberg.com, www.bloomberg.com/apps/news?sid=a1frueBejyV4&pid=20601087.
2. "Mexico Estimates Flu Cost Economy $2.2 billion." *Wall Street Journal* and *Associated Press*, May 5, 2009.
3. Larry Barrett, "Cisco's $2.25 Billion Mea Culpa." *Cnet News*, May 9, 2001.
4. The handling of an uncertain risk posed to or by a single person or investment by combining it with the same risk affecting a large group, which can be calculated. Source: http://encarta.msn.com/dictionary_701709476/risk_pooling.html.

5. Yaroslav Trofimov and Peter Wonacott, "Terrorists Paralyze India's Business Capital." *Wall Street Journal*, November 28, 2008; Sumit Sharma, "Mumbai Hotels, in Spotlight After Attacks, Struggle to Recover." Bloomberg.com, December 18, 2008.
6. Mandyam M. Srinivasan, *Streamlined: 14 Principles for Building and Managing the Lean Supply Chain.* South Western Educational Publishers, 2004.
7. "Cereal Box Typo Sends Callers to Phone Sex Line." *Associated Press*, April 2, 2009.
8. Vanessa O'Connell and Rachel Dodes, "Saks Upends Luxury Market with Strategy to Slash Prices." *Wall Street Journal*, February 9, 2009.
9. John Ruwitch, "Coke Says Two-Thirds of China Suppliers Fail Audits." *Reuters*, August 21, 2008.
10. "Risk Talk, Supply Chain: Risk and Responsibilities." WebEx, Marsh, 2008.
11. Melissa S. Hersh, "Preventing and Mitigating Contamination in the Food Supply Chain from Farm-to-Fork." Marsh & McLennan Companies, 2008.

CHAPTER 6

Law #5: Never Set Up Your Suppliers for Failure

Bad News Rolls Downstream

During the second half of 2008, 296,000 people throughout the world, mostly children, suffered kidney-related illnesses. More than 50,000 were hospitalized. There were 11 suspected deaths (3 confirmed), 60 people were arrested in China, and two people were sentenced to death. The cause was believed to be adulteration and subsequent contamination of milk and milk-derived products such as infant formula. Melamine, an industrial chemical, had been added to raw milk and/or animal feed somewhere upstream in the food supply chain. The health and social consequences were enormous, and so were the economic consequences from this single point of failure.

The Sanlu Group the largest dairy supplier in China, had been implicated and later found guilty of the adulteration. But the problem was not isolated to San Lu; 21 organizations were found guilty (but to a lesser degree), while economic consequences began to mount. Demand for Chinese-produced dairy products dropped as public confidence waned and 11 countries went as far as banning all imports of mainland Chinese dairy products. Supply shrunk as well, as authorities seized 2,176 tons of milk powder in San Lu's warehouse and recalled an estimated 9,000. The supplier of the protein powder produced 800 tons of the tainted mixture, which was eventually confiscated and/or destroyed. Traders, cattle farm owners, milk collection centers, and milk purchasers were also arrested and removed from the supply chain. Critical interdependencies in the supply chain began to evaporate, and as a result, an estimated two million Chinese farmers had nowhere to sell their milk, nor the means to support their dairy cows because of this single point of failure. The Chinese Dairy Association

(continued)

estimated that sales fell by 30 to 40 percent. Fonterra, one of the top dairy companies in the world and 43 percent owner of the San Lu group joint venture, was forced to write off its estimated 2005 investment of $107 million. On September 24, 2008, Fonterra recognized an impairment charge of $139 million against the carrying value of its investment in San Lu, 69 percent below its previous carrying value. The write-down included product recall costs, liability claims, and the impairment of the San Lu brand (this does not include an estimated $700 million in compensation claims). San Lu went into bankruptcy on September 27, 2008.

The ramifications to the supply chain network design were even more widespread as suppliers and distributors were redefined and/or replaced. Mengniu-Arla, a joint venture between Danish/Swedish cooperative Arla Foods and Mengniu, halted production. Mengniu, milk supplier to Starbucks, was replaced by Viatsoy and suspended by Kentucky Fried Chicken. The Tokyo headquartered Lotte Group recalled Koala's March cookies in Hong Kong; Unilever recalled its Lipton milk tea powder from Hong Kong supermarkets; Wellcome and Park 'n Shop as well as Dutch and Slovakian distributors also cleared their shelves of these products. Heinz recalled baby cereal in Hong Kong; France destroyed nearly 1,200 tons of poultry feed (Chinese soy meal); Vietnam recalled and returned 26 milk and dairy products imported from China; and Cadbury withdrew all of its 11 chocolate products made in three Beijing factories.[1] In November of 2008, melamine was discovered in eggs in Hong Kong and animal feed in China. More than 3,600 tons were either confiscated or destroyed.[2]

Supply Chain Risk Management Program

Are you prepared for this scenario and is your organization's supply chain risk management program robust, intelligent, and resilient enough to absorb a failure of one or more key suppliers? Does your enterprise risk management program include the monitoring and measurement of supply chain and supplier risk? If your organization is like most, then suppliers and material providers concealed behind your first-tier suppliers are probably considered not within the scope of your supply chain risk management program. However, as we have learned by the milk contamination example, any supplier (third party) that assists with the creation, production, delivery, and/or servicing of the products must be considered "in scope." That view extends to the farthest points upstream, back to the raw material and commodity suppliers; they fail, you fail. Their inaction or incorrect action, at any point in the supply chain, could cause financial loss or adversely affect your brand. Which relationships should be categorized as a supplier? A simple but often overlooked reality is that almost anyone or any organization can be a supplier. Remember the Laws of the Laws? Everyone, without exception, is part of the supply chain, including infrastructure providers (power and utility, sanitation, communications, public safety, public health, customs—including government/public sector organizations), raw material providers, consultants, port operators, insurance carriers, financial institutions, IT service firms, contract maintenance workers, human resource consultants, suppliers (subassembly, assembly), third-party logistics companies, transporters, distributors, and the list goes on and on.

Self-Assessment Action

Ask yourself the question "What entities do I rely on to deliver value; from the inception of the product or service to delivery (including ongoing service, maintenance, and eventual disposal)?" Paint the picture, draw the map, and be sure to include anyone who comes in contact with your supply chain. Don't forget to monitor change and the impact it has to these relationships.

When evaluating a supplier, the scope of your organization's activities must include a view of the fully extended supply chain. Avoid prejudgment, bias, and blinders.

- Do not assume that upstream suppliers are adequately addressing risk. And if they say they are, believe it, but not until you validate it. The reality is that most have less financial capacity, experience, and training to understand and address the tough supply chain risk management issues. Most possess the desire to do so, with the exception of those that command the marketplace as a primary supplier, one that multiple organizations depend on. Their risk interests are their own, such as quality, as they tend to be less interested in servicing the individual needs of the thousands of organizations they supply. Although this might appear intuitive, many extremely intelligent business managers that I've worked with over the years have fallen victim to this trap, usually because they have been distracted by other immediate priorities.

- Here's an example of working with blinders. While I was on assignment with a large high-tech organization in Asia, the Senior Sourcing Executive confessed to me that he had never looked beyond his first-tier suppliers. When asked why, he responded by saying, "I don't want my suppliers to think that I am questioning their sourcing practices—they might get upset." He went on to say, "They should be managing their upstream risks—it's their problem." This was not the first time I had witnessed this kind of behavior and potential for a single point of failure. The point of this is obvious: If one link fails—all links fail!
- Managing supplier and supply risk should not be limited to variations in demand. It should also include the broader universe of unexpected, low-probability, and potentially catastrophic events.
- Do not assume the cost-benefit analysis that was used to justify the outsourcing or offshoring shift still applies (you know, the opportunity versus risk analysis that should have been performed many years ago). The costs have changed significantly and so has the risk profile (threats more pervasive and vulnerabilities more prevalent in these long tailed and highly complex supply chains—see Law 1). The average wage inflation from 2003 to 2008 in Brazil and China was 21 and 19 percent, respectively (versus 3 and 5 percent, respectively, in the United States and Mexico), and the cost of shipping has tripled during that period (it dropped significantly when oil prices fell in 2009).[3] When in doubt, push for a cost-benefit reassessment of the supply chain strategic network design (location of suppliers, material and component providers, manufacturing and distribution sites, and customers) and the cost-benefit analysis to be reassessed. Consider volatility in the assessment, especially key supply chain costs such as commodity, energy, labor, and foreign exchange prices. Establish thresholds to act as a trigger or tipping point for configuration redesign. Also, do not assume the criteria (if any) used to measure supplier risk are static or all inclusive.

To reduce complexity, organizations should avoid trying to encapsulate all of their supply chains and associated suppliers into one view. This grand approach is simply unachievable due to time and resource constraints. Instead, the process can be simplified by first identifying the product and/or product lines that represent the greatest value to the organization. I refer to this process as "segmentation and rationalization." For example, an organization that produces and distributes semiconductors might select a short list of catalog numbers (products, stock keeping units/SKUs) that represent the greatest revenue, brand, cash flow, and strategic value to the organization. In another example, a consumer product company that produces chips, bottled water, juices, and carbonated beverages might choose bottled water as the product representing the greatest value. The supply chain and associated suppliers used to produce bottled water are significantly different from the supply chain used to produce orange juice. This distinction is essential and complies with the Laws of the Laws—it's all in the detail. Once the product or value driver is indentified, you can then profile all suppliers that are critical to deliver this value—from the source, for example, dairy farmers, to the destination, the consumers. This process can be quite revealing and scary.

Here's a question to ask: Can the value/product be produced and delivered to the market without this supplier? An inadequate risk practice is one where the organization considers only the top 10 percent of suppliers (usually determined by the level of spending) or just the sole source suppliers. The exception is when parts or materials are considered "discretionary" and do not impact the material value of the product. For example, an auto manufacturer might produce a vehicle that contains 24,000 parts, which are provided by 4,000 suppliers. Some of these parts, such as a cigarette lighter or floor mat, might be considered discretionary. As a result, the supplier can be categorized as a lower priority than the other suppliers. However, if you are manufacturing electronics sets or medical devices, then all parts and suppliers are essential, up to and including those who provide the specialized shipping material. To repeat our earlier theme—if one link fails, they all fail (the infamous *single point of failure*).

Risk Sourcing Policy

Once the supplier base is understood and documented, you can begin to communicate your expectations and deploy the risk sourcing policy. The risk sourcing policy is more than just a checklist of criteria that are used to evaluate your suppliers. When I refer to the *policy*, I am including the standards, technology, products, and procedures that drive service level agreements, code of conduct contracts, and are included as part of any comprehensive program. Remember, the supplier base is multilingual, multicultural, and not necessarily aligned with your risk expectations. For that reason alone, the organization must put structure in place to define expectations and a way to measure success or failure (of course, prior to an incident like the one in the beginning of this chapter). Supplier diligence typically evolves over time, beginning with contractual language and joint expectation setting, then evolving active monitoring and more active collaboration.

Over the years, I have come to appreciate the value of policies and standards. However, I also realize what a long and tedious process it can be to get them defined, endorsed, and deployed. A good starting point is to agree on common risk terminology. Here are some suggestions and examples, not rocket science but rather a necessary tool in the risk solution arsenal. Let's begin with some basics. The (supplier) *policy* represents the overarching risk objectives; it's brief and addresses the question of why you are doing this and what you are trying to accomplish. A supplier risk management policy might contain statements about being a "proactive process for identifying and managing risks—threats and vulnerabilities—to the upstream supply chain" and "reducing the severity and frequency, if applicable, by clearly articulating risk expectations." The policy might also reference the commitment of the organization to educate suppliers. Next are the *standards*, which bridge the gap between "what are we trying to achieve" and "how will we achieve (via a common framework) and who will own the responsibility." The risk standards must map back to the policy. Standards are typically structured into four major categories:

1. Roles and responsibilities
2. Processes
3. Baseline risk controls
4. Additional, impact-driven risk controls

Critical roles should be defined, along with expectations, such as the role of the supplier, materials providers, transportation carriers, and, of course, organization roles such as procurement and legal (contracts). Processes that should be included are:

- Qualifying suppliers (criteria/requirements definition, compliance)
- Monitoring suppliers (performance, triggers, access, compliance, collaboration, feedback and escalation, measures, mitigation)
- Classifying suppliers by contribution/importance and current risk status
- Promoting supplier collaboration (continuous improvement, collective intelligence, root cause analysis)

The baseline due care standards represent a minimum expectation. The impact-driven additional standards are driven by the risk assessment process. A baseline requirement might define minimum documentation, criteria to evaluate suppliers and the environment that supports the supplier, creation and storage of vital records, traceability expectations, no foreign sourcing (e.g., defense contractor), and labeling. In some instances, the risk assessment process might require additional needs for a particular geography, supplier, type of risk, or market condition (e.g., additional supplier diligence and higher standards could be enacted if a part of the supply base was at risk, such as what we witnessed in the auto industry in 2008 and 2009). To simplify communication about a particular supplier-based risk issue, for example, labor practices, the organization may create an interpretation of the policy and standards for that particular item. I've found that the so-called interpretation can be a valuable tool for communicating and presenting the technical requirements of the policy and standards rather than just presenting the requirements in a dry, functionally oriented document. Finally, the *technology, products, and procedures* portion of the overall policy provide guidance for execution. They address the how, when, and where questions when implementing a policy and can be either a standard or guideline. Exhibit 6.1 illustrates the policy structure.

Communicating expectations is critical. A successful practice deployed by Campbell's, a multibillion-dollar global manufacturer and marketer of food products, is to post to its Web site what is expected of their supplier. Campbell's "Supply Base Requirements and Expectations Manual"[4] contains policy guidance as well as ownership, behavioral expectations, and technical requirements. Policy and standards are necessary but do not frequently change. The policy

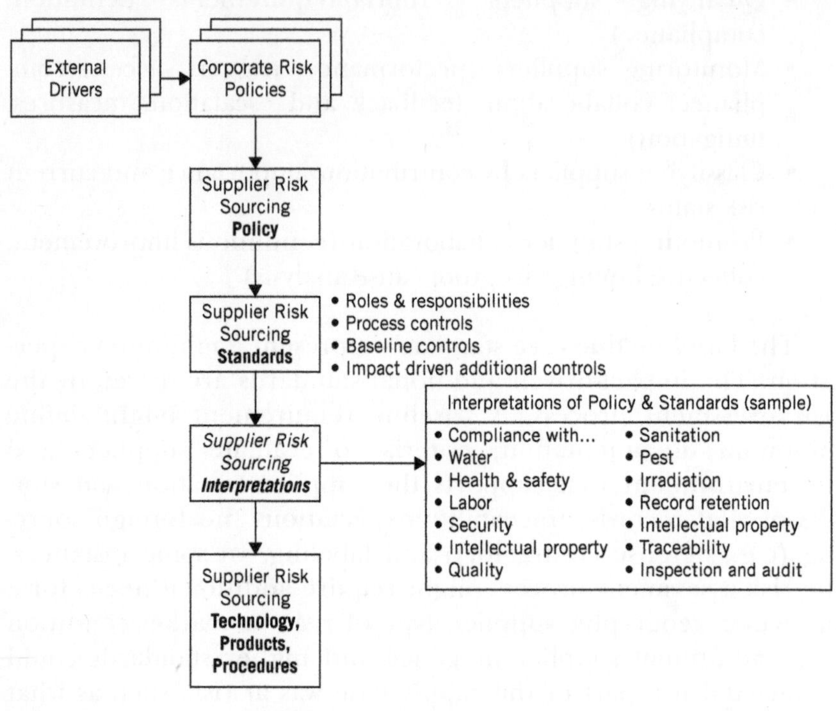

Exhibit 6.1 Policy Structure Illustration

interpretations, technology, products, and procedures change with greater frequency and evolve as relationships and the risk program evolve. At the end of the day, compliance and structure are needed and a supplier policy framework can be the vehicle that helps deliver, but above all, the organization must understand the response to these three questions:

1. Who are we doing business with and how do they make money (business model)?
2. Where do they operate and whom do they interact with (geography, operating environment, and interdependencies)?
3. What are the behaviors and motivations of all those that participate along the entire supply chain?

The supplier risk policy provides a structure to define and communicate expectations, but to be effective, the technology and procedures must follow. Risk triggers and sensors should be deployed (supported by process and technology), key performance and quality indicators monitored, volatility thresholds established (indicating when risk appetite is about to be or is exceeded), and the environment continuously monitored. Applying some of these practices to our earlier example might reveal the flashing of a few warning lights. For example, a mapping and subsequent analysis of the dairy supply chain would have revealed that the industry model relies on the use of small-scale farmers for product. In fact, these farmers account for over 90 percent of the production capacity, creating an aggregation risk that applies to the small-farmer business model. For most farmers, business consists of a small herd of dairy cows, the income from which represents their sole source of food for their family. A sick or unproductive cow translates into no income at all. This type of business model requires these farmers to be extremely sensitive to cost. If given the choice of the higher price, potentially healthier feed versus lower-priced substandard feed, most farmers would opt for the latter. Additionally, some of these farmers are not aware of how to feed and care for the dairy cows, and as a result the milk will fail the dairy company's standards. Hence, some farmers are motivated to add a cheap additive to boost the perception of protein content (melamine), convinced by others that they are doing no wrong. Of course, this issue is not unique to the dairy industry; there are similar examples in the chemical, minerals, food, and pharmaceutical industries. The opportunity is presented way up the supply chain, close to the original source of raw materials and then later disguised as the product. Finally, there were several claims by competing dairy farmers, those who decided not to use melamine, that this practice was pervasive. A visit to the farms might have revealed some of the warning signs and triggers prior to wide-scale contamination.

How Does a Supplier Fail? Let Me Count the Ways

A supplier's failure—such as that of the melamine example—is not a simple problem to evaluate or understand. The cause is not simply negligence on the part of the farmer, but also includes culpability up the chain, including those who insist on tighter margins and impose restrictions on suppliers who are already barely making it. It also includes the risk of the unscrupulous others who see the opportunity to take a shortcut and who exploit the system, such as the dairy trader knowingly moving (and promoting) contaminated milk. Simply stated, the entire business model that is supported by the extended supply chain must be included in the scope of the analysis. Fortunately, the trader in this instance was later convicted of wrongdoing but that was of no consolation to others in their supply chain that lost their only source of revenue (and did not have insurance). This was also the case of a U.S.-based arsenal provider. The company in question, AEY Inc., was accused of providing 49-year-old ammunition in decaying boxes to an Afghan government that was heavily dependent on the U.S. logistics and military support.[5] A supplier does not operate in isolation, but suffers consequences when decisions beyond their control change their entire paradigm. For example, take a look at what has happened to U.S. auto parts suppliers.

These suppliers suffered along with their big customers, the U.S. auto companies. In the trend toward auto manufacturer bankruptcy, the potential damage went far beyond these well-known companies. Auto parts suppliers faced dire outcomes if the automakers failed. For example, in January 2009, Visteon Corp., a major parts supplier to Ford, hired legal and financial consultants to prepare for bankruptcy. The fear in the industry was that any Big Three bankruptcy would have a ripple effect throughout the parts manufacturing industry, resulting in the loss of tens of thousands of jobs. The problems were many, but overcapacity was among the top problems in the auto industry. One thing was clear: The fallout from the problems in the auto industry goes far beyond manufacturing jobs in the Big Three.[6]

The global market has brought much advantage but also contains disadvantages. Non-U.S.-based auto dealers also faced oversupply problems beginning in 2008, and it may take years for the industry to catch up and stabilize. This points out a stark reality about supply chain risk: Although demand begins with the customer downstream in the supply chain, the detailed, tedious work is often focused on the supplier side of the equation, whether local or remote. Today, the trend continues as previously outsourced and offshored supply chains are now being extended even further to emerging countries with labor costs (e.g., China +1 strategy where the plus 1 represents countries like Vietnam and Cambodia).

All too often, the theme established by the central office is intended to curtail threats, but the organizational view is limited to only what is seen and heard. As a consequence, many of those who manage risk attempt to limit their interests in a parochial way. This is only the beginning of the supply chain errors. In other words, by limiting the organizational view, a manager can only deal with the most immediate problems and can only address them as far as his or her vision extends. The real irony in this: By addressing only the immediate, local, and known supply chain risk, managers may easily transfer the risk and the blame to suppliers. This sets up your suppliers for failure. As one senior executive of a multinational consumer product organization explained it, "How the heck can someone assess supplier or contract manufacturer risk from afar, unless they've seen the operation with their own eyes?" He went on to say, "An auditor asked if our contract manufacturers (third-party suppliers) had taken the necessary precautions to protect against the threat of bird flu, such as not shaking hands. I asked him whether he had been to any of the facilities in these lesser-developed countries. There are dozens of birds living in the rafters of the facilities—that's the harsh reality of our globally disbursed supply base and supply chains!"

The recession of 2008–2009 highlighted the especially severe problem of supplier risk. A majority of companies suffered some form of supply chain disruption in 2008, for example. Is this the fault of the supplier? No, but it is a reality that the system relies on outsourced manufacturing and production and has a tendency—on the part of the primary organization—to create high expectations for their suppliers. A survey in 2008 revealed that 99 percent of companies reported one or more disruptions during the year, and 58 percent had financial losses as a result. The most commonly cited cause of supply chain disruption was that supplier capacity did not meet demand, cited by 56 percent of respondents. This issue is exactly the same one faced in China by milk suppliers in the same year. So the problem occurs in good times and bad, and to any number of vulnerable suppliers. When your suppliers cannot meet immediate demand, that is going to cause disruptions and loss; and when revenues are falling, overcapacity (as in the auto industry) creates an equally serious problem. The bottom line, however, is that less than one-third of companies have taken steps to manage supplier risks.[7]

The supply chain is not limited to a beginning and an end within your organizational view. Failure at the genesis of the supply chain moves throughout the entire system, and failure can mean a specific delay, damage, or price increases; or it can mean overcapacity problems that could last for years. Failure can be caused by, but is not limited to, poor economic and financial conditions. The many risk triggers described in the first Law (e.g., environmental, quality, operational, hazard, etc.) can also lead the supplier down the path of failure. In addition, the failure of the environment in which the supplier operates, such as an infrastructure caused by a natural hazard or a geopolitical event, can also result in severe consequences. This was the case in China when food costs soared more than 23 percent after severe first-quarter 2008 snowfall froze transportation and destroyed crops. Suppliers were paralyzed and the shortage fueled price increases in pork (up 63 percent from a year earlier) and vegetables (up 46 percent from prior year).[8] The fact that most companies take no action to manage these risks reveals that the entire supplier risk problem is poorly understood. However, it is likely that most companies place expectations on suppliers that are often not going to be met. Look once again at the extreme consequences of these very issues on the Chinese milk industry to better understand the severity of this problem. If you infect your suppliers with the risk parasite, it works its way through the system until you can feel it gnawing away at your organization—at systems, profits, human resources, morale, effectiveness, competitiveness, and even at the ability to achieve the most basic of tasks, delivering quality goods to the customer. Anyone who has seen the erosion in the auto industry understands all too well how this reality plays out.

Sourcing Strategies That Create More Risk, Not Less

Most people want to accomplish good things, create success, and solve problems. Ironically, however, many of the prevalent risk strategies actually create *more* risk rather than less.

To make a system work efficiently, you need to find innovative ways to revolutionize how your organization deals with suppliers. No longer does it make sense to set up suppliers to fail or behave badly. Here are two guidelines:

1. *Remember, lower costs = something has to give; for example, substandard quality practices.* It cannot be avoided or changed with

wishful thinking. It is simply a fact: When you lower costs and impose tighter margins on your suppliers, they are going to strive for ways to maintain their margins. It is not realistic to expect suppliers to accept lower margins or to lose their profitability. It is ironic that today's organizational leaders continue to focus their efforts on budgets, including the lowering of costs by mandate and without considering the consequences. Lowering costs puts a squeeze on your suppliers and forces them to cut corners, resulting in a higher cost due to supplier failure. This is the most common form of setting up suppliers for failure.

The conflict between lower costs and lower quality cannot be resolved, but it can be modified so it is possible to find ways to lower costs in partnership with your suppliers and through improvements to the supply chain that benefit both your supplier and your bottom line. The time is now to become more intimate with your key suppliers, as supplier consolidation continues to accelerate due to the economic downturn and opportunity for greater efficiency. But that requires trust that comes from long-term relationships, empowerment and visibility on the supplier side, collective intelligence and analysis (both parties), trigger-based risk identification systems, and on-site systems analysis and improvement. Of course, that is an investment on your organization's part but many of the lessons have already been learned as part of evolving supply chain management practices (e.g., collaborative and collective, technology enable, supply chain practices such as Vendor Managed Inventory and Collaborative Forecasting and Planning). You gain great advantages by identifying what has worked before and exporting it to other places in the supply chain. It pays dividends over the long run, but it is still a hard sell to the less than enlightened leadership whose only case is focused on cost cutting and whose considerations never touch on how cost cutting affects risk.

In fact, the conflict may be managed by encouraging greater freedom to innovate rather than trying to restrict suppliers. In the United States, for example, smaller firms and younger companies develop far more innovations than larger organizations. One promising solution to the problem of supplier risk may be to focus on creating a local base of entrepreneurial suppliers, rather than continuing to focus on lowest-cost outsourcing in other countries. Diversifying your supplier bank makes sense. However, as the former CEO of Pepsico stated, in 2007, diversity is the solution. The "strategic imperative of supplier diversity is not immediately obvious to many businesspeople . . . Companies succeed best in a flourishing economic climate, and small-business entrepreneurship provides critical engines for innovation and job growth."[9]

2. *Changes in credit and financing mean belt-tightening throughout.* The effect of losing short-term financing and credit insurance on suppliers, organizations, and trade flow can be disastrous. The supply chain design itself will change as a result, and not always in positive ways.

You must develop procedures for early detection of problems and fast-response internal controls. Just as the effective auto assembly plant has enabled Japanese workers to stop the assembly line once a defect is spotted (*jidoka*), anyone in the supply chain should be empowered to raise a red flag for the same reasons. The parasite raises its ugly head and can be spotted at once, but all too often people say nothing or just assume it's someone else's responsibility. In some instances, your organization might even need to provide funding to suppliers to keep them viable, even to make sure they are able to stay in business (many that I have spoken with over the past six months already have). It's in everyone's interest to think like a team rather than like insiders and outsiders. This step takes the concept of partnership beyond lip service and makes it a reality.

Engaging early is one of the keys to successfully spotting problems early. Edscha, a German auto accessories manufacturer, filed for insolvency and presented its primary customer, BMW, with a problem. It would take at least six months to replace the supplier. BMW provided help to keep their supplier afloat, but also introduced a new initiative to prevent similar supply chain disruptions in the future.

This new program includes several key components. These are:

- *Communicate (deploy sensors).* It seems like an easy and simple step to just keep in touch with suppliers. Sadly, many do not begin with this and it creates problems later on. If a supplier problem takes your organization by surprise, there is no excuse.

- *Set up a rating system (establish priorities).* Examine ownership structure, cash flow, and profitability to ensure that your suppliers are able to maintain going concern status.
- *Create an early-warning system (define demand and supply triggers).* You need to be able to monitor your suppliers to identify emerging issues before they become large problems.
- *Know your suppliers' suppliers, or distributor's suppliers (gain visibility).* This is crucial. Too many organizations rely on a first-tier supplier only to discover (too late) that these suppliers were outsourcing their manufacturing, meaning the whole supply chain is out of your control.
- *Recognize that multiple sourcing is no panacea (avoid fragmentation . . . focus, focus, focus).* If you try to diversify but your suppliers all rely on the same logistics or manufacturing, then you do not eliminate risk. Just as investing in several different oil drilling companies does not diversify your investment risk, diversifying among interdependent suppliers is ineffective. To truly diversify, you need to create entirely independent and separate supply chains.[10]
- *Be careful what you wish for.* When asked what the most challenging risk of globalization is, many supply chain managers will respond, "Exiting a country where you decided to set up shop" (contract manufacturers). What might appear as a brilliant, cost savings sourcing strategy today might translate into the organization's worst nightmare as they attempt to shut or wind down operations. The problem is simple when your organization represents a significant source of tax revenue (or significant concessions had been made to attract the organization to this location), or the resistance and brand penalties that you will incur when withdrawing may represent a significant brand and financial cost.
- *Educate and empower.* One of the goals of Nike and a best practice is to become more intimate with its suppliers and as a result, educate, enable, and empower. In most instances, the genesis of supplier risk issues is only visible within the local geography or organizational lens. Teaching the suppliers to communicate risk issues early and then enabling them with the tools, protocol, and knowledge is not only an effective way to enhance the supplier risk program but also a realistic way.

Show Me the Money: The Financing Issue

Too many companies, when faced with financial restrictions due to tightened credit, first think about how suppliers have to change *their* operating model and *their* profit margin. This is an error because, remember, everyone operates in their own self-interests. No one is going to be willing to "take one for the team" by accepting lower profits or giving up profitability altogether. The solution to financial-based problems is to sit down with suppliers and figure out effective solutions; to consider reducing the costs of the extended supply chain by shrinking its scope; and by looking for methods to reduce existing costs. For example, create transportation groupings from proximate international suppliers, delay regular shipments for bigger bulk and lower unit cost alternatives in exchange for increased local inventory and warehousing. This goes against the concept of lean and just-in-time goods handling, but if it costs less to abandon these ideas in a shrinking economy, reality has to serve as the decision point.

By the end of 2008, belt-tightening slowed traffic down to record low levels in the usually robust Port of Long Beach. The recession was blamed generally, but the root cause was a credit crisis, with loans to export-dependent companies brought to a standstill. The 2008 slowdown was the worst since 1971. The problem was international, seen in coal from the Maputo, Mozambique port, Brazilian auto exports, appliances, and more. The Port of Singapore, the world's biggest container port, posted its first monthly decline in seven years in November 2008. The continued trade credit problem threatened at least one-fourth of the $54 trillion global economy by the end of 2008.

The problem is not limited to unavailability of credit. Financing costs grew more than six times pre-crisis levels. Exporters fell short by $25 billion in global trade credit requirements, and trade credit insurance, which normally protects about 40 percent of European trade and 5 percent in the United States, became much harder to get under any circumstances. For example, Atradius NV, an Amsterdam insurer providing one-third of global trade receivables insurance, raised prices by as much as 50 percent while reducing coverage on 12,000 policyholders in the United Kingdom and all of the suppliers to the Big Three U.S. auto manufacturers.[11]

It is not all bad news. Demand eventually returns (or the organization fails), even though global manufacturing production fell nearly 20 percent in the fourth quarter of 2008. By January 2009, the prediction was somewhat more promising: "Trade financing is beginning to flow. Firms cannot run down stocks forever: eventually, they will empty their warehouses. But the damage is done: those temporary factors triggered a collapse in global demand that has now spread way beyond the Anglo-Saxon economies at the heart of the credit crisis."[12]

Tough times demand outside-of-the-box thinking. Is it really cost effective to rely on suppliers based halfway across the world? It might be necessary to change or diversify your supplier base. Given the transportation and timing costs of remote processing, would your overall costs be lowered by contracting with alternate suppliers residing closer to home? Can you reduce costs by expanding your supply chain to avoid risks related to known threats? Conversely, is a limited local supplier base causing the problem? Can this be resolved by expanding to a broader, international supplier base? The actual diversification can require localization or globalization, depending on the circumstances.

For example, when gas prices rose to record high levels in mid-2008, Great Britain saw its domestic supplies of gas fall to dangerously low levels. The U.K. addressed this problem by relying on European pipeline suppliers or outright purchase of shiploads of liquefied natural gas (LNG). The U.K. economy is especially vulnerable to high gas prices, with 85 percent of homes heated by gas and 40 percent of its electricity generated via natural gas. Diversification helped somewhat, but the U.K. had to shop for the best prices and compete with Asia, where many countries were willing to pay higher prices, making the shortfall even worse.[13]

Also consider the potential for higher or lower risks in your supply chain resulting from making a change. No idea should be off the table, but the trick is going to be finding ways to reduce overall costs without placing all the burden on your suppliers. This means developing systems and processing improvements in the supply chain that maintain current profit levels while keeping risk levels in check, but at a lower expense.

The Credit Insurance Problem

Some new realities have to be overlaid on the supplier issue. In recessionary times, like the 2008–2009 period (and probably to continue for a few years beyond), trade credit is likely to dry up or be dramatically reduced. We all know that banks are restrictive on lending more than ever before. But even if you can find a financing source for your supply chain (and especially for international supplier reliance), you are not going to get any lending help without carrying trade credit insurance.

Credit insurance protects your organization against default or insolvency—the credit risks you live with—and may even include a political risk clause when you rely on suppliers in countries subject to the threats of currency exchange losses, political instability, and expropriation of private assets by the government. The importance of credit insurance arises when it serves as an alternative to COD (cash on delivery) terms that will otherwise apply, especially in unstable countries; and let's face it, many of the most affordable supply chains extend into many of these third-world nations.

One problem with reliance on trade credit insurance in place of COD or more liberal financing is that your suppliers are required to assume the nonpayment risk. This is complex when you also consider the variances in laws internationally concerning trade and contractual obligations, customs, currency exchange fluctuations, and time delays involved. So when financial terms are not favorable, the first tendency is to transfer risk to the supplier. Considering that some domestic organizations have actually refused delivery of international product shipments and turned ships back to their origin (due to lack of credit and very slow markets), this risk is very real.

The insurance alternative may work for some, but not for all. But the reality remains: Trade credit tends to dry up in recessionary times, so how do you manage your supply chain and its inherent risks without also seeing those risks grow tremendously? In the past, lenders often failed to perform due diligence on payment obligations because, in their view, the risk was simply transferred to insurers. Does this solve the problem? It's unlikely.

Insurance can be withdrawn without any notice, making the situation high-risk for many industries. When insurance was cut off to many suppliers of bricks, nails, and wooden frames in Britain's construction industry early in 2009 (a risk trigger, requiring immediate, in-depth analysis), widespread bankruptcy became a very real possibility. Aggravating the falling demand for homes in the U.K., the industry suffered from the lack of choice. Three companies provide 85 percent of all credit insurance globally (the leader is Paris-based Euler Hermes SA, a unit of Allianz SE). Banks used to allow merchants to carry as much as £2 billion in unsecured loans, but those same banks suddenly did away with this credit provision, resulting in many companies' inability to work in markets where goods are not paid for at the time they are provided. Hardest hit in this type of arrangement is, of course, the construction industry.[14]

Among the changes you can expect to see in coming years is the requirement that banks and other lenders perform more risk assessment before simply demanding that your organization carry insurance. This will mean more supervision by your organization, lenders, regulators, and even the federal government with its newly acquired equity stake in the major banks. At the same time, given the heightened claims risk, the trade credit insurance market is going to become more restrictive as well. How will this change?

Carriers typically have performed some due diligence in the past, but they have been accused of receiving premiums equivalent to the turnover of a medium-sized business to protect more that 20 percent of the output of the entire British economy. The Association of British Insurers reported that there were £334 million sterling of premiums written by the insurers in 2007, covering £282 billion sterling of sales by British companies.[15]

Your suppliers normally cannot wait 30, 60, or 90 days to receive payment. They continue to need trade credit just to make their own cash flow, so increasingly you are going to see a demand for advance payments in cash before shipping. As a consequence, your organization is going to be squeezed for cash, especially if banks continue to withdraw overdraft protection and short-term financing for goods provided and not yet paid.

Declare a Supply Chain Risk Management Strategy but Walk before You Run

Should you declare a risk strategy? Of course, but it should not be limited in any sense of the word. Think big, think comprehensively. In this section, I will provide some examples of how companies have enacted a risk strategy that was both affordable and effective.

Your supply chain risk management program will only work if it extends all the way from beginning to end. Putting this another way, the question has to be: How far up the supply chain do you look for solutions? You must look upstream to identify solutions to supplier risk, and you need to also understand that a supplier's risk is not external; it is part of your organization's overall supply chain ecosystem and cannot be transferred away. This is not just lip service to a concept; it is the one element essential to creating an excellent strategy that is also sustainable.

What good is excellence on only one leg of the supply chain if what occurs before is shoddy, defective, or dangerous? What good is excellence if what comes after is failure? You cannot solve the supply chain problems in your organization unless your program reaches all segments of your supply chain. This is a point of emphasis you need to bring to everyone's attention, especially to the decision makers, movers, and shakers who ultimately decide these matters.

Among today's trends in supply chain risk management, a few major ones are relevant to this argument. Risk expectations on the part of key external stakeholders have increased sharply in recent years. So your organization needs to be aware that customers, investors, underwriters, and trade partners demand that you *are* managing risk. Two-thirds of all companies surveyed are failing in this. This increased demand is occurring at a time when supply chain risks are growing, often beginning with or associated with suppliers. One promising trend is that many organizations are beginning to include their suppliers in risk management education, but this has to be coupled with working programs as well.

First: Develop a Clear Line of Sight As long as your internal analysis is limited to first-tier suppliers, you do not have a clear line of sight. For this primary reason, it makes sense to consider eliminating second-tier suppliers, simply because their risks are not controllable, but your exposure continues and worsens as more outsourcing occurs. Imagine how you would feel upon discovering that the private school to which you send your children was outsourcing its education to a substandard school in a different city. The point is not limited to the financial issue; the real question is whether or not your child is getting the quality of education you thought you were paying for. In this situation, you would not have a clear line of sight because:

- You have no way to know what is being taught.
- You do not know whether the teachers are certified or even qualified.
- The curriculum you thought was being taught might not be in effect.

- You might be speaking in different languages, interpreting the messages in a different way, or dealing with conflicting priorities.
- You have no way to know whether the school you are paying has any processes to monitor the second-tier school and its results.

The same general problems relate to second-tier suppliers and raise exactly the same questions. Without a clear line of sight, you have no control. This begs the question of whether you should continue the policy of even allowing first-tier suppliers to subcontract.

Because your suppliers are probably no more ready than your organization to deal with supply chain threats, the solution is to incorporate suppliers into an all-encompassing risk management and response program. This is where systems have failed so often. By excluding suppliers or assuming that their risks are separate from yours, the chronic problems never get addressed.

Next: Take Up the Cause of Your Suppliers Challenge yourself to crusade for a comprehensive risk management program. Stop the blame game and become a champion for your suppliers. The blame game, a favorite in many organizations, does not solve problems—even if the blame is placed properly. Instead, push for a change in culture and promote a *solutions game.* Once you recognize that the risk parasite exists, blaming the suppliers does not remove or neutralize the parasite. You have to work for solutions and remove the parasite from the entire supply chain. This cannot be limited to statements, but has to include specific policies. By creating a working partnership with suppliers, you can work together on the necessary solutions to the inherent problems faced by the entire supply chain and you can get away from the unproductive practice of trying to decide who is at fault, who has failed, and who has to take the blame.

In your efforts to develop a strategy to improve the supplier's role, where do you begin? Realizing that the organization's whole environment has changed with globalization, improved communications, and the development of a complex and multifaceted supply chain, how do you define the role your supplier provides? Remember, if you think of a supplier as functioning outside of your quality arena and as a separate supply chain that is not part of your job, then nothing is going to get done.

Finally: Incorporate Your Supplier as Part of Your Supply Chain in a Very Real Sense There is often a sense that the supplier is an outsider in every respect. It is in a foreign country, it is part of a different culture, and its problems (risk profitability, deadlines) are outside of your supply chain. This is a huge mistake.

Imagine how all of this would change if you made your primary suppliers a true part of your organization. This could include several initiatives, including permanent on-site internal audit departments within your supplier organizations, and consisting at least partially of employees of the primary organization; consultation with supplier executive-level personnel within your organization, perhaps even including membership on your board of directors; and ever-present cross-communication and in-person meetings, not only at headquarters but in your suppliers' plants and offices.

These concepts can revolutionize your supply chain and the key is a simple one: Stop thinking of suppliers as outside of your organization and supply chain and bring them into it directly. While communication is essential in a remote situation, it can go only so far. You are eventually going to need a physical presence at the supplier's location. An enlightened approach includes the opposite and equally essential element, supplier presence in your location. Remember, *you* are your supplier's customer, and if you simply assume that you and your suppliers are sharing the same demand paradigm, you are mistaken. You can overcome this major stumbling block only by taking proactive steps to begin talking the same language.

Finding a Common Language

One effective approach to this ever-present issue was developed by Avon Products. The very first observation made by the company in addressing supplier risk was "We speak different languages." Acknowledging that risk management is not a part of the supplier's vocabulary or strategy, this leads to a second realization: Suppliers may not see risk management as a priority and may even see it as an impediment.

The study compared supply chain drivers to risk management drivers and identified many areas of conflict. These were:

Supply Chain Drivers	**Risk Management Drivers**
Consolidate vendors	Alternate vendors
Reduce inventory to just-in-time	Build in redundancies
Outsource warehousing services	Control your inventory
Streamline logistics	Pre-negotiate alternate carriers/routes
Lowest cost suppliers	Quality vendors over low cost
Unwind complexity	Testing suppliers' products/ingredients
Focused manufacturing/distribution	Multiple sources for manufacturing/distribution

Risk managers need to respond to these conflicts by fully understanding the supply chain organization, learning the language of the supplier, and studying their priorities and challenges. Avon undertook the task of consolidating its supply chain, fusing a series of chain links to manage its global supply chain. The goal: to create a supply chain that was both interdependent and interactive.[16]

The lesson of Avon's initiative is that management cannot control suppliers as outsiders but have to become true partners.

Trust but Verify

Doverey no poverey (Trust but verify)

—Russian proverb

In the mood of creating an effective partnership with your suppliers, you need to get your organization thinking in a different way about the whole supplier relationship. For example, your suppliers are not really *outside* of your supply chain or your organization. Like the demand side of the equation, managers tend to view their organization in terms of matters within their direct "equity realm." This assumes (wrongly) that management has complete control over both its demand and supply generators. This also assumes that anything generated on the outside is not part of the supply chain. This is a mistake of the first order. An enlightened and holistic view accepts the simple reality: You cannot separate your organization from its suppliers. It's part of the same risk paradigm and cross-reliance.

In this newly recognized partnership between yourself and your suppliers, you need to adopt a new view of the entire system. A "trust-but-verify" concept has to replace one of the two more common points of view: trying to completely control suppliers and imposing restrictions on them without corresponding compensation, or ignoring the risks entirely and considering those risks as belonging to someone else. Neither of these models work, but "trust but verify" is more likely to help make the supply chain operate more smoothly, with less risk, and in a win-win environment.

Here are two ideas for reform going along with this:

1. *Financial consolidation.* Create joint venture partnerships rather than strict vendor relationships with suppliers demonstrating strong financial positions. By entering into relationships with solid companies, rather than with questionable suppliers offering low cost but low stability, you avoid the unpleasant surprises that are most likely to come up during recessionary times.

   The strong financial position is only half of the equation. The other half is involvement on a joint venture basis. This may include stock swaps, creation of a jointly owned subsidiary (with shared risk incentives), or membership on boards of directors (not only yours on the supplier's board, but also suppliers on *your* board). This new view of the supplier relationship may solve many of the problems you have to face, many of which are based on self-interest or lack of complete trust, and gives both sides an equity interest in making sure the supply chain succeeds without higher risk exposure. One imaginative proposal during the Cold War was that the leaders of the United States and the U.S.S.R. should send their own children to be educated in the other's country. This would ensure that any nuclear attack would be very personal. The object lesson in this is that developing a vested interest in your suppliers (and vice versa) goes a long way toward building a real relationship.
2. *Increased exposure for customers.* You may need to contend with the problems of recessionary times by simply requiring customers to live with longer lead times for some products. This affects your

ability to compete and may also directly affect your markets, notably when your products are sole-sourced. But unless you can solve the problems of sole sourcing and financing issues, this could be the only alternative left to your organization.

Remembering as well that you are your suppliers' customers, you may need to accept the same limitation and restriction. As a customer, you might have to accept the same longer lead times. In other words, if you place this expectation on your customer, you should naturally assume that your supplier has to live with the same recessionary problems and will have the same expectations of you.

Can these problems be solved without eroding profitability or ruining your markets? Your organization is under pressure to demonstrate that it comprehends and can manage supply chain risks. But at the same time, the always-present demand to maintain or improve profits is becoming increasingly difficult. This is why managers often choose to ignore the higher risks that are inevitable when cutting costs.

In any change to existing systems, one step often overlooked but essential to success is testing of your basic assumptions throughout the supply chain. This starts with the very beginning of the chain itself. And incidentally, this is not restricted only to systemic issues that are normally focused on process alone. So many internal folks want to focus on the question of how the process can be made more efficient. I propose that the kinds of questions you should be asking go beyond this, as you look for ways to reduce waste, mitigate risks without additional costs, and even more basic questions. For example, it is time to abandon many assumptions and review the whole thing from the ground up. Are you really saving money overall in your current supply chain? Are there more cost-effective alternatives?

Of course, the assumptions you will test are much more extensive than this very basic one and may involve a detailed internal audit; development of revised minimum standards; joint venturing, revisiting transportation, inventory, and lean policies; and taking a fresh look at how you can diversify the supply chain from start to finish. Rely on aggregate data to test geography, buyer preferences, and costs at all levels.

You gain a lot of insight into the workings of your supply chain when you examine the supply chain from top to bottom. This is like taking the back off of a watch and seeing how the gears turn. On the face of the watch, it seems like a simple device with three hands, each one denoting hours, minutes, and seconds; but when you look inside, you realize that the watch is far more complex than a sundial.

To really start the process of reevaluating your supply chain with fairness to your suppliers in mind, you are going to need to map the process all the way back to your sources. Your suppliers understand at the raw materials level how to create greater efficiency through location of inventory, warehousing buffers, and management of goods in transit, and they understand and can demonstrate greater efficiency where you place inventory and buffers—raw materials, work in progress, goods in transit, and finished goods. Don't forget that your suppliers are the experts here, and not your CFO or CEO.

A poll of several leading Global 500 organizations revealed the following standard supplier and site risk evaluation criteria:

- Organization (structure, chemistry, financial management, strategy, customers, product composition and diversity, communication flow, pricing history, educational and training practices, interaction, subcontractor management, growth)
- Financial health (quick ratio, debt/equity, distribution of top five customers, cash flow, ratings)
- Labor practices (health, safety, compliance, security, hazard)
- Capability and capacity (space, facility, adequacy and maturity of equipment, qualified resources, after-sales service, manufacturing flexibility, and SCRM technology)
- Quality systems and processes (track record product quality, metrics such as return ratios, certified quality processes, certifications, methodology)
- References (customers, industries, compliance track record)
- Brand strength (market awareness, experience)
- Social responsibility (sustainability, green supply chain initiatives)
- Geopolitical (political, social, infrastructural, environmental)

Model simulated supply chain disruptions in cooperation with your suppliers to identify the weak links and most likely single points of failure as a premise for making overall improvements. These must be done cooperatively and not as imposed demands made on the supplier. However, the IT company's outline brings another issue to the front: Why would any multinational company expose its supply chain to the risks inherent in allowing first-tier suppliers to outsource to second-tier or third-tier suppliers? The need for setting standards, auditing, incentives, and enforcement beg the question. Your organization can only expect compliance to minimum quality standards if you are allowed top-to-bottom auditing rights and partnership. The second-tier situation completely sabotages this desirable result.

Restricting your supply chain to first-tier suppliers is a logical, obvious, defensive move to eliminate many of the more serious risks. Take the threat-based approach along with the impact-based approach to develop a revised supply chain process. Focusing on threats helps to identify how and where the supply chain is most vulnerable (my infamous explanation of uncertainty), and impact-based analysis (exposure to uncertainty) tells you where the greatest costs are likely to occur.

The threat of using the wrong suppliers was the focus of Nike when it decided in 2009 to stop ordering from four Asian footwear contract factories. Nike uses more than 600 factories, so the decision represents a minute part of its overall supplier base. However, the company had been trying to streamline its supply chain since 2007, and closing out relationships with some suppliers was part of the consolidation effort. The reason cited for cutting off work with the four factories was streamlining, and no further explanation of why these four were selected was provided by Nike.[17]

Contracting the supply chain by streamlining—that is, reducing the sheer number of suppliers—is one of many ways to at least reduce the potential for supplier-based risk. Keep in mind that:

- Supplier failure or change is just another example of what can go wrong and what can't be predicted.
- To spend a lot of time trying to predict a threat—especially of large magnitude—is futile. It makes more sense to develop the supplier processes cooperatively to mitigate potential disruptions and financial effects of known risks.
- Impact of failure at this point—both at the individual supplier level and aggregate level—helps you to model the impact of both. This is the better way to analyze and make financing and mitigation decisions about the risk.

Threat analysis is useful if you are going to create stress scenarios to test your decisions, verify assumptions, and optimize your resource allocations. As previously mentioned in the Laws of the Laws (it's all in the detail), paying attention to the details, the warning lights, will return huge results. Here are a few examples: violations (environmental, labor, government), claims, management turnover, packaging, increasing quality issues, escalating shipping, delays and shortages, and incidents.

The sheer magnitude of key indicators relating to suppliers is overwhelming, including marketing/finance, buying/procurement, replenishment/order fulfillment, merchandising, information systems, supplier capability/support, logistics/distribution, supply chain management, and operations. Where do you begin? Look for ways to reduce the size of your supply chain in terms of supplier outlets. More is not always better.

Establish minimum standards and enforce them. Consider eliminating all suppliers who outsource to second-tier providers. Insist on the right of quality control audits and other forms of direct monitoring. Taking these initial steps will do away with most of the serious threats you face from your suppliers along with the implementation of more dynamic, integrated, and active risk systems (e.g., sensors and triggers). Working in cooperation with your supplier base takes care of most of the remaining risks. Remember, you cannot completely eliminate risk, but you can identify the root cause and whittle away the list of issues over time.

These steps are never going to be easy or simple; some are going to be quite disruptive. The key point to remember is that you need a two-pronged attack of the supplier-specific risk parasite. First, you need to ensure that your contact with the supplier is excellent (communication, analysis, standard-setting, follow-up, perhaps even financial assistance). The relationship must be a partnership in every sense of the word. Second, you need to simplify your supply chain. This involves creating effective and properly structured supplier diversification, elimination of second-tier participants, and perhaps even contracting your supply chain to a smaller, more controllable, less-risky size (both geographically and logistically). The supply chain is driven by demand, but that demand does not matter unless you are in control of the supply chain. You need your suppliers and they need you. Unlike the status quo in too many international organizations, you and your suppliers need to work as a partnership.

Notes

1. Multiple sources: www.guardian.co.uk/world/2008/dec/o2/china; Fonterra Co-operative Group Ltd press release, 2 December 2005; www.businessday.co.nz/industries/4704082; Jenny Wiggins, "Unilever Recall over China Milk" FT.com, October 1 2008; Scott McDonald, (22 September 2008). "Nearly 53,000 Chinese Children Sick from Milk,"*Associated Press*; Jane Macartney (22 September 2008). "China Baby Milk Scandal Spreads as Sick Toll Rises to 13,000."
2. Gordon Fairclough, "Tainting of Milk Is Open Secret in China," *Wall Street Journal*, November 3, 2008.
3. Ajay Goel, Nazgol Moussavi, and Vats N. Srivatsan, "Time to Rethink Offshoring?" *The McKinsey Quarterly*, September 2008.
4. Campbell's "Supply Base Requirements and Expectations Manual," www.campbellsoupcompany.com/supplier_requirements.asp.
5. C.J. Chivers, "Supplier Under Scrutiny on Aging Arms for Afghans," *New York Times*, March 27, 2008.
6. John D. Stoll and Jeffrey McCraken, "Bankruptcy Fears Grip Auto-Parts Suppliers," *Wall Street Journal*, January 26, 2009.
7. Allison Manning, "Economy: Supply Chain Disruptions Plague Most Companies," *Modern Materials Handling*, October 1, 2008.
8. Kevin Hamlin and Li Lanping, "China's Inflation Surges to 8.7% as Food Prices Soar," Bloomberg.com, March 11, 2008.
9. Tim Laseter and Greg Fairchild, "Supplier Empowerment and the Bottom Line," *Strategy + Business*, Issue 53.
10. Richard Milne, "Early Warnings in the Supply Chain," *Financial Times*, March 24, 2009.
11. Michael Janofsky and Mark Drajem, "Frozen Ports from Long Beach to Singapore Presage Bleak 2010," Bloomberg.com, December 23, 2008.
12. "Accelerating Downhill," *Economist*, January 15, 2009.
13. "The Gas Market—Flaring Up Again," *Economist*, July 26, 2008.
14. Scott Hamilton, "Travis Poised to Benefit as Insurers Shun Building Merchants," Bloomberg.com, January 16, 2009.
15. Robert Peston, "Insurance that Worsens Crunch," BBC News.
16. Gary S. Lynch (Marsh) and Pamela Britt Schneider (Avon), "Improving Supply Chain Resiliency and Investments in Light of Increased Risks," April 28, 2008.
17. Wing-Gar Cheng and Stephanie Wong, "Nike to Halt Orders with Some Asia Contract Factories," Bloomberg.com, March 25, 2009.

Law #6: Managing Production Risk Is a Dirty Job

FOCUS ON MANAGING THE ENDLESS RISK OF MANUFACTURED WEAKEST LINKS

How did Western society advance from the meanness and turmoil of the Black Death era, when bodies piled high in the streets, and mass graves were thinly covered by hastily piled earth, leading to the horrid stench of the simultaneous decay of thousands of bodies? . . . the Black Death accelerated the decline of serfdom and the rise of a prosperous class of peasants, called yeomen, in the fifteenth century. With "Grain rotting in the fields" at the summer harvest of 1349, because of labor shortage, the peasants could press for higher wages and further elimination of servile dues and restrictions. The more entrepreneurial landlords were eventually prepared to give in to peasant demands.

—Norman F. Cantor,
In the Wake of the Plague, 2001 (202–203)

Going Global with the Production of Risk

How vulnerable are your production processes? The unheard of labor shortages that were seen in Europe for 200 years after the worst of the Black Death era had much to do with the Industrial Revolution. Before that time, artisans manually crafted products, such as clothing, furniture, and jewelry. They relied on common and precious metals, glass, wood, leather, ceramics, and textiles for their products. As the masters of their trades and sole producers, they were also the single point of failure to themselves as well as to those they served. Since artisans produced their own products, they were exposed to many health and safety risks, even without the Black

Death, which killed at least one-third of Europe's population. These artisans sometimes created risk to those who purchased or traded for their products. The impact was especially severe for the artisan, the customers they served, and the community they operated in; it is virtually certain that the Black Death mortality rates for those in contact with many others suffered higher death rates than average, according to historians of the era.[1]

As Europe entered the era of the Industrial Revolution, mass production had a multiplier effect, allowing an infinite number of products to be produced in a fraction of the time. However, with mass production came mass risk: labor abuse, contaminated products, air and water pollution, rapid depletion of sources of energy and materials, and environmental disasters. These risks replaced the Black Death as a multifaceted risk paradigm rather than a deadly but singular one. As the impact became more widespread, so did public awareness and outrage. The groundswell of concern led to a wave of environmental, health, safety, and security regulatory frameworks as well as public oversight. The impact to manufacturing was significant and the cost of compliance high. Organizations began to search outside their geographic and jurisdictional borders for ways to lower compliance and thus production costs. Once contained, globalization led to globalized risk as production processes were outsourced to countries with poor or nonexistent environmental, health, labor practice, product quality, and safety frameworks and regulations. Production was outsourced but the risk certainly was not.

As discussed in my previous book (*At Your Own Risk*, John Wiley & Sons, 2008), and in the first Law of this book, the media and nongovernment organizations (NGOs) pounced on the wide-scale inequity and abuse. The practice of violating individual human rights and the exploitation of the environment by manufacturers in Asia, Latin America, and elsewhere set off alarms and varying degrees of response around the globe. Market and regulatory pressure followed and although many of these practices are still prevalent, progress has been made—but not without great sacrifice of human life and economic loss. Manufacturing, one of the two dirtiest jobs in the supply chain (the other being the extraction, mining, and cultivating of materials, minerals, food, energy, and water), will forever be fraught with significant internal and external risk. As discussed in previous chapters, the risk parasite is embedded in all its processes; the parasite knows no geographic or physical borders. The consequential damage of an adverse event during the production process can materially impact the brand and financial standing of *all* those that were linked together in the supply chain. An example of this occurred when the WCNC news channel in North Carolina reported that two people purposefully contaminated fast-food pizzas during the production process. Unfortunately, the video was posted on YouTube and quickly made its way around the world. Although the extent of incident to the brand remains unknown, it goes without saying that there was some degree of consequential damage.[2]

Why Is Managing Risk Such a Big Production?

What precisely is production risk management? Leveraging our original definition of risk, uncertainty, and exposure to uncertainty, we can better understand the challenges of managing supply chain risk during the production process. Let's begin with uncertainty (threats). What are the risks relevant to the manufacturing, fabrication, construction, assembly, or subassembly production processes, resources, and systems such as the enterprise or manufacturing resource planning applications? Here are a few, but keep in mind this is just a subset of a very long list. It includes labor strikes, workplace violence, cyber attacks, rising water, wind damage, machinery failure, obsolete technology and inventory, failed relationships, shifting earth (including liquefaction), sabotage, pandemics, intellectual property theft, material and product shrinkage (theft), and infrastructure failure (power, water, public safety, health, energy, sanitation). The list of threats appears to be endless, but that's only part of the issue. We must also take a closer look at all that can be exposed to uncertainty (vulnerabilities). The scope of resources is far-reaching and includes, but is not limited to, labor, intangibles (knowledge, experience, corporate memory), process, technology, data, communications networks, relationships, machinery, boilers and other physical assets, hand tools, vital records and public filings, inventory, and relationships.

Now that's just the risks internal to the manufacturing portion of the supply chain. What about the risks that the manufacturing process presents others—the community? In December of 1984, a Union Carbide (now part of the Dow Chemical Company) plant in Bhopal, India, leaked 42 tons of toxic gas. The actual death toll has been disputed, but Greenpeace cites a conservative number of 20,000.

The reason for the failure (accident, equipment failure, or human sabotage) was disputed and the final report never released. In the end, the presence of this manufacturing facility in Bhopal resulted in significant loss of life and damage to the environment.[3] The list of other potential adverse external impacts does not stop there; it also includes climate, energy use, water, biodiversity and land use, chemical toxins and heavy metals, air pollution, waste management, ozone layer depletion, oceans and fisheries, and deforestation. Sites that support production operations—especially manufacturing, processing, and construction—are ground zero for environmental disasters and the rapid reproduction of the risk parasite.

As if the list of threats and vulnerabilities is not long enough, we also have to remember about the reality of big business. Their survival relies on a network of globally dispersed owned or contracted manufacturing sites numbering in the hundreds if not the thousands. Another *multiplier effect*—risks that were once isolated to a single production facility and its operations—now explodes into a list of thousands or even tens of thousands. Nike, for example, leverages over 600 contract manufacturers, all of which must comply with strict manufacturing supply chain risk requirements. (Note: The number of contract manufacturers dropped since I began this book, thus the reason for the differing number from Chapter 2.) Managing risk now becomes at least 600 times more challenging as Nike deals with physical, language, legal, cultural, and environmental differences. Nike is not alone. All global organizations are faced with similar risk complexity challenges—Unilever, BP, Procter & Gamble, Fonterra, IBM, Johnson & Johnson, Toyota, Shell, Acer, Barilla Group, Rio Tinto, Emerson Electric Company, Cisco, General Electric, LVMH Moët Hennessy. To address this challenge, many of these organizations have established the office of Corporate (Social) Responsibility (CR or CSR). The office typically reports annually to the board and external stakeholders on the state of their environmental, health, safety, security, inspection, and other manufacturing risk practices.

Nike's case is instructive and augments the methods needed to manage the multiplier effect. Paul Ranta, Nike's Compliance Manager, explains the company has a "four C's" strategy: compliance (including worker rights, code of conduct even for outsourced processes, leadership standards, environmental enforcement); community (sometimes called this corporate governance, and done right it reduces and eliminates many forms of risk); climate (energy use, corporate footprint, long-range planning for responsible global actions); and considered (evaluation of the impact in processes used, notably chemical and design). Craig Bartol, Nike's Global Risk Manager, accepts the reality that issues come up every day and that the learning process never ends. Never. He explains: "We learn, continuously improve, and build on our experiences; we have extensive corporate knowledge and memory. We nurture and improve the asset." He went on to say, "By the time you publish this book, we will have most likely evolved this strategy even further—we are on the mission, not just the assignment."

Think about this for a moment. It is profound. In too many organizational cultures, the paradigm is viewed as something that comes and goes. Risk rises up, costs money, and is handled. And then it goes away. The job is done. In this approach, no one learns anything at all. But Nike has advanced to the point of acceptance of risk as ever present and, more important, the company knows that it can learn valuable lessons about improving in the future from the risk realized today. This is the key.

With eyes wide open, any organization can advance to the same stage. There is a good reason that the United States remains number one in the world of production: It is a culture of forward thinking, success, free markets, and *doing the right thing* even when that is difficult or expensive. Nike has shown that the answer is to acknowledge risk and turn the liability into an asset.

This raises a question we all have to address: Are production risks isolated or do they affect just emerging and lesser-developed nations? Hardly. The top 12 manufacturing countries in 2007 (by output) were the United States ($1,831 billion), China ($1,106b USD equivalent), Japan ($926M), Germany ($670M), Russian Federation ($362M), Italy ($345M), U.K. ($342b), France ($296M), Korea ($241M), Canada ($218M), Spain ($208M), Brazil ($206M), India ($167M), Mexico ($144M), Indonesia ($121M), and Turkey ($101M). If output to the two largest (U.S. and China) were curtailed, that would equal 40 percent of the world's total.

Ours Is Not to Question (or See) Why

The Imperial Sugar disaster makes another point: Manufacturing has become the most overlooked aspect of the supply chain. This

Production Does Not Operate in Isolation. Imperial Sugar Explosion, Direct and Indirect Impacts (How It Unravels)

A refinery explosion at Imperial Sugar's Georgia plant in 2008 killed 13 people and injured 42 more. This directly impacted the production supply chains for many huge concerns, including Piggly Wiggly, General Mills, and Wal-Mart, to name a few. But the impacts were much more far-reaching.

There are always multiple and unforeseen impacts from production failures. The Imperial Sugar disaster resulted in a 60 percent reduction in its own capacity and 9 percent of U.S. production capacity. The rebuilding of Imperial Sugar's Port Wentworth refinery following the explosion is expected to total $200 to $220 million.[4] The Coast Guard closed off rivers to mitigate the damage of a minor oil spill resulting from the explosion, and shipping was delayed. Effects were long-term as well. Cargill, Inc. and the Louisianan sugar co-op had been supplying 90 percent of Imperial's factories with raw cane but began building a competing refinery. Imperial retaliated by entering into an agreement with a Mexican sugar refinery. One thing is clear: The sugar supply chain was about to be redefined and so was the risk profile. In the end there were OSHA fines, operating losses, wrongful death suits, federal investigations, and new regulation—not to even mention the damage done to the brand.[5]

The lesson here: In production, there is no such thing as a contained disaster. It inevitably has far-reaching and long-term consequences, many permanent. It doesn't matter what you produce; even an isolated disaster like the Imperial explosion is going to have a ripple effect.

is ironic, considering that it is where the whole process begins for virtually all of the tangible products people end up buying. And the problem is not isolated, either. As an example of where process manufacturing risk can become disastrous, you may remember the Mattel toys case. In 2007, Mattel was forced to recall 83 products, numbering more than 900,000 units. This occurred when it was discovered that the products contained toxic lead paint. Even Mattel's extensive audits did not uncover the problem in its China-based suppliers until after one-third of the tainted toys had been shipped to stores. Making matters worse, a Mattel spokesman said the factory that produced these toys was a 15-year supplier and not a newcomer, and that "They understand our regulations, they understand our program, and something went wrong."[6]

It might be more easily explained if the factory had been a new supplier, but this was a long-standing relationship, and Mattel had conducted audits. Most alarming of all in this story is that Mattel did not seem to know exactly what went wrong.

This type of problem is not isolated to a single industry or company; it can happen anywhere. For example, one of China's largest pharmaceutical companies released a contaminated anticancer drug in 2007, injuring a five-year-old child rather than curing her leukemia. Many Western pharmaceutical companies rely on Chinese-produced drugs even though quality control problems are often severe. Dozens of Chinese patients may have also taken the tainted medicine and the Chinese government has accused the manufacturer of covering up its quality problems. Many companies in China rely largely on unregulated factories where sanitation may be minimal or nonexistent. Also in 2007, the former head of China's drug regulatory agency was sentenced to death for accepting bribes.[7]

Why does this occur and, more to the point, why does it recur? Here are a number of reasons:

1. *Manufacturing is often invisible in the boardroom.* The emphasis in the organization's power center is more likely to be on budgets and stock prices than on the nitty-gritty of manufacturing. Little thought is given to lead paint or poisoned milk. This is due to the training of many executives and managers in the financial arena and not so much in supply chain processes. This is true even in accounting, where corporate management and forecasting gets greater emphasis than cost accounting.
2. *Nearly all U.S.-based companies have outsourced the process.* The ruling view of manufacturing is that "it's not my problem." This is because the overwhelming majority of manufacturing operations are now offshore, handled in remote factories and farms in other countries. The home office probably does not even own its manufacturing operations, but has come to rely on the interaction between foreign factories and foreign suppliers. In other words, the product does not even appear until it arrives ready to market; and quality control at home rarely considers that lead paint is still in use anywhere, or that margin-squeezed farmers might contaminate a food product. So if there are problems in this portion of the supply chain, it is due to errors made by someone else. This failure to embrace the entire

supply chain (including the outsourced portion and its very real potential single points of failure) is one of the most serious flaws in modern supply chain risk management.

3. *Managers tend to view the supply chain as beginning when the process enters their immediate view.* The myopic view of supply chain is that it only begins to exist when it arrives locally. This is oldthink, however, because everything is interconnected today, and that implies a revolutionized level of responsibility. We are living in a world of advanced technology and primitive controls, of environmental awareness side by side with dangerous levels of environmental pollution. But everyone is responsible for managing risk; the new view of supply chain is like the new and modern view of everything else. Your organization cannot afford to think of supply chain management *only* within the organization. Effective supply chain management demands extending the process all the way to the factory floor and even farther back to the field, forests, and farms where raw materials are derived.
4. *Many finance-trained managers are clueless about the process.* The Achilles' heel of modern industry is also one of its greatest strengths. Thus, a financial executive would ask, "Why would you use lead paint in a toy?" rather than asking the more important question: "How did we miss this?" For many reasons, organizational management is dominated by people trained and educated in the financial industry. However, this also means that many of today's top management have never been to a factory floor or, if they have, the visit was on a catwalk above the work area and visitors wore coat and tie and a yellow hard hat. Few of today's top managers have ever worked on the floor itself, and they simply don't know what is involved in the genesis of a supply chain. They can only speculate about how supply chains work at the origin. Furthermore, most executives are going to think of manufacturing as a large-scale, modernized, antiseptic, and fully automated facility, including robotic assembly, computer-controlled environment, and close, continual oversight. Many pharmaceutical executives may not even realize that their suppliers consist of hundreds of extremely small, poor, and uncontrolled pig farms in rural third-world regions. So a vast educational effort needs to extend knowledge beyond the higher floor of buildings and

down into the factories and farms where the work begins. There must be a realistic understanding of how these basic suppliers operate on thin margins and are at the mercy of the financial interests they serve.

A New Collaborative Effort

The challenge of enlightening and educating today's finance-oriented management to adopt an informed view about production is a daunting task. But by looking at the whole issue with supply-side risk in mind, it is not difficult to quantify what needs to be done and why simple cost-cutting is not going to fix anything.

The way to retrain management to truly appreciate what the supply chain risks are is to enter into an entirely new and different business model than the one assumed to apply in past venues. In the days when manufacturing was done domestically, customers rarely if ever existed outside local boundaries, and the entire market was fairly simple; it was easy to simplify and even ignore production supply chain risk. Today, however, with the production activity often two steps removed from management (who often deal to a degree with suppliers but rarely with companies actually building and assembling product), it is quite difficult to make this point, but it is essential.

For a manufacturer of printed circuit boards and electronic components, understanding the relevance of different risks was critical to the management team. Production-related risks were classified into eight specific categories, and identifying these, as well as the most serious threats, is a good starting point in the process. With the distance between production and management, the criteria you develop can be applied to identify steps needed immediately to reduce risks; these may include the imperative of shrinking the supply chain in order to eliminate the twice-removed risks associated with the second tier problem. The eight areas and their most severe risks are as follows:

1. Economic
   Labor/skills shortages
2. Informational
   Loss or disclosure of proprietary/confidential information
   Information integrity issues
   Technology failure

3. **People**
   Oversight, accidents, errors, and other process failures
   Loss/defection of key employees
4. Psychopathic, criminal, and terrorist
5. Weather
   Hurricane, typhoon, cyclone, wind, hail, tornado
6. Environmental and man-made
   Biochemical and radiation release
   Fire and/or explosion
7. Political and social
   Government policy and/or attitude change
8. Reputational
   Product liability, failure, recall

A value in listing these primary and highest-priority risks is that it allows you to reduce the threat universe to a quantified level, as well as adding relevance. A limited number of high-priority risks can be addressed more readily than a broad range of known and unknown threats. A highly useful approach is to develop a scenario and then decide what the losses would be to the organization and how to respond (or, more to the point, how to change the current supply chain operating environment to better respond or to remove the threat). In one example, the company assumed that a catastrophic event occurred after working hours at one of its key facilities; that equipment, inventory, and vital records as well as processing capabilities became unavailable for an extended time; and that records were either destroyed or damaged. In a second version of the hypothetical event, the assumption was that the incident occurred during working hours. In this version, key personnel were unavailable for many hours and some portion (less than one-fourth) of employees were not able to return to work within 30 days.

This exercise defined the priorities and consequences of the incident. Tolerance levels were clearly defined in terms of performance at several levels, including organizational, product line, production, and resources. The outcome of the event included observations by many employees. For example, one conclusion was that the company could survive a five-day plant outage (some estimates extended this to two weeks); another pointed out that employees needed to know what corporate was willing to tolerate as to down time (in other words, what is a maximum acceptable limit of loss?). Perhaps the most important observation was that an outage of one month would require nine months of recovery time.[8]

The value in the exercise was that it defined exactly what losses would create in terms of cost, down time, and response. This led to recognition that the organization needed a supply chain continuity plan, organized under a coordinator who was given the task of holding a strategy planning session with executive management and key process owners. Various recovery options were identified and subjected to a cost/benefit analysis. In this extensive analysis and study, the most valuable result was that the organization was able to prioritize both risk exposure and appropriate response/investment. This mitigates the potential loss and, of great interest, also led to evaluation of how to reduce the down time and lost productivity that could result from a disruption to the production side of the supply chain.

How do you create a collaborative and interdependent environment in the modern fast pace of business, where keeping costs down is often the highest priority? This is the big question. Even companies that audit their suppliers and demand minimal quality standards often completely ignore the real sources of problems, which often are the manufacturing process and those companies doing the work. Does this mean that it's not the supplier's problem, but the manufacturer's? No. It is *your* problem if you don't extend your quality audits, standard-setting, enforcement, and assistance all the way to the source. In other words, the revolutionary idea may seem contrary: Your company has spent years outsourcing and offshoring as much as possible. But now it is becoming evident that you need to extend your reach and accept responsibility for the entire process, even beyond the authority of your organization, and all the way to foreign suppliers *and* manufacturers, and including large factories as well as small farms and assembly plants.

For example, a single nuclear reactor at Chalk River, Ontario, is the sole source for the world's supply of technetium-99, an isotope used in medical diagnosis. This isotope is injected into U.S. patients 20 million times per year to create images for diagnosis of many ailments, including heart disease and cancer. An extended shutdown of the reactor in November 2007 created a severe shortage of this vital ingredient. The problem includes the fact that it cannot be stockpiled because it decays rapidly (in about six hours), so the reliance on a single source for such a vital diagnostic tool is a huge problem for the medical community.[9]

The usual solutions to this type of production problem would include diversification (creating a relationship with a second provider) and stockpiling. Both of these solutions are impossible in this situation.

Some production problems do not have good solutions and, in the case cited, shortages led to delays in diagnosis. Most production and material issues can be solved by a more holistic approach, including a wider view of the supply chain and its elements, with production a driving force that creates many of the risks you have to address.

In trying to enact this new and holistic approach to the supply chain, with its all-inclusive interest from A to Z, a different management problem arises. There are going to be a large number of participants in this process, so the question comes down to how you are going to manage manufacturer and supply risks within and beyond expectations, within imposed budgets in a tight economy, and with the assurance of effective results. Making this even more challenging, you face critical review from the finance-oriented management in your organization.

This is not limited to restrictions within your budget. Remember, a completely effective supply chain risk management program will be invisible. It is only when threats materialize that management can actually come to understand the cost of a weak system. So the losses you prevent are not going to appear anywhere on that familiar budget report. In fact, the increased cost that inevitably arises will be criticized as unnecessary primarily because of the dazzling success—and invisibility—of the program.

Is Change a Catalyst for Improved Production Risk Management?

If you hope to manage change, don't try to deal with the full scope of it because there is just too much to think about. Start with a blank piece of paper and begin listing the greatest impacts you can imagine. Keep the list short, to the three to five events your organization cannot manage or needs to take steps to avert, and then list the steps you can take to reduce or avoid those risks.

A weather disaster cannot be avoided, but your supply chain can be effectively diversified so the whole thing isn't shut down as a result. Other means include many ideas that some consider revolutionary today. For example, should you consider deglobalization, the shrinking of your supply chain to a smaller logistics range and more manageable, closer to home, first-tier suppliers? Should you also reverticalize, completely eliminating the risks of second-tier outsourcing, and work only with suppliers you can monitor directly and close to home?

Your short list of disasters and their possible solutions, if put into action, will eliminate the most expensive and catastrophic production risks to your organization. And it can happen quickly. But to do so, you first have to go through the steps to make sure your management really understands its supply chain. If your organization is like most, you are not there yet.

So to seriously address this issue, it is essential that management gains education about the full extent of its supply chain. The enlightened manager of today may proudly point to the decision to send experts to suppliers overseas to impose high standards, train suppliers' employees, and enact enforcement and quality control actions. The same executive may even have met with CEOs of supplier organizations to discuss these new and innovative outreach programs. But remember, a supplier today often outsources its own manufacturing, often to another country. So your supplier in China may be working with a factory in Vietnam or Bangladesh. Now the question arises: Is your primary supplier enforcing quality standards with its own supply chain? Of course, you have no way to know the answer, and therein lies the problem.

To take responsibility for the entire supply chain, management needs to take a step back from the financial aspects of its task and assess the risks to the production process of the entire supply chain, including not only foreign suppliers but *their* supply chain and outsourced manufacturing as well. So the supply chain is truly global in nature and is not limited to the immediate office or store, and not even to the first-rung supplier. It extends to the supply chain of your supplier as well; and another problem is that from the point of view of the source manufacturer, their reporting interest is to the supplier and not to you.

This broad responsibility has to take into account the ramifications of long-standing practices. For example, among the many causes of water shortages in western states, some uses of water resources have been questionable, and a solution has to include involvement of many agencies, municipalities, and individuals. The water shortage in Las Vegas has led to some of these solutions. For example, a superintendent of a golf course tore out turf and replaced it with rocks, with over 65 acres transformed in five years. Western cities fine homeowners for excessive water uses. Phoenix has begun using technology to recycle wastewater. Tucson has begun requiring new businesses to collect rainwater for irrigation. California developers have to prove that they have sufficient water available for the number of houses they want to build. And major hotel-casinos in Las Vegas have adopted green building codes aimed at slashing water use by 40 percent.[10]

The whole process has to change. If your supplier outsources any portion of its manufacturing operation, your agreement has to extend your responsibility and authority to the real origins of your product. So you will need to impose a requirement on your suppliers, specifying that your organization must be granted access and authority throughout the supplier's secondary supply chain.

Because the true genesis of any product may involve multiple levels of manufacturing, assembly, warehousing, and delivery, you need to extend the reach of your supply chain as far as it needs to go. It is no longer enough to audit first-tier suppliers in one country if they are relying on other manufacturing sources in locations remote for them. The new supply chain risk management program has to reach as far as it needs to in order to ensure that all known single points of failure are monitored and risks are mitigated.

Weak demand among steelmakers led to renegotiation of contracts with many suppliers in 2008, due to falling prices for scrap metals, among other causes. Suppliers are required to delay shipments or lower prices, or face having no outlet at all. The decision to cancel contracts makes sense when commodity prices are down, but the causes and effects of production slowdowns ripple throughout the economy.[11]

Why Is Production So Critical?

Invisible problems are easily ignored. However, they are all too real in many cases, and manufacturing-level supply chain risks are a good example. If any threats are realized at this level—including contamination, theft, natural disaster, and anything that will stop the supply chain in its tracks—it moves rapidly through the entire supply chain. The risk parasite that is born in the factory infects the entire body of the supply chain right to its end, where your customers buy the product.

The task you face in bringing this critical problem to management's attention, and, equally important, the authority to devote time and budget to solving it, faces many obstacles. Not the least of these is the financial burden you will demand of suppliers and their subcontracted manufacturers. Among the problems you might encounter are:

- Financial limitations at the manufacturing level
- Lack of budget to make improvements
- Outdated or insufficient business and operating models for the changes required
- Cultural differences, varying level of experience
- Competing priorities (with other suppliers)
- Limited leverage

In other words, for all of these reasons, you have to be aware that the old problem—imposing demands on suppliers and manufacturers without also providing the financing, education, incentives, and/or empowerment for those changes—becomes an operating model. Thus, you are back where you started. You may discover that some models for fixing supply chain problems only create more and bigger problems. This is why the changes you need to make throughout your supply chain are going to require financial resources as well as education, new quality-based rules, and enforcement practices. The education portion is challenging because remote manufacturers may define risk in vastly different ways than you do and because so many of these resources exist beyond your tier-one contacts. Quality control is equally challenging in many situations because it is viewed primarily as a new cost imposition that often is perceived to slow down processes and add to costs (thus reducing manufacturer profits). Enforcement rules and practices may be equally resisted at the manufacturing level for the same reasons. And financing of all of these changes has to come from your organization, where you can expect even greater resistance. You will be asking management to fund a fix for problems that have not occurred, may not occur, and, if prevented, are invisible and cannot be measured.

Getting over the budgeting hurdles is a significant problem in itself. But even if you are able to accomplish that, you still face the problems of resistance from both suppliers and their subcontracted manufacturers. In designing new enforcement rules along with improved standards, what are the incentives and what are the penalties? Ultimately, you have the power to switch to different suppliers for noncompliance, but that should be viewed as a last resort. It is much better to think of suppliers/manufacturers as partners than as adversaries, which, while not always possible, does lead to better relationships over the long term.

However, material shortages can turn partners into adversaries, depending on the root causes. In 2007, Boeing, which has a multiyear backlog of orders, found itself facing a shortage of nuts and bolts. This occurred as the company was trying to meet a deadline for completion of its first Dreamliner jet. Boeing's primary fastener supplier, Alcoa, produces the specific quality of titanium bolts for use in aircraft manufacturing (a single one-inch-diameter bolt could support the weight of 50 automobiles). However, Alcoa is one of only a few providers of these pieces. Boeing has always had the attitude that these high-tech bolts were readily available because it had never faced a shortage before. Ironically, the problem grew from a series of causes and effects. After the 9/11 attacks, the airline industry cancelled hundreds of orders and Boeing laid off 35,000 workers. As a result, Alcoa laid off 41 percent of workers at its fastener division. More than five years later, the resulting bolt shortage was a direct result of these events. It took that long for the shortage to develop, but it demonstrates the vulnerability Boeing faced.[12]

How could Boeing have anticipated and prevented this problem? Because there had never been a shortage in the past, the bolt problem took Boeing by surprise and affected the more than 600 orders for 2008 and 2009, when Boeing delivered only about 112 jets. Learning from the past, inventory policies should be altered to ensure that a minimum required number of months of parts—even parts believed to be readily available—are on hand at all times, even though this means investing more money in building up the stock. In other words, it is a fairly simple short-term problem that can be resolved easily. But like so many production issues, this problem was not anticipated by anyone.

These unexpected problems are not limited to companies relying on single sources of supply and based on the idea that the supplier is taking care of business. The most common interpretation of supply chain risk management is typically limited in scope to an assessment of the risk management practices of first-tier, or primary, suppliers. Remarkably, the assumption by many organizations is that these suppliers are effectively managing their supply chain risk. Ask yourself: If your organization is not effectively managing its own contract manufacturers and job shops, why would you assume that the same are effectively managing their own production risks?

Wal-Mart set up a series of new and more stringent requirements for its suppliers in 2008. Included was a requirement that all manufacturers selling directly to Wal-Mart must provide a complete list of their suppliers. The company also announced it would begin requiring third-party certification that all suppliers are meeting safety, labor, and environmental standards required by local law. Categories Wal-Mart assessed included a wide range of issues: environmental, chemical, and pesticide management; health and safety; labor practices; and right of inspection (including subcontractors to whom production had been outsourced). All of these categories had dozens of subcategories. The point is, Wal-Mart's 2008 initiative was comprehensive, aggressive, and designed to eliminate the kinds of risks that could damage its supply chain and reputation.

Wal-Mart also began requiring outside audits for supplier labor law compliance. Increased environmental regulation and labor law enforcement have led to closure of thousands of factories in southern China, and Wal-Mart's requirements are only a small part of the larger picture.[13] However, few organizations possess the leverage of a Wal-Mart, Carrefour SA, IBM, Cisco, Nokia, or Tesco.

Worse yet and more scary, these same organizations often believe or assume that their supplier's suppliers, or upstream contract manufacturers (tier two or beyond), understand and are effectively managing their risks to expectations up the line. And even worse, some organizations assume that the manufacturers in their extended supply chain somehow now *own* the risk; that is, by some miracle the management of supply chain risk was assigned to the manufacturer and that further diligence was not necessary.

This defensive trend applies to every organization and to every product, at times with unintended consequences. Consider the case of consumer electronics company Best Buy. As the economy slowed down in 2008, Best Buy reduced inventory levels of PCs. So all of the subassemblers, assemblers, and manufacturers—Dell and

Hewlett-Packard, for example—also had to bring their inventories down. This trickled down to Intel and AMD, dominant players providing the guts of the circuitry for PCs. Then UMC and TSMC, dominant chip manufacturers, were also affected. But when these companies have to restart as demand grows once again, how long does it take to ramp up production? Restarting an idled line in the high-tech manufacturing world is not as simple as flipping a switch. It involves calibration, priming, reengaging the workforce, and restarting the broader supply chain resources.

The complexities of cyclical changes in production and inventory require a higher effort in scenario analysis and modeling. The questions are: What happens when demand spikes, and what happens when demand evaporates? How will the supply chain react to these events, and what lead times are required to respond?

Where Does It All Begin and What Is the Proper Scope?

The determination of where the supply chain management issue begins requires mastery of several different (and often geographically diverse) resources, including human skills, materials, the efforts of suppliers and manufacturers, technology, data, inventory, and even customers. I cannot emphasize this enough: The issue of logistics is never simple, and the time demands for recognition of change and response to it involve the entire length and width of the supply chain, from farm to factory to ship and to customers.

This case history demonstrates the complexities of supply chain breakdown due to unforeseen circumstances. Wherever the truth lies, the implication is clear: No one knows whether the world supply of heparin is safe. No one can say that standards are enforced and the evidence indicates that, in fact, few if any standards exist in the source villages of China.

The problem specific to imported drugs and drug ingredients led the FDA to launch a pilot program in 2009 to improve quality and safety of drug imports. The FDA planned to select 100 participants for its Secure Supply Chain program. The goal: to identify what is needed to ensure safety of products imported from China and other countries. Michael Chappell, acting Associate Commissioner for Regulatory Affairs at the FDA, explained, "With the increase of drug products produced outside the United States, it is critical that the FDA concentrate its resources on companies

The Invisible Danger

A case study demonstrates how a critical supply chain can be more vulnerable than anyone thinks. The drug heparin is derived from animal liver cells and is a vital anticoagulant (formula $C_{12}H_{19}NO_{20}S_3$). It prevents blood clots and is used to treat acute coronary disease, a trial fibrillation, thrombosis, and pulmonary embolism; clinical trails for treatment of arthritis, asthma, cancer, and even organ transplants are promising. It is also used in bypass and other heart surgery operations. In other words, it is a vital drug. David Strunce, president of Scientific Protein Laboratories, Baxter Lab's main supplier of heparin, says that the Yuan Intestine and Casing Factory is not in his company's supply chain. Scientific Protein can't trace its supplies in China in as much detail as it can in the United States. "We're all dealing with the China collection system," Mr. Strunce reported.

China is the world's largest heparin exporter, shipping more than $100 million of the substance a year. China's lack of consistent oversight of its heparin industry highlights a regulatory gap that's opening as drug makers increasingly go shopping globally for ingredients. The raw heparin made by China's myriad small producers ends up in the hands of about 50 export companies, which sell to customers overseas. In the first half of 2008, more than 85 percent of these heparin exports went to the United States, Austria, France, Italy, and Germany, according to an industry trade group.

An ideal system for tracing heparin back to the barnyard would involve tagging individual pigs, then keeping files detailing each animal's record of vaccination, feed, and overall health. That record could follow the animal to the slaughterhouse, providing a paper trail that a drug company or the FDA could later tap into. Many heparin processors, including Changzhou Scientific Protein Laboratories (SPL), the plant that supplies Baxter, are registered as chemical or agricultural-byproducts companies and weren't checked by health authorities. Abraxis Pharmaceutical Products, or APP Pharmaceuticals, Baxter's main rival, says its Chinese supplier, Shenzhen Hepalink, is able to trace refined heparin back to individual pigs. Shenzhen Hepalink also says it requires suppliers of raw heparin to follow rules designed to minimize the chances of contamination.

The agency did, at most, 21 inspections of Chinese drug-making facilities annually in fiscal years 2002 through 2007, according to the U.S. Government Accountability Office (GAO). That represents a fraction of the 714 Chinese facilities that, as of the end of fiscal 2007, the GAO says were involved in making drugs or drug ingredients for the U.S. market. FDA Commissioner Andrew von Eschenbach has said he would like to station inspectors in China.

Because heparin is derived from living tissue, companies that purify raw heparin follow a range of steps—filtration, heat treatments, and other processing—to reduce the risk that it may contain active viruses or bacterial toxins. Since

(continued)

mid-2006, China's pig herds have suffered serious outbreaks of porcine reproductive and respiratory syndrome, a viral illness commonly known as blue-ear disease. Sick animals are supposed to be rejected by slaughterhouses, but enforcement can be lax. Also, infected animals may be slaughtered before symptoms are recognized.

Some drug makers say it's important to be able to trace back to the pigs that served as raw materials. That way, if patients have adverse reactions to a drug, the root problem can be discovered and other possibly tainted batches can be pulled from the market. Many Chinese heparin manufacturers say this is a very difficult standard to meet in China's business and agriculture environment. Wang Shengfu, manager of another raw-heparin maker in China's Shandong province, Linyi Meiyuan Seasoning Co., notes that unscrupulous businesspeople and middlemen can easily "provide buyers with fake records."[14]

By 2010, China is expected to produce nearly 25 percent of the world's pharmaceutical ingredients, according to a recent study by the investment firm Credit Suisse. "If you haven't been in a plant for the last two or three years, you don't have any clue what's going on in those places," said a congressional source familiar with investigative work into the FDA by the House Commerce Committee's subcommittee. "They could be running monster truck rallies on the plant floor, and we wouldn't know about it."

"The computer infrastructure is outdated, it's not stable, there is insufficient security and capability," said Dale Nordenberg, a Science Board member who specialized on the computer systems. "The FDA is still relying on an amalgamation of paper-based records and poorly integrated electronic platforms." The two main FDA databases cannot agree on how many foreign companies are subject to FDA inspection. One claims the number is 3,000, the other 6,800. Compounding the confusion, the FDA uses corporate names, rather than identification numbers, to track production plants and registration information. For an agency monitoring the operations of companies in dozens of countries worldwide, this creates confusion. Indeed, Scientific Protein's China operation slipped through the FDA's inspection regimen primarily because of confusion over the company's name. But Nordenberg is hardly encouraged by the agency's admission this was at the root of the FDA's failure to inspect the plant. "That's just another heparin timeline," he said.[15]

One expert says as much as 70 percent of China's crude heparin—for domestic use and for export—comes from small factories in poor villages. One of the biggest areas for these workshops is in coastal Jiangsu Province, north of Shanghai, where entire villages have become heparin production centers. In a village called Xinwangzhuang, nearly every house along a narrow street doubles as a tiny heparin operation, where teams of four to eight women wearing aprons and white boots wash, splice, separate, and process pig intestines into sausage casings and crude heparin. The floors had large puddles and drainage channels; the workshops were dilapidated and unheated; and steam from the production process fogged up the windows and soaked the walls. There were large ovens to cook ingredients and halls lined with barrels to store enzymes, resins, intestines, and wastewater. "This is our family-style workshop," said Zhu Jinlan, the owner of one heparin operation, who stopped sorting pig intestines and invited visitors to a back room, where she lives with her husband and child. "We've been doing this about ten years."

Experts say the small, unregulated factories could pose dangers because they do not have the same controls and rules as large slaughterhouses, which also produce crude heparin. "If you don't control the incoming source, it's very hard to get rid of the contaminants," says Liu Jian, a heparin expert at the University of North Carolina. Mr. Strunce of SPL says his company never buys directly from the crude-heparin producers, only through its wholesalers, which he called "consolidators"—Changzhou Techpool, its Chinese joint venture partner, and Ruihua. His company, he said, has records documenting all the transactions. But in Rugao, producers of crude heparin tell a different story. A sales manager for a major supplier, Nantong Koulong, said he sells directly to SPL without going through either of the two wholesalers. "We provided crude heparin to Changzhou SPL," said the sales manager, Chen Jianjun. Some of Koulong's stock comes from the unregulated workshops, he said. The owner of one such workshop, Ms. Zhu in Xinwangzhuang, said she sold to SPL two years ago. She also sells to Koulong. "We are really a traditional family-style plant," she said. "We have no certificate."

After an outbreak of blue-ear pig disease swept through 25 of China's 31 provinces and regions in 2008, prices soared and many drug suppliers had to look to the small workshops. The epidemic, said Cui Huifei, a heparin expert at the Shandong University School of Medicine, "made those biotech companies inevitably purchase from the family-style plants, for cheaper prices."[16]

that pose the highest risk of importing products that don't meet the FDA's standards and violate U.S. laws."[17]

The guidelines that the FDA announced that it will use to monitor pharmaceutical risks could be applied to other imports as well and could vastly reduce the incidence of contamination and other supply chain risks. However, such programs may be more effective when instituted by importers rather than by government agencies. If the program succeeds, it could present an actionable model for organizations to apply in nonpharmaceutical imports.

The same level of threat can exist for any product and for any company doing business internationally. It makes the logistics approach essential in order to protect your organization's name and reputation. It is not just a public relations problem if something goes wrong. Whether it's melamine in milk, lead in children's toys, or other poisons in pet food or meat products, the threat at the source—the risk parasite you live with every day even if you don't see it—threatens the health of the entire supply chain.

Part Two of the Double Whammy: Labor

I have previously noted that among the most serious known threats, high-priority economic threats include labor shortages and people threats—first, oversights, accidents, or errors; and second, loss or defection of key employees. These two threats pose serious potential disruptions in the production and logistics ends of the supply chain; the possibility of labor strikes and slowdowns is an additional potential threat that every manager needs to think about. The solution may be to create adequate supply chain diversification so that a labor-generated threat in one location does not bring the entire supply chain to a complete halt.

The labor problems can grow from any number of causes, many beyond the most obvious disputes over wages. For example, in the U.K., Prime Minister Gordon Brown faced the problem in 2009 of hundreds of workers walking off the job at oil refineries and power plants. This was a protest against the U.K. policy of using foreign labor, which is a growing international problem. In Spain, the government began offering immigrants money to return home, and France has devised stimulus programs aimed at granting government-sponsored programs to French companies. In the United States, the widely publicized stimulus package restricted project funding to U.S. companies only, banning foreign suppliers from even bidding on infrastructure projects. Even though the often-tried "Buy American" approach has invariably led to higher costs and has not achieved the desired results, politicians find the scapegoating of foreign labor a favorite populist trick. German Chancellor Angela Merkel criticized the United States in its efforts to provide rescue funds to the auto industry, saying U.S. measures "constitute protectionism." A WTO assessment warned that the U.S. trend toward protectionism "would only worsen the economic situation for all and diminish prospects for an early recovery in activity."[18]

Labor unrest, the downside of protectionism, strikes, slowdowns, and workplace walk-outs are the best-known labor threats. However, there also appears to be a growing problem toward workplace violence. Numerous stories in the past decade document the incidence of disgruntled and mentally unbalanced employees or ex-employees entering the workplace and killing or injuring workers. The consequences move beyond workplace safety, even though that should continue to pose one of the highest priorities. However, organizations also face an additional form of risk: lawsuits resulting from the failure to provide a safe working environment.

In 2005, a story emerged about a lawsuit against Lockheed Martin resulting from a 2003 incident in which five workers were killed and eight more injured. The incident, motivated partly by racial tension and partly by a conflict between husband and wife, followed months of harassment of black workers by the shooter, Doug Williams. On July 8, 2003, Williams left a diversity training class and returned with a shotgun and semiautomatic rifle. A 20-year employee, Williams was a troubled man, and others said that the warning signs were there, and that led to the lawsuit.[19]

This was not an isolated or unusual incident, either. A 2008 study noted that on an average workday, three people are killed on the job. Annually, more than one million people are assaulted at work, and homicide is the second highest cause of death on the job (number one is motor vehicle accidents).[20] In one year alone, nearly five percent of the 7.1 million private industry business establishments in the United States surveyed had an incident of workplace violence within the 12 months prior. The danger of workplace violence is a major problem, but only part of a larger and complicated issue. The combined production-related and labor-related supply chain risks often are the weakest link in an organization's supply chain. Among the problems are the size and complexity of the supply chain itself. Solutions may involve not only improved working conditions, threat scenario analysis, and outside-of-the-box thinking. A more expansive supply chain is not always a better supply chain. So a possible way to reduce production and labor risk may include shrinking the size of the supply chain while, at the same time, creating diversification in the routes of the chain itself. The solution should be based on where vulnerability exists and how big a priority the organization assigns it. That solution has to include, at the very least, these six absolute requirements:

1. Don't centralize warehouse and manufacturing or single point of failure manufacturing processes.
2. Never outsource without knowing where and who is involved, and without inspecting thoroughly and regularly.
3. Don't sleep (in other words, don't assume you can fix the problem and then walk away; you cannot).
4. Don't assume that you are the most important player in your suppliers' supply chain. This may occur in regions where prices are low, but the countries involved are IP theft or piracy-friendly.
5. Never assume that insurance will make you whole or protect your reputation after a loss; it will not.
6. Expect to be on your own locally for the first 24 to 48 hours after a disaster, and longer if the disaster involves regional outages as well. You need an emergency plan to offset the down time and loss of productivity, protect valuable assets, and ensure worker safety, just to name a few of the steps your emergency plan needs.

These steps are only a starting point; you need more specifics and you need to flesh out the steps you need to prevent the kind of loss your organization cannot afford. Remember, local disasters focus your attention, but bigger, global disasters are always possible and may eventually happen. We can learn a lot about the two-pronged risk paradigm in production, and especially taking into account the combined economic and people issues, from the extreme example of Europe for 200 years after the Black Death in the fourteenth century. There were simply no skilled workers to create products, plow the fields, or even bury all of the bodies. This disaster ended serfdom and led to the Industrial Revolution, out of pure necessity. But from the disaster came changes that remain with us today, and many of these changes have been progressive and beneficial. When tackling your production supply chain risks, remember the Black Death children's rhyme:

Ring around the rosies,
A pocketful of posies
Ashes, ashes,
We all fall down.

This rather morbid reference to Black Death symptoms (skin discoloration) and the usual aftermath (death) is a reminder of worst-case outcomes. As a worst-case scenario, this history provides you with an instructive and cautionary conclusion: A seemingly small event at the production end of the supply chain can have far-reaching and expensive effects. So you need to literally come to terms with the very real issues, plan for the worst case, and identify the steps you need to take to avoid the "ring around the rosies" in your production supply chain.

Notes

1. Norman F. Cantor, *In the Wake of the Plague: The Black Death and the World It Made*, New York: Harper Perennial, 2001.
2. YouTube, http://www.youtube.com/watch?v=OhBmWxQpedI.
3. Ingrid Eckerman, *The Bhopal Saga—Causes and Consequences of the World's Largest Industrial Disaster.* Universities Press, 2004; and Greenpeace, *International Nightmare in Bhopal*, www.greenpeace.org/international/news/nightmare-in-bhopal.html.
4. Dan Chapman, "Sugar Refinery near Savannah Determined to Rebuild," *Atlanta Journal-Constitution*, April 13, 2008.
5. Caroline Scott, "Explosion costs impact on Imperial Sugar's full year results," *Food Navigator-USA.com*, December 2008.
6. Louise Story, "Lead Paint Prompts Mattel to Recall 967,000 Toys," *New York Times*, August 2, 2007.
7. Nicholas Zamiska and Avery Johnson, "China Drugs: A Cautionary Tale," *The Wall Street Journal*, January 31, 2008; and Audra Ang, "Chinese Regulator Sentenced to Death," *Associated Press*, July 7, 2007.
8. "Business Impact & Gap Analysis Briefing," defense contractor, undisclosed organization, 2005.
9. Ian Austen, "Reactor Shutdown Causing Medical Isotope Shortage," *New York Times*, December 6, 2007.
10. Tim Gaynor and Steve Gorman, "Fast-Growing Western U.S. Cities Face Water Crisis," *Reuters*, March 11, 2009.
11. Robert Guy Mathews, "Steelmakers Squeeze Suppliers," *Wall Street Journal*, November 18, 2008.
12. J. Lynn Lunsford and Paul Glader, "Boeing's Nuts-and-Bolts Problem," *Wall Street Journal*, June 19, 2007.
13. Ann Zimmerman and Mei Fong, "Wal-Mart Suppliers Face Energy, Other Mandates," *Wall Street Journal*, October 22, 2008.
14. Gordon Fairclough and Thomas M. Burton, "China's Role in Supply of Drug Is under Fire," *Wall Street Journal*, February 21, 2008; Bruce Japsen and David Greising, "Baxter Unaware Plant Not Inspected," *Chicago Tribune*, February 21, 2008.
15. The Centers for Disease Control and Prevention; the Missouri Department of Health and Senior Services; the U.S. Food and Drug Administration; David

Barboza and Walt Bogdananich, "Twists in Chain of Supplies for Blood Drug," *New York Times*, February 28, 2008.
16. Debra Sherman, "APP Pharma Unveils Plans to Safeguard Heparin Supply," *Reuters*, December 5, 2008.
17. "FDA Launches Pilot Program to Improve the Safety of Drugs and Active Drug Ingredients Produced Outside the United States," www.fiercebiotech.com, January 14, 2009.
18. Neil King Jr., Alistair MacDonald, and Marcus Walker, "Crisis Fuels Backlash on Trade," *Wall Street Journal*, January 31, 2009.
19. Holbrook Mohr, "Lockheed faces suit over '03 killings," *Honolulu Advertiser*, March 21, 2006.
20. "Workplace Violence Statistics," www.workplacevisions.com, April 11, 2008.

CHAPTER 8

Law #7: The Logistics Risk Management Rule: Managing the Parts Does Not Equal Managing the Whole

(IMPROVEMENTS CAN ONLY BE GAUGED BY THEIR IMPACT ON THE ENTIRE SUPPLY CHAIN)

A cargo vessel is seized by pirates and held for ransom. Weeks go by. Aboard the ship was ore needed by a refinery where plate steel is made. But because of the piracy incident, there is nothing available to fabricate into components. Without components, there is nothing to assemble, so the factory has to be closed, putting hundreds out of work. With no finished goods coming from the factory, the retail stores have nothing to offer to consumers. Without anything to buy, Christmas has to be canceled.

Is this scenario far-fetched? The problem is not apparent because the global economy operates with thousands of supply chains, shipping lanes, factories, and stores. It may be transparent to some of us in the supply chain business, but behind the scenes the scope of what is needed to support the flow of goods and information is astounding: ocean carriers, highway systems, customs, freight forwarders, TL/LTL (truck load and less than truckload), and parcel carriers, rail systems, logistics networks and technology, security, warehousing, regulatory authorities, air traffic controllers, port operators, and unions, to name only the most obvious. The more disbursed and extended the supply chain, the more complexity is involved; and as astounding as it sounds, most people remain blind to the essential upstream providers (the source to your organization's back door). Imagine the catastrophic outcome if the flow of critical agricultural products, commodities, or energy were brought to a standstill. This means that delivery of many commodities—not only ore, but grain, oil, copper, gold, and cotton—are exposed to unexpected disruptions caused by a handful of pirates, a government that decides to nationalize an industry and then restrict all international suppliers from doing business (e.g., Venezuela), a natural disaster, a terrorist strike, or a large ship sinking in a narrow supply corridor. Life, safety, health, and security—all are at risk without the supply networks that support the flow of vital metals and minerals, medical and food supplies, or heavy factory and construction machinery.

What Is Logistics Risk?

It was going to be another long night. An endless stream of planes scattered across the tarmac, 40 or so, all waiting for the ground stop to be removed at Newark Airport in New Jersey. What a logistical nightmare! Logistics is the flow of goods and information and other resources, including energy, water and people, between the point of origin and point of consumption.[1] I wondered, "What has to be done to get these planes and their passengers out of this log-jam and back on schedule?" Here are just a few of the many considerations: (1) adjust hundreds of flight schedules, (2) rebook passengers with connections, (3) advise baggage handlers that overtime will be needed, (4) recalculate fuel capacity to accommodate the three hours of idle time, (5) recalculate flight plans for new departure times, and (6) validate that the flight crew still has enough available hours to fly. Oh, then the planes have to be funneled from multiple locations into the only outbound runway, all at a time when inbound planes are landing every two to three minutes. Coordination and movement, scheduling, fueling, and compliance are a few logistics issues that must be managed, with no margin for error (risk management).

But this is what logistics management is about: moving information, people, and goods in the most effective and efficient means possible (plan, implement, and control the efficient, effective forward and reverse flow and storage of goods, services, and related requirements). Most of us probably think of logistics management in terms of transportation such as air, rail, motor (truck), water, and pipeline. It's more than just the simple but high-priority job of getting goods from point A to point B. Logistics management involves the integration of information, transportation, inventory, warehousing, material handling and packaging, safety, and security.[2] A ripple effect of missing a logistics target never diminishes in severity; it always increases as it spreads throughout your supply chain.

Remember the first Law: Risk management would be easy if supply chains were static. However, the movement of goods creates uncertainty and logistics is all about movement. Before goods become final product, raw materials are extracted from the ground, forests, water, and fields and then transported to suppliers. The goods (materials, component parts, liquid) are later shipped to manufacturers, assemblers, or refineries. The goods are typically converted into work in progress or finished products. These goods are constantly moving through the product life cycle, with an occasional stop in a warehouse, distribution center, or factory (Exhibit 8.1). The speed, frequency, and size in which the goods move through the supply chain are dictated by demand and controlled and coordinated via logistics networks.

During the journey, goods are exposed to a continuous barrage of risks, including theft, destruction, delays, spoilage, and even obsolescence; thousands of vulnerabilities, single points of failure, are presented throughout the life cycle of global supply chains. For example, in December 2008, Russia responded to a pricing dispute with Ukraine over the cost of gas by threatening the rest of Europe with a supply disruption. The dispute about prices started as far back as 2005. The natural gas monopoly OAO Gazprom cited Ukraine's unauthorized diversion of gas supplies from a pipeline going through its territory. The problem, according to Gazprom, was that Ukraine owed $2.4 billion in debt, posing what the Russian authorities considered a threat to one-fourth of Europe's natural gas supplies. At the heart of this dispute is Russia's anger at Ukraine's interest in joining NATO and residual anger at Ukraine over its short-lived war of August 2008. So political disputes in remote

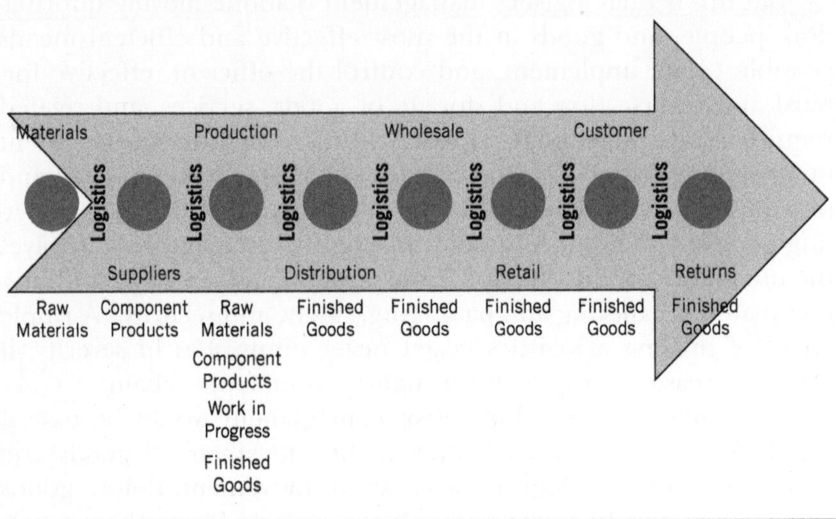

Exhibit 8.1 Logistics Flow in Manufacturing

regions can directly impact entire continents dependent on the logistics of energy pipelines among other supplies.[3] In January 2009, the dispute elevated and, as a result, 18 European countries reported major falls or cut-offs of their gas supplies from Russia transported through Ukraine.[4] The logistics chain had been broken and a single point of failure was created, one that impacted much of Europe.

In another example, harsh summer weather resulted in extraordinary flooding in the U.S. Midwest in June 2008. The impact of the severe rain and flooding brought the logistics chain of corn, cement, coal, scrap metal, fertilizer, steel, and soybeans to a halt when barges were idled along the Mississippi and railway lines were washed out.[5]

Logistics risk can be attributed to the failure of an obscure resource—one that is critical to the supply chain (remember, it is all in the details; that is, clear understanding of all resources that are needed to support your organization's supply chain networks). One such example occurred in the late 1990s, when the enactment of an executive order led to a shortage of shipping pallets.

The U.S. president was forced to enact an executive order to address the threat of invasive species being transported into the country.[6] The Asian Longhorn Beetle was finding its way into the wood pallets used for bulk transport of products. The single point of failure was the pallet itself. So in this case, the risk parasite and the biological parasite were one and the same. As the regulatory change took place, wooden pallets were phased out. Fortunately, the regulation did not immediately terminate use of the pallets. Shippers, consumer product companies, and others, for the most part, were able to avoid a catastrophe. However, the executives at several large consumer product companies had experienced pallet shortages and it was a serious problem. Bottom line: Goods cannot be shipped or trucked without pallets, nor can the supply chain operate without organizations such as CHEP USA that manage the logistics of these pallets (availability, quantity, quality, location). If this event had occurred in October 2007, when Chinese imports into the United States were $31.5 billion for the month versus $8 billion in October of 1999,[7] the impact from the regulatory change would have been catastrophic. The shortage of pallets would have severely delayed shipments and led to potential spoilage (food and agriculture) or obsolescence of goods and a significant decrease in fill rates. The supply chain of those organizations affected, as well as the supply chains of others in a chain of interdependencies would have come to a crashing halt. The possibility of systemic failure was initiated by a single parasite, a single point of failure.

Are pallet providers and other third parties included in the scope of your supply chain (logistics) risk management practices? Even in a small country, such as Malaysia, the considerations are extensive (see Table 8.1).

This shows how something as simple as infected wooden pallets can have a devastating effect on many supply chains. As a side note, the substitution of plastic pallets for wood presents yet another risk; the commodity classification within the facility (e.g., warehouse) is potentially higher. Plastic pallets burn much hotter than wood, which in turn threatens the integrity of the fire suppression system. The increased combustion must be factored in when sizing fire suppression equipment. But logistics risk is not limited to safe shipping methods and devices. You also have to be deeply concerned with managing logistics risk in the security of goods in transit and even at rest.

Cargo and Warehouse Theft

Cargo theft is one of the biggest risks facing logistics managers and their organizations, and one of the more difficult to contend

TABLE 8.1 Number of Companies Providing Ancillary Transportation-Related Services in Malaysia

SERVICE	NUMBER OF COMPANIES
Cargo handling	165
Freight brokerage	13
Cargo clearance	52
Logistics management	50
Shipping agency	733
Stevedoring contracting	24
Storage	28
Freight forwarding	1,084
Customers clearance	71
Warehousing	222

Source: www.equideglobal.com.my, as of December, 2008

with given cost constraints and volume of goods movement. One estimate states that cargo theft costs Americans $60 billion annually. Another report cites that 5 percent of all container movement in the world results in loss through theft, damage, or delays. The report stated, "With more than 675,000 registered interstate motor carriers moving 65 percent of the freight in the United States, the opportunity for theft is at an all time high." And the National Cargo Security Council estimates that cargo theft accounts for up to $25 billion in direct merchandise losses each year. The problem is global. In 2007, a report cited direct losses from the theft of trucks and cargo at 8.2 billion Euros between 2001 and 2005. Romania, Hungary, and Poland suffered the heaviest losses, but the Netherlands, Britain, France, and Italy also have high-risk highways, the report said. In the United States, the top states for theft were Texas and Georgia; top products stolen were consumer electronics, food and food products, clothing and footwear, computer technology, metals (cooper and nickel), and pharmaceuticals. Most thefts happened on the weekend (and the least on Friday). Truck and parking stops are at the top of the list, plus modal yards and unsecured areas, drop lots, motels, restaurants, malls, and casinos.[8]

The impacts include value of goods, business downtime, reputation, loss of opportunity to market seasonal goods, and total loss of product sales. Theft is the fourth-largest cost of business after equipment, fuel, and labor.

A lot of risk emphasis is focused on known threats, notably within warehousing facilities and stores or factories. But this is only one of the logistics challenges. Today, in the twenty-first century, a scourge of the seventeenth and eighteenth centuries has returned: piracy.

The Piracy Risk

Protecting goods once they get to your warehouse is essential, of course, but how sure are you that these goods can even arrive safely? Considering only one transit risk—increased piracy—many industries may want to seriously consider moving their supply chains closer to home or to regions not at risk. Coincidentally, I presented this issue in my last book, *At Your Own Risk* (John Wiley & Sons, 2008), and the response from one former CEO was "Pirates, are you kidding me?" Beginning in 2008, an unprecedented rise in piracy incidents brought chaos to international logistics and negatively impacted the global supply chain.

The majority of problems come from Somalia and Nigeria, but piracy generated from Indonesia makes ships leaving from major Asian ports just as at-risk as those passing through the Indian Ocean. In the first nine months of 2008, 199 incidents were reported to the International Maritime Bureau (IMB) and its Piracy Reporting Centre (PRC). These included 115 boarded vessels, 31 hijackings, and 23 vessels fired upon. Plus, 581 people have been taken hostage, nine kidnapped, nine killed, and seven missing and presumed dead. These are no longer random attacks, and crew safety is a problem equal to the potential disruptions to the supply chains of many organizations. Because the Gulf of Aden is at a strategically important point in the supply route between Asia and Europe, the problem has to be solved—either by eliminating the piracy risk or choosing to take a longer shipping route around Africa.

The top four chokepoints in the world are located in the region. These are the Suez Canal in Egypt, which connects the Red Sea to the Mediterranean; Bab el-Mandab Djibotty/Eriteria/Yeman, which connects the Red Sea with the Gulf of Aden; the Straits of Hormuz; and Bosphorous, the connector between the Black Sea and the Mediterranean. The director of the IMB observed in 2008 that

> The increased frequency of piracy and heightening levels of violence are of significant concern to the shipping industry and all mariners. The types of attacks, the violence associated with the attacks, the number of hostages taken, and the amounts paid in ransoms for the release of the vessels have all increased considerably.[9]

Complicating the many transportation-related risks in the supply chain is the unexpected risk that occurs during shipment. In 2006, a ship transporting 4,703 brand new Mazdas came close to sinking in the Pacific when it was caught in rough seas. Because the ship listed at 60 degrees for an extended period while in danger, the possible damage to the automobiles became an issue. Possible damage to engines could be caused if corrosive liquids seeped into various chambers and so, rather than live with the risk resulting from selling damaged cars, Mazda decided to destroy the approximately $100 million worth of new cars. To do so, the company had to create what was termed a "disassembly line," which took over a year to create to everyone's satisfaction. The city of Portland, Oregon, where the shipment ended up, wanted assurances that antifreeze, brake fluid, and other hazardous materials would be handled properly. Insurers covering Mazda's losses also wanted assurances that the company would not sell off parts and profit from the mishap after receiving its settlement dollars. So every wheel had to be sliced, battery rendered inoperable, and even CD players smashed in the disassembly process. The cost was significant. For example, rendering the six airbags per car unusable (a 30-minute process for all six), multiplied by 4,703 cars, required over 2,000 labor hours. And that is only one step in a very expensive process, all caused by rough seas.[10]

The irony in this matter—with costs resulting from insurers' concerns about post-losses profits—is that the expense and time required to destroy products as a consequence of a transportation loss created an even higher loss for the company. The insurers' concern was understandable. They did not want to pay a claim only to have the company profit from selling off tires, CDs, and other components. Ironically, had Mazda and their insurers been able to work together cooperatively, the size of the claim could have been reduced. Tragically, however, the cost-benefit ratio was not promising enough to take this route. In times of weakening demand for both autos and auto parts, it may be that the benefit of partial recovery was not as great as the cost of total destruction.

At the other end of the logistics risk spectrum are disruptions caused by failed infrastructure. In early 2009 when commodity prices soared, thieves in Oxfordshire, England, struck overhead power lines carrying 11,000 volts, pulling the cable down by felling a tree onto the lines, short-circuiting the power supply with a chain and resulting in a loss of power at Ramsden. The FBI reported that in April of 2008, when tornadoes were threatening Jackson, Mississippi, many residents were not alerted to the severe weather because five tornado warning sirens didn't work. The reason: The sirens' copper wiring had been stolen.[11]

The point is that all communications, power, and other logistics are vulnerable to accidents, theft, and many other threats.[12] The FBI report went on to state:

> Late last year, vandals removed 300 feet of copper wire from a Federal Aviation Administration tower in Ohio, threatening to interrupt communications between in-flight aircraft and air traffic controllers. The demand for copper from developing nations such as China and India is creating a robust international copper trade, and as the global supply of copper continues to tighten, the market for illicit copper will likely increase. From 2001 until 2008, the price of the metal has increased by more than 500 percent. Transformers contain approximately 50 lbs. of copper with the potential to yield $200 for copper thieves and if stolen, result in thousands of dollars in damages, replacement costs, and environmental clean-up.

Clearly, this type of risk is going to grow in the future, or at least as long as metals prices continue to rise. It is easy to ignore many risks you face because, if you are like most people, you see a limited version of the supply chain, often a singular one. In reality, you are part of a much larger complex, and the logistics risks of invisible chains threaten your very visible chain as well.

What's at Risk?

Once you begin studying logistics with a realistic point of view, you quickly realize that the entire supply chain is at risk and the option of taking no action invites disaster. New Orleans had many supply chains just for operating its municipal responsibilities, and *all* of them failed at the same time due to the single point of failure (the weak levee). When you study the spiraling losses, delays, and human suffering that followed—all of which was preventable—you realize that the whole supply chain will go down when a catastrophe strikes.

If you think of your logistics supply chain as though your organization was the city of New Orleans before Katrina hit, you will immediately understand what I mean.

The city was below sea level and the levee wall was weak due to age, poor maintenance, and virtually no disaster planning. The hurricane highlighted the poor planning all around, on the part of the city, the state, and the feds. The Federal Emergency Management Agency (FEMA) was not able to respond appropriately, the mayor of the city did not move people out when he had the chance, and no one really thought the city would ever get flooded (in spite of its topography). Now try to imagine the logistics challenges for your organization. But remember three points:

1. To date, the problem with the weak levee has *not* been addressed and this means that flooding will happen again.
2. The city is just as unprepared today as it was before Katrina.
3. Budget money given to the city was spent on other things and not where it was needed.

Think about your own logistics risks. Have you had a loss in the past that could recur and has not been addressed? Has your organization forgotten to perform its logistics-based disaster planning? Has budget money gone for other priorities and, more to the point, can you afford not to take care of these risks?

Frankly, many organizations are ignoring their logistics risks, either because they are not aware of them or because they simply don't know what to do. In this regard, many of us are living 12 feet below sea level and pretending that no more hurricanes are ever going to come through.

What were some of the invisible logistics risks associated with the New Orleans disaster?

- Major truck, rail, and maritime cargo routes were shut down. CSX Transportation, a major rail carrier in the region, was not able to restore full service until February 2006, five months after the storm. The company had to restore six major bridges, more than 40 miles of track, and its major rail yard in New Orleans. Eighty percent of energy production in the gulf area was shut down, increasing gas prices.[13] New Orleans and the surrounding gulf ports are a major import and hub for food and agricultural products, including the ports of Gulfport (tropical fruit, poultry, and grain) and Pascagoula (fish, frozen foods, and grain) in Mississippi. The Port of New Orleans was also a major import center for metals, rubber, coffee, forest products, and cement, and an export hub for aluminum, iron, steel, and forest products.[14]

- Twenty-five percent of the U.S. stock of green coffee beans is held in the port of New Orleans. A quarter of the entire U.S. stock of unprocessed coffee—211 million pounds' worth—is stored in New Orleans. More than half of the Folgers and Millstone brand coffees sold by Procter & Gamble are made at two plants in New Orleans.[15]
- Fifty percent of London Metals Exchange's reserves of zinc were housed there.
- Retail sporting goods and apparel companies were unscathed directly, but they relied heavily on Gulfport, Mississippi, as a transportation hub. This port lost 40 containers.
- The forestry industry in Mississippi was also affected, as 1.3 million acres (5,300 km^2) of forest lands were destroyed.[16]

A similar hurricane example demonstrates that the level of logistics devastation was, like that of Katrina, unexpectedly severe and far-reaching. Hurricanes Gustav and Ike interrupted the flow of oil and natural gas, destroying 60 drilling platforms. Another 31 platforms were extensively damaged by the two storms. The Interior Department explained that there were 3,800 oil and gas platforms in the Gulf of Mexico—2,127 of these had been exposed to Gustav's hurricane-force winds. Katrina destroyed 44 and Rita destroyed 64.[17]

Responding to the losses, insurance companies increased rates, provided new sublimits, excluded exposures altogether, excluding platforms built before a certain date, increasing retentions for direct damage to property and waiting periods for business interruption insurance; and including a complete schedule of all property in policy wording that exempts "windstorm" coverage.

In other words, the real impact of the Katrina disaster went beyond the news stories of a broken levee. That was serious, but it was only one of many problems. The logistics for most of the U.S. economy suffered in some way, and many people and businesses were hurt catastrophically, often by invisible consequences. This is the real nature of your logistics risk: far-reaching, expensive, and invisible.

Supply Chains Frozen Solid

In late January 2008, a catastrophic weather event froze China's transportation, electrical, telecommunications, energy, food services, hospitality, and logistics networks. The factory floor of the world came to a screeching halt for nearly three weeks because of unexpected cold temperatures, heavy snow, and ice. By the time the ice began to thaw in early February, more than 223,000 homes had been destroyed and another 862,000 damaged. A 500-meter-long auto plant in Xiangtan had its entire roof collapse.[18]

The logistic challenges in nearly all industries were enormous:

- *The flow of electricity stopped* in many areas. Chenzhou (population 4.6 million) lost power for more than two weeks. Snowstorms also toppled 330 major power lines and 96 electricity towers.
- *Power generation was threatened.* Coal reserves were down to emergency levels and stockpiles were only sufficient for eight days of power. Approximately, 78 percent of China's power is derived from coal-fired plants. Without trains and trucks to deliver coal freight, the National Power Grid says its latest coal inventory has fallen to just 16.58 million tons, an all-time low that was barely sufficient for seven days' worth of production.
- *Industrial production was slashed.* Dong Tao, a Hong Kong–based economist, estimates the snowstorm cut industrial production growth by 25 percent and may have wiped out 10 percent of national farm production in January alone. Production of steel and aluminum was scaled back due to a significant shortage of raw material, and loss of production of about 50,000 tons of lead and zinc was forecast in Hunan.

- *Water supply equipment was damaged,* caused by bursting and frozen water pipes.
- *Agriculture and farming was devastated.* Approximately, 870,000 pigs, 450,000 sheep, and 65,000 head of cattle were killed by the storm. Food shortages were reported.
- *Transportation was paralyzed during the busiest travel season,* Chunyun, which precedes the Lunar New Year. At one point, somewhere between 500,000 to 800,000 people were stranded at railway stations across southern China. Eight thousand cargo trains were delayed. Heavy fog on February 3 caused further delays in Hunan. Main highways, including Jingzhu Expressway (which connects the capital of Beijing with Guangdong province), were shut down. Seven of the eight highways connecting Hunan and Guangdong (two major industrial centers) were closed. Ten boats at Shanghai port with their container goods were stuck and unable to unload because of sea levels. At one point, 19 major airports were closed in ten cities. About 3,250 flights were cancelled and another 5,550 delayed. Provincial bus services in Jiangxi were halted. Telecommunication companies had significant repair costs as about 10,000 kilometers were affected.

Losses are not due only to hurricanes and snowstorms, of course. For example, gas supplies to Western Australia were disrupted due to an explosion at an offshore plant that supplies 30 to 40 percent of the state's gas needs, including large industrial users (mining companies). The federal government had to authorize the release of emergency fuel reserves.

As you can see by now, the types of risks vary but one thing is for sure: Someone, somewhere along the supply chain will be impacted. A study conducted in 2006 to ascertain the economic impacts on 12 APEC economies of a U.S. port shutdown concluded that "the estimated economic impact—measured in export and GDP loss—is significant, where the magnitude of the economic impact increases dramatically with the length of time of the trade disruption . . ." After a protracted period of diminished trade activity due to closures, the estimated impact measured in loss of GDP increased substantially to nearly $500 billion. Using the 30-day equivalent scenario, the ripple effect on the 12 economies alone was estimated to be $137 billion in lost GDP and $159 billion in reduced trade.

Single Points of Failure and Aggregate Risk

Logistics is also characterized by bottlenecks, either geographic or process specific. The so-called bottleneck can exist upstream, at the source or beginning of the supply chain—farms, mines, fields, and forests. These commodity, energy, and agriculture sources represent a mega point of failure and, unfortunately, much of the resources are concentrated in a specific region or controlled by a handful of countries. The root cause of these bottlenecks can be network design (e.g., configuration of suppliers, production facilities, distribution centers, and customers) operational issues or external factors (e.g., natural hazards). Exhibit 8.2 illustrates this point.

Another typical bottleneck can be a busy airport or port, which when closed down prevents the movement of people and goods. Exhibit 8.3 illustrates these bottlenecks, as well as the aggregate exposure in Asia (specifically, Southeast China region).

The chart of the world's business airports and shipping ports demonstrates that international logistics are very much a house of cards. With most of the manufacturing in today's economy being generated in Asia, you cannot ignore the very real and constant logistics risks involved. Big companies like Wal-Mart ship almost all of their product from Asia. Even smaller concerns often rely completely on such logistics. The solutions involve rethinking the whole question of where you get product, what costs are involved, and what the real costs are, compared to a vastly reduced supply chain and its lower risks.

Why Logistics Risk Is Difficult to Manage

Why is there not greater urgency in mitigating the logistics threats to critical supply chains? In the case of logistics, consequences are typically understood but there is a belief that output can be controlled. This is not the case. In fact, exposure is typically not quantified and control is relinquished. Who owns the risk? Everyone dabbles in managing supply chain risk, but ownership in almost all instances is not clear. Ownership typically is assumed at a functional level and seldom extends across the entire supply chain.

What is logistics risk and why is it so difficult to manage? The special consideration is that when a logistics-based risk is realized, the failures ripples out into virtually every other part of your supply chain. A risk isolated to a warehouse, such as broken machinery or a safety issue, tends to remain isolated both geographically and in other terms (personnel, cost, time element, and inventory). But

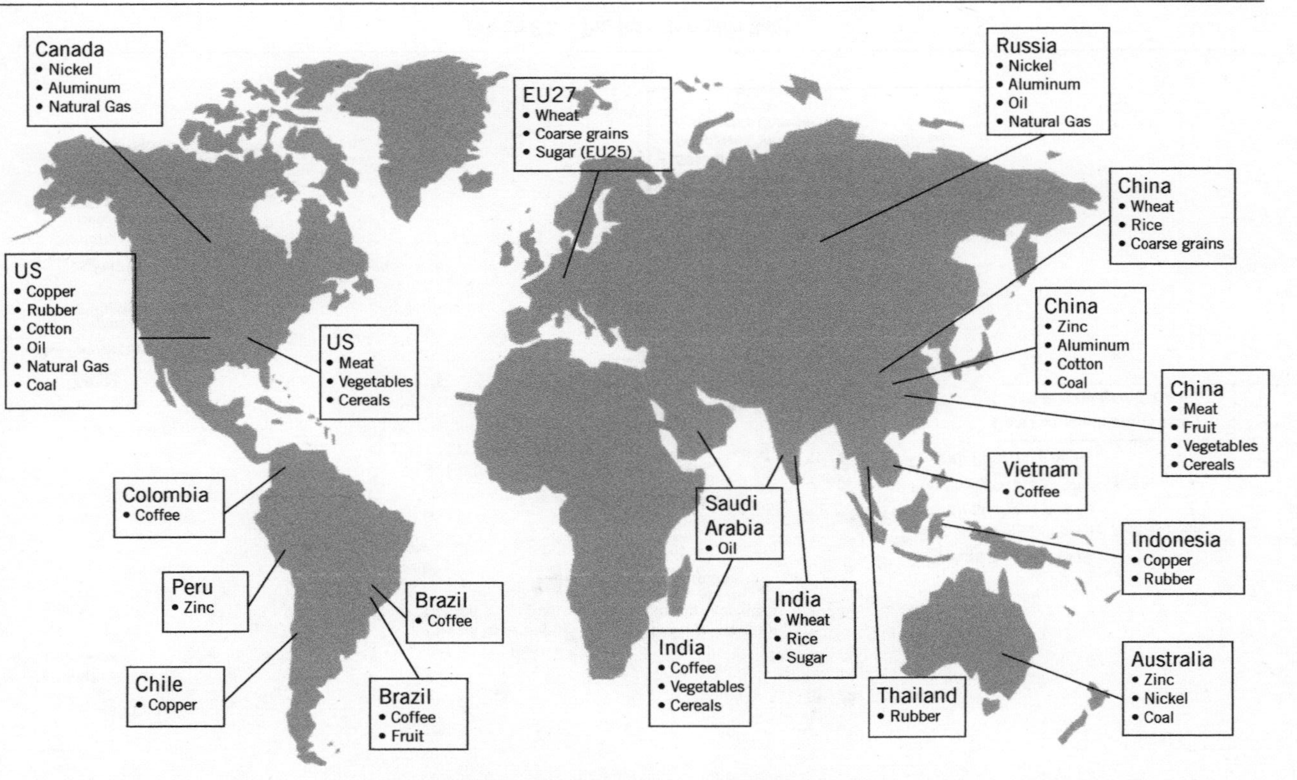

Exhibit 8.2 Top Three Producers—Commodities, Energy, Agriculture

Source: "Pocket World in Figures," *The Economist,* 2008.

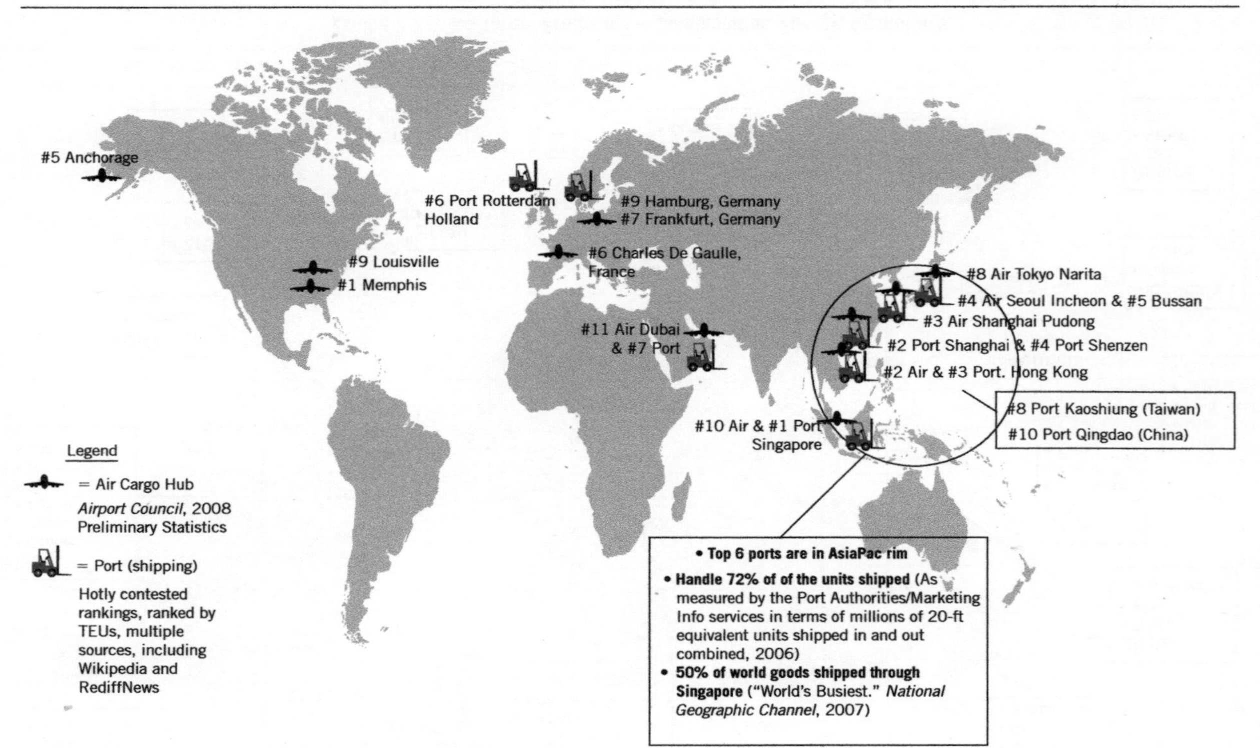

Exhibit 8.3 Top Transportation Hubs

a logistics loss cannot be contained any more than a category five hurricane. If your organization suffers a logistics-based loss, you are going to find yourself underwater and without immediate resources to fix the problems. So you need to develop a disaster recovery program, diversify your dependencies, and take all the steps you can to either avoid the risk or speed up recovery time.

Logistics risks often point the way to solving problems as widespread as competing with larger, better capitalized companies. For example, Best Buy, based in Minnesota, is the market leader in consumer electronics, with over 700 stores in 49 states. But in 2003, big competitors (especially Wal-Mart and Target) were taking a share of Best Buy's primary product markets—consumer electronics, home office equipment, entertainment software, and appliances. Management realized that they could not compete with Wal-Mart by trying to be all things to all customers, so the company developed a new strategy it called "customer-centricity." The success of this marketing strategy was found in vastly improved logistics. It involved changing focus by moving non-sales activities away from the on-floor sales staff, improving sales staff autonomy to serve local market needs, and improved information flow.

But the real crux of Best Buy's improved program was based on logistics changes. These included:

- *More frequent but smaller shipments of product*, with distribution centers located close to retail outlets. This represented a contraction of the supply chain in a big way. Asian imports are warehoused in Seattle and Long Beach and then shipped to regional distribution centers. In addition, when products come off the trucks, they are ready to be put directly on the sales floor.
- *Better access to information.* Store sales staff can easily determine the status of shipments en route, and they are also updated on delays such as slowdowns at ports.
- *Improved forecasting*, including combined data from departments and partners into a single consolidated product forecast.

These changes are both sensible and logical. By improving the logistics of the most basic requirement—getting products into the stores in time to sell—the entire supply chain works much better. More to the point, these logistics changes, coupled with improved empowerment of associates on the sales floor, improves customer response and eliminates many basic but chronic risks.

The same tactical analysis and action plan can be applied to virtually every logistics chain. Contraction and diversification, improved efficiency, and more rapid deployment of products not only improve overall logistics, they also reduce the larger logistics threats coming from hurricanes, piracy, port strikes, terrorism, and unknown dozens of other potentially catastrophic risks. In other words, taking these steps to improve the entire logistics flow enables a business to better compete and also mitigate many other risks.

This provides you with the strongest possible argument to management: By taking these specific steps, we improve profitability and customer response—and, by the way, we also reduce our logistics risks. This approach makes sense. Had the City of New Orleans had a risk management program in place, someone could have argued that fixing the levee improves revenues from tourism and retail business in the city, while also preventing logistics problems on an untold scale.

The trick, of course, is in creating a program in your organization that will effectively improve logistics as the Best Buy initiative did. You need to first develop an improved strategy and then convince management that it works. So you face a daunting task, which has to be executed in two ways at the same time. The first avenue is to develop a coherent scope and sequence of activities that have to be addressed. Second is the difficult task of providing guidance, education, awareness, and strategy throughout your organization. If you are able to overlay on this a convincing argument that your ideas also improve profits, it makes the whole argument much more convincing. It addresses the questions decision makers are going to ask: How much is this going to cost? Is it a priority? Why should we spend money to prevent something that probably won't happen? Best Buy did increase profits while improving efficiency and eliminating logistics risk. The same strategic approach will not work in every case, but it does provide a worthy goal.

Supply Chains Don't Survive on Product Flows Alone; Information Flows Are Essential

Much has been said about risks to the flow of products through the supply chain. Equally important is the flow of critical information, such as orders, compliance filings (customs), inventory levels, forecasts, product and materials locations, and funds. A failure of information flows is a failure of the supply chain.

Seemingly small threats, when realized, may pose a far more serious international logistics problem. In February 2008, an underwater fiber optic cable was severed between the UAE and Oman. Two additional cables were cut near Egypt, believed to be caused by a ship's anchor. As a consequence, shipping was halted awaiting repairs, and shipping between the Middle East and India became very difficult. In addition, Internet and phone traffic from Egypt to India was hopelessly slowed down. So the temporary loss of maritime cables affected both communications and shipping for several days.[19]

This type of communications logistics is not limited to undersea cables, either. Many countries have control over threat levels. Cutting underwater cables by dragging an anchor is careless and unintentional. In comparison, countries in control of natural resources exert great power over others.

While logistics also has to involve communications, distribution, and border-related problems, most of the costs and risks are related to the basic transportation requirements within the supply chain. Church & Dwight Co., Inc., manufacturer of Arm & Hammer products, faced this challenge and relied on software provided by JDA to vastly improve its forecasting of both inbound and outbound shipping traffic. The forecasting enabled the company to accelerate shipment consolidation and manage semi-fixed trips. By automating carrier selection, for example, efficiency was improved vastly. Rather than asking for bids from several carriers, the automation of this process evolved so the company was able to pick the best carrier based on service levels, capacity, and cost. Church & Dwight's supply chain planning manager reported, "We have successfully reduced days of supply by several million dollars . . . enabling us to set safety stock levels, which indicate when to produce at the correct times."[20]

Logistics is perhaps the most complex of supply chain risks, for numerous reasons. Many vulnerabilities, such as customs and trade restrictions, language barriers, differences in regulation, exchange rate fluctuations, natural perils, affect what used to be a fairly simple fulfillment cycle.

In the nineteenth century, for example, years before the home use of refrigeration, perishable goods such as ice cream, ice, and milk were delivered to a household every day, and they were consumed within 24 hours to prevent spoilage or simple melting. The biggest cost of delivery was feed for the horse, and the biggest threat to this supply chain was also based on logistics. For example, if the horse fell and broke his leg, no delivery could take place. If you think of this as a model for the level of vulnerability in modern-day supply chain risks, you get a fair picture of what you face. In the past, the horse could break his leg. Today, a vast array of risks can also stop the supply chain cold. Without a smoothly running logistics system, nothing else happens. The supply chain breaks just like that horse's leg.

This type of serious vulnerability exists in all supply chains. We all have at least one horse's leg at risk that can bring our entire operation to an immediate halt. It is not enough to wrap the horse's leg because that is only one of many risks (the deliveryman's cart could lose an axle, the supply of feed might be halted, or weather could prevent completing the route). So it is not cost-effective to try and prevent losses alone; you need to keep costs down, but is that enough? No. You also need to create efficiency and reduce exposure at the same time.

Minimizing costs is a huge issue in logistics management, and this is why you need to combine logistics risk management with an argument for greater supply chain optimization and, ultimately, higher profits. Two revolutionary changes to your supply chain will resolve many of the logistics risks you face when you rely on international suppliers. This is especially true when these vendors outsource to second- and third-tier manufacturers in other countries. In these common situations, you have virtually no control over logistics risks. The first change you can expect to see more in the near future is *reverticalization,* or a return to the vertically integrated supply chain (organization relying on primary suppliers, who in turn rely on second-tier manufacturers). Much of the logistics risk is reduced when organizations insist on working with a limited number of suppliers that are subject to internal audit and standards that can be checked and enforced.

The second change is *deglobalization.* On the surface, it appears to make simple economic sense to move manufacturing operations to another country where labor is quite cheap and material costs are often lower. But the landed costs can be substantial. The supply chain risks, notably logistics risks, that have grown from the complexities of global supply chain management, raise questions as to whether it is really cheaper to continue verticalization and globalization. It may prove cheaper to restrict the size of the supply chain and move single suppliers into one tier, closer to home, and subject to more direct supervision, audit, and standards enforcement. It may

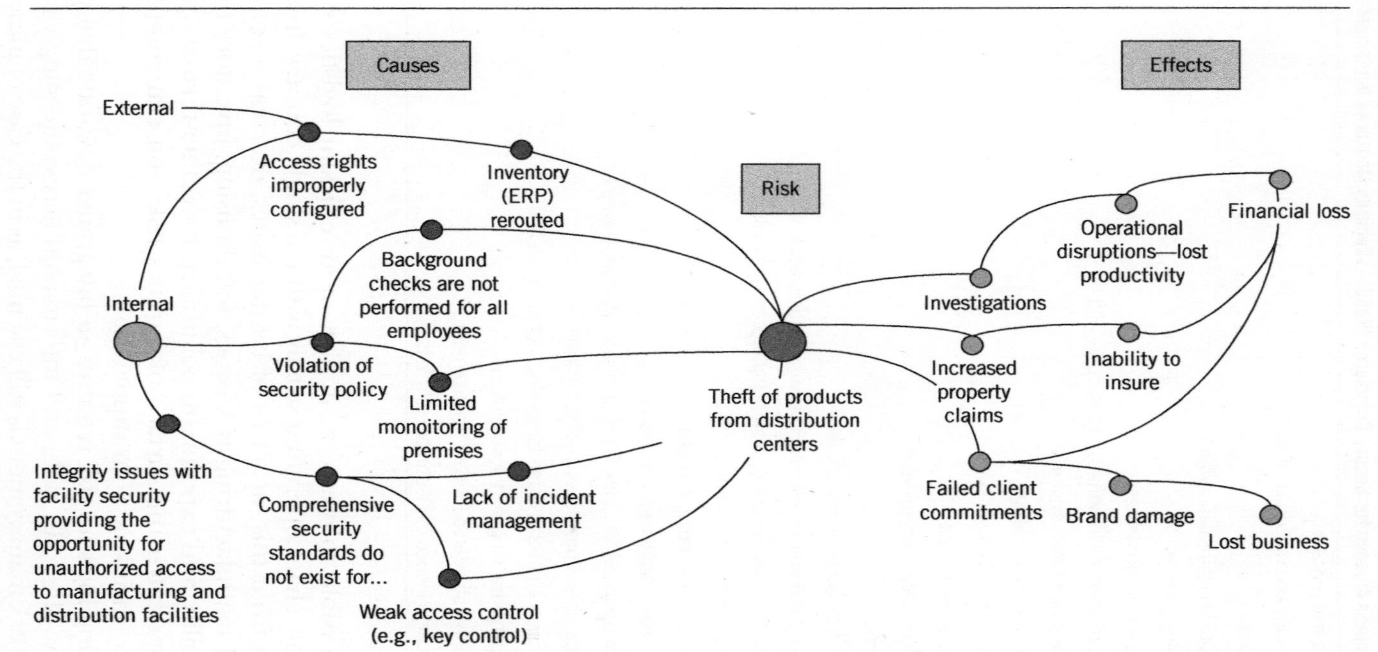

Exhibit 8.4 Root Cause Analysis—Product Theft

TABLE 8.2 Business Alliance for Secure Commerce (BASC)—Security Measures Implementation [21]

Employee hiring/exit process
Organizational roles and responsibilities
Facility protection
Protection of business information/data
Personnel training process
Information dissemination process
Recordkeeping of shipping information for security audits
Business partners evaluation systems
Warehouse/terminal layout design
Company security management system
Security culture development
Quality information/data management
Facility monitoring
Logistics systems designed to reduce risks
Establishment of collaborative relationships with customs actions
Prevention, detection, and reporting of shipping process anomalies
Inventory management and control
Inspections during the shipping process
Data exchange with customs administration
Logistics system designed for quick eventual disaster/failure recovery
Access/presence control processes and technologies
Exploitation of cargo and vehicle anti-tampering technical solution
Exploitation of cargo tracking technical solutions
Use of international standards for data management
Exploitation of cargo inspection technical solutions

even be possible to create a simpler, more efficient logistics system with a supply chain operating strictly within a single country. Imagine the savings from this, in terms of border issues, overseas second-tier supply and manufacturing risk issues, warehousing, inventory timing and availability, and exposure to political- and weather-related threats. These only scratch the surface of logistics risks you can completely eliminate by shrinking your supply chain.

Managing logistics risk requires an integrated view, one that parallels the flow of goods, cash, and information across the supply chain. Functional risk management is still essential, as in the case of managing cargo security. But the functional elements must be integrated into the risk intelligent supply chain (see Chapter 9 on mitigation). One technique for managing product risk is to conduct a root-cause analysis to identify sources of risk (see Exhibit 8.4). The organization can then assign responsibility to the appropriate functional unit for additional analysis, measurement, and resolution.

Once the risk analysis is completed, successful practices can be implemented such as those recommended by the Business Alliance for Secure Commerce (BASC) (see Table 8.2).

In the End It's All about the Priorities and Economics

Selling your concepts about risk management—those invisible threats that, once prevented, cannot be quantified—is a formidable task. The decision makers inside and outside the organization who are dealing with budgets always demand measurable results, and in risk management you simply cannot produce them. You need to demonstrate why the organization cannot afford to ignore the problem. But convincing these decision makers is like trying to sell faith to a bunch of heathens. The organizational graven images based on old ways of thinking are difficult to overcome because so many managers continue to worship them. These graven images of organizations include beliefs such as:

- If you can't measure it, you don't need to fix it.
- Money spent to eliminate threats that might not happen is a waste.
- Risk is simple. You get rid of it with insurance or transfer.
- Your responsibility exists in a very limited space, only a tiny portion of the larger supply chain.

Keep in mind here that the goal of logistics risk management is not to try to eliminate the insurmountable number of risks that exist throughout the supply chain network. Instead the goal is to effectively and efficiently allocate precious risk resources against the greatest priorities—the single points of failure that will have the greatest impact. Simply stated, it's a case of economics—getting the greatest return from limited risk investments (resources allocated to the task). To address this objective, one must define impact along product and/or SKU (stock keeping units) lines. Once this segmentation is completed the extended line of sight can be viewed and mapped, then failure points quantified and qualified in order to prioritize investments. Chapter 9, on mitigation, will explain this process further.

Notes

1. CNN (4 February 2008). "New devastation emerges in China." CNN.com. http://edition.cnn.com/2008/WORLD/asiapcf/02/04/china.weather/index.html.
2. Hernandez, Vittorio (2008 02 01). "Three-Week Massive Snow Storm Costs Chinese Economy $7.5 Billion." All Headline News. http://www.allheadlinenews.com/articles/7009905178.
3. "Russia Again Warns of Gas Supply Disruption," *Associated Press*, December 28, 2008.
4. "FACTBOX—18 Countries Affected by Russia-Ukraine Gas Row," *Reuters*, January 7, 2009.
5. Alex Roth and Thomas M. Burton, "Midwest Floods Cripple Shippers," *Wall Street Journal*, June 16, 2008.
6. The Executive Order was signed into action on February 3, 1999, by President Clinton.
7. U.S. Census Bureau, "U.S. Trade in Goods (Imports, Exports and Balance) by Country," www.census.gov/foreign-trade/balance.
8. Chubb Group of Insurance Companies, "Rethinking Security and Logistics Can Help Reduce Risk of Cargo Theft," www.chubb.com/corporate/chubb8937.html; Cargo Security International, "UNITED STATES: LoJack Supply Chain Integrity Releases First Annual Cargo Theft Study," www.cargosecurityinternational.com/channeldetail.asp?cid=16&caid=10687; "Cargo Theft a Problem on European Highways," Manufacturing.Net, May 12, 2009.
9. Capt. Pottengal Mukundan, Director, IMB, "Unprecented Rise in Piratical Attacks," ICC Commercial Crime Service, online at www.icc-ccs.org, October 24, 2008.
10. Joel Millman, "A Crushing Issue: How to Destroy Brand-New Cars," *Wall Street Journal*, April 29, 2008.
11. Federal Bureau of Investigation, www.fbi.gov.
12. "Thieves Steal Power Line Cables," BBC, February 4, 2009.
13. Fleet Owner, "CSX reopens Gulf Coast line," Jan 26, 2006, http://fleetowner.com/news/csx_gulf_coast_line_012606/.
14. Ports in a Storm: Katrina Tests Resilience of Nation's Supply Chain, Knowledge@W.P. Carey, September 28, 2005.
15. Thomasnet.com, "Functional Matters: Hurricane Katrina and the Supply Chain," September 14, 2005, http://news.thomasnet.com/IMT/archives/2005/09/functional_matt.html.
16. Pervaze A. Sheikh, "The Impact of Hurricane Katrina on Biological Resources" (PDF). Congressional Research Service. October 18, 2005. Retrieved on June 5, 2006.

17. "Gustav, Ike destroyed 60 Energy Platforms," Yahoo! News, November 26, 2008.
18. CNN (February 4, 2008). "New devastation emerges in China." CNN.com. http://edition.cnn.com/2008/WORLD/asiapcf/02/04/china.weather/index.html, http://en.wikipedia.org/wiki/2008_Chinese_winter_storms.
19. "New Undersea Cable Cut in Mideast Compounds Net Woes," *Xinhuanet*, February 2, 2008.
20. "Aiming at Industrial-Strength Supply Chain," JDA Software Group, 2008.
21. Ximena Gutierrez, Juha Hintsa, Philippe Wieser, and Ari-Pekka Hameri, "Voluntary Supply Chain Security Program Impacts: An Empirical Study with BASC Member Companies," *World Customs Journal*, September 2007.

Law #8: Mitigation: If Supply Chain Risk Management Isn't Part of the Solution, It Will Become the Problem

GOOD ANSWERS OFTEN RAISE BIG QUESTIONS

It was 3 A.M. when my BlackBerry vibrated, alerting me to a 6.9 strength earthquake in Mexico. My immediate thought was, "Oh no! I hope the loss of life and property is minimal." As the U.S. supply chain manager for a large consumer electronics company, I had lived through similar catastrophic events in Japan, Turkey, and San Francisco. I quickly began to work the resiliency checklist in my head. "Are any of our people affected? No, fortunately we do not have any employees working in the affected area, unless of course they were meeting with customers or vendors." I took this as a follow-up action, to ensure we have full accountability for our people. "Do we have any operating facilities or branch offices in the area?" Again, the answer was no. "Okay, do we depend on any critical suppliers in that area?" I had to stop and really think about this one. "No, I think we are okay." I concluded that our exposure was limited, so I went back to bed. It was Friday night; I decided to send off a few e-mails and make follow-up calls on Monday. After all, we did not have a footprint in this area, nor did we rely on any suppliers in the affected area.

I arrived at work on Monday to find the Head of Procurement and three other senior operations managers hunkered down in his office. As I entered the office, the expression on their faces told the story. It appeared that production of our new television set had come to a halt on Friday night; however, we could not confirm the report. We were operating a lean supply chain with little excess inventory, so we could not afford to loose the 24x7 line for more than a day.

(continued)

Knowing that we did not have a plant in the region, I had to assume that we lost one of our critical suppliers. So I posed the question to the group: "Which supplier did we lose?" The head of Procurement responded, "The manufacturer of the plastic injection mold for our yet to be announced, cutting-edge new TV." He went on: "It's worse. You see, we decided to sole source the plastic injection mold to keep the cost low and control who can produce this unique flat design." This is a characteristic of a lean, well-tuned supply chain that relies heavily on a limited number of known third parties. He continued: "We believe our supplier's plant was destroyed." Although this might have been disruptive, I felt a bit relieved, since I knew we could avoid catastrophic consequences by quickly sourcing with other suppliers that could produce the plastic injection molds. "So is that it?" I asked. The head of Procurement responded, "We believe that our first-tier supplier's building collapsed, the location where the actual molds were stored. Worse yet, the specialized contract mold maker was only a few blocks away and we believe that building was demolished as well" (the supplier's supplier).

We were now looking at an event with disastrous consequences, a single point of failure. Without the chromium steel master molds, the plastic molds cannot be produced (with nothing to inject the plastic into). The Procurement Manager continued: "We believe we will be starting from scratch—I think we are looking at least at a three-to-six-month delay to get back online." The impact would be market crippling, we would miss the holiday window of opportunity, and our leading competitor, who was supposed to be launching a product a month behind ours, would now have competitive advantage.

Supply chain risk management, the solution—correct? But what problem is the organization trying to solve? The best way to address this question is to fast-forward to the end of the script, when the uncertainty (event) and exposure to uncertainty (risk) become one. This is the time, place, and circumstance when risk has become a reality and the threshold for pain has been exceeded, or at least threatened. Forgetting about the story in between, let's jump ahead to the potential impacts and outcomes. The possibilities are limited to four:

1. No brand, financial, strategic, or compliance impact: This is a non-event.
2. Slight but manageable negative impact—our resiliency or agility allows us to avoid more significant impact.
3. Significant initial negative impact, but the outcome of the disruptive event presents an opportunity (e.g., the game-changing

event provides the organization with an opportunity to change its cost basis).

4. The event the organization least desires (or avoids at all costs): significant or severe impact, one with no upside, often referred to as having catastrophic consequences.

So how does your organization attempt to alter the odds and avoid the catastrophic outcome? Supply chain risk management, of course! Not so fast—let's not forget our *Laws of the Laws*: It truly is all in the details.

Supply Chain Risk Management: I have the hammer, wood, and nails.

Now What Do I Do?

> When the only tool you have is a hammer, it is tempting to treat everything as if it were a nail.
>
> —Abraham H. Maslow,
> *The Psychology of Science*, 1966

Even with my tools in hand and ready to go, I have to be very careful that I "fix" the right problem. I have to make sure I understand what it is I am trying to prevent before I start banging away. This applies to anyone trying to manage risk. This lesson is well understood by Bob Murphy, VP of Operations and leader of the Supply Chain Enterprise Risk Management program for Rockwell Automation and a 30-year industry veteran. In an interview conducted for this book, he summed up the risk challenge as follows:

> As a multi-billion enterprise that is responsible for supplying manufacturers with industrial automation controls and information solutions, we are committed to managing risk. Over the past decade we have focused on an integrated enterprise risk management program that includes routinely assessing and validating that we understood strategic, financial and operational risks. But where we fell short was the need to create a structure, process and way to execute and resolve gaps. Exposure needed to be resolved at the detail level, deep in our multi-national extended supply chains. Of course that raised the question, "Where do we begin?" Now the good news is that we have not

experienced a major catastrophic failure in our supply chains in over 100 years. However, that doesn't mean we don't think about it or prepare for it each and every single day.

We began by identifying assumptions that would eventually affect our supply chain risk profile. One such assumption was to acknowledge the reality that their business is not a high volume business and as a result their leverage with third parties was limited. We are not Wal-mart or Best Buy so our ability to gain risk leverage on any large vendor, or commodity material provider, is severely limited. It is for this reason that we need to be even more diligent in the way we manage risk with our upstream supply chain providers. As a next step we decided to lay the foundation and began a three-tier effort that reflects immediate, short-term and strategic needs.

Our immediate need was to ensure that the facility and function based business continuity plans for our central distribution center were up to date. While this was underway our next activity (short-term) was to enhance the supplier risk evaluation, vetting and monitoring process. We wanted to be sure that we were considering the entire risk profile of our critical third party providers. They are blood that passes through veins, they fail—we fail. Finally, we wanted to lay the foundation for an extended supply chain risk process that was aligned by critical product streams. That was fairly easy to identify, we know our markets and what throws off the greatest revenue and profit. Our focus was to measure impacts, prioritize exposure, price the risk investment options (against the exposure/impact), and then plan and deploy a portfolio of risk mitigation and insurance solutions. We needed a process and protocols to gain scale and ensure longevity of the approach.

How do we measure success? Here are a few simple metrics besides the detailed program metrics. Did our preparation and plan work when we experienced an event; that is, were we able to recover within our desired recovery time objective? Do we have a process that effectively and efficiently maintains currency (adaptable and flexible) to stress testing? Did we achieve the desired level of resiliency regardless of the risk event?

—Bob Murphy, Vice President of Operations and leader of the Supply Chain Enterprise Risk Management program for Rockwell Automation

The Rockwell story highlights many of the key attributes of a successful supply chain risk management strategy and a way to increase the chance of success. Here is a summary of a few:

- Does a culture exist that supports an enterprise-wide risk philosophy?
- Have I aligned supply chain risk activities with market driven priorities—value (product and SKU, stock keeping units) rationalization?
- Does the program address market, client, and operating realities and assumptions?
- Is my program multidimensional and reality based to reflect immediate needs (e.g., continuity for critical distribution facility) and strategic needs?
- Is program ownership assigned at the executive leadership level and is a senior leader driving the execution of the overall program?
- Is there a systematic approach for execution, one that works in all kinds of conditions, to manage risk throughout the extended supply chain?
- Is resiliency built into the response or mitigation plan?
- Does the program include measurements, such as key performance indicators, monitoring capabilities, and validation?

Enter the Risk Intelligent Supply Chain

The Rockwell experience defined the proper approach. Another variety of this approach was expressed by a large-scale change and organizational design expert, David Nadler, Vice Chairman of Marsh & McLennan Group and founder/CEO of the Delta Consulting Group, Inc., which consults with the Marsh CEO and board. In an interview with David, he raised the following key points that can be applied as a foundation for a successful supply chain risk management program:

- How are you expanding your way of thinking about problems? How do you gather information and react to it?
- Have you created communities to think about risk—a learning organization?
- Have you considered social networking technologies and techniques to promote and support the risk community?
- Do you understand the social topography: risk interactions from top to bottom within the organization as well as interdependencies and relationships across the vast external supply chain network and market/clients served?
- Are you able to mimic open systems design, leverage the power of the community and the collective intelligence?

These important questions, when overlaid with the attributes defined by the Rockwell approach, round out a discussion of how risk should be approached and conquered. But the approach has to be integrated into the existing operational mode of your organization. Remember, organizations do not live and breathe by supply chain risk management solutions alone. A key point: Supply chain risk management is an *overlay* to the bigger, broader business and supply chain and operations picture. It sits at the intersection of business/supply chain design and supply chain risk management philosophy. Exhibit 9.1 illustrates the business construct, supply chain, and supply chain risk management overlay.

The point here is that there is an overlay; the SCRM philosophy has an effect on every layer and as such must be incorporated into the design.

We need to know the why and what we are trying to accomplish. To address this, we will need a process and protocols, but before we get into the how, let's begin by looking at the following three critical why and what supply chain risk questions:

1. Can I see it, do I understand it, and can I quantitatively and qualitatively assess its impacts (risk identification)?
    - Is it relevant to your business value?
    - Do you have listening posts, ways to collect stakeholder expectations and external influences?

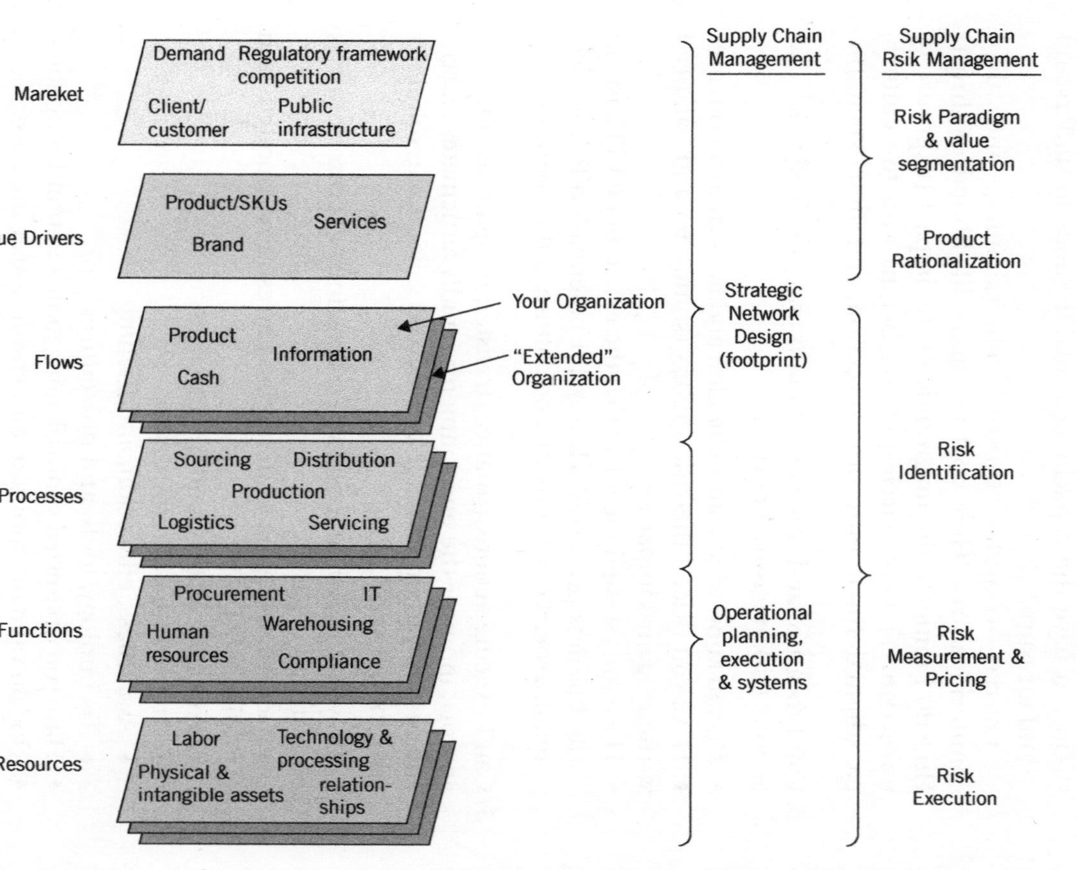

Exhibit 9.1 Business Construct, Supply Chain, and Supply Chain Risk Management Overlay

- Can you prioritize risks by impacts?
- Are you aware of what is already being done (current risk program), what works, what doesn't?
- Do you have the capacity and qualifications to understand and measure?

Overlay—consider threats, vulnerabilities, and then countermeasures. How do I minimize likelihood of threat? How do I mitigate the magnitude of the impact (exposure to uncertainty)? Three-circle picture: Begins with the culture, paradigm defined, enterprise direction, and then execution.

2. Can I measure and price investments and prioritize risk actions (risk measurement)?
   - Do you know what your mitigation and financing options are?
   - Have you priced the risk options (solutions) and balanced these against impacts?
   - Have you assessed the effect that the risk solution will have on the business processes? How will it potentially affect service, quality, social environment, and culture of the operation?

3. Can I execute actions (finance/transfer, mitigate, avoid, accept); monitor the environment; rapidly anticipate, react, and respond to undesirable events; and validate the solutions (risk execution)?
   - Do you know what it takes to successfully execute your risk strategy?
     - Governance, financial/business investment (model), and alignment
     - Policy, standards, and organization
     - Architecture and processes
     - Awareness, education, and training
     - Technology, tools, and procedures
   - Have you optimized your risk mitigation and transfer options?
   - Do you validate, monitor, and continuously improve?

Another way to look at the three major supply chain risk management elements is through a subprocess level (i.e., what are key processes that support the three major supply chain risk management processes). I refer to this design as the "Risk Intelligent Supply Chain, as illustrated in Exhibit 9.2.

Risk Identification			Risk Measurement & Investment		Risk Execution		
Value Alignment	Prioritization & Allocation	Gap Recognition	Options & Alternatives	Pricing & Measurement	Execution of Risk Strategy	Optimization	Monitoring & Diagnostics
• Risk paradigm set, listening posts, client & market alignment • Value segmentation & SKU/product rationalization • Flow analysis	• Line of sight (business process & resource mapping) & scoping • Impact failure analysis & modeling • Relevance & threat analysis & modeling	• Current state evaluation • Risk tolerance index (current state & benchmark) • Risk effect analysis (current state & benchmark)	• Risk option analysis & modeling (finance, alternate finance, mitigation, acceptance) • Integration impact analysis & modeling (cost, service, social, quality)	• Investment solution pricing and modeling • Business case creation with road map • Decision modeling	• Governance & alignment • Policy, standards & organization • Architecture & processes • Awareness, education & training • Technology, tools & procedures • Note: The above categories consist of four phases: Planning, doing, checking, and acting	• Risk transfer optimization analysis & modeling • Risk mitigation optimization analysis & modeling • Aggregate risk portfolio optimization analysis & modeling	• Overall program assessment, validation, continuous improvement

Exhibit 9.2 Processes and Subprocesses of a Risk Intelligent Supply Chain

Economic Change—A Catalyst for Redefining Resiliency Management

A detailed analysis and study of the SCRM in your organization is valuable, but always keep in mind that when the economy changes, business priorities and perspectives must change, too. This is not only crucial in order to survive, but also to persevere. Though maintaining liquidity might seem like the most important organizational priority, a company needs to fortify itself against ongoing disruptions as well as the fallout of initial change. Though putting risk management aside while tending to daily survival is expected, as the dust settles you have to realize that other disruptions are inevitable; economic volatility makes it more likely that an event will occur.

The goal of resiliency or continuity risk management is to minimize an organization's exposure and to keep business running smoothly during disruptive situations, while constantly adjusting to changes outside your organization's immediate influence. What could be more unsettling than the failure of business partners, deterioration in quality standards, consolidation of facilities, loss of corporate memory via reductions in the workforce, and offloading assets—all symptoms of changing economic times? And what if all this happens at a time when threats (geopolitical, hazard, terrorist, and health) have become more relevant and vulnerabilities (quality, security, intellectual property theft, and counterfeiting) more prevalent?

Change has been thrust upon us—industry change, business change, regulatory change, supply chain network change, operational change, third-party relationships change, even customer demand change. These changes have put your supply chain risk management and resiliency practices (including continuity, crisis, emergency, and disaster plans) at risk or, worst case, made them obsolete.

An example: Warning lights were flashing in late 2008 and again in early 2009 in boardrooms around the world as demand rapidly declined, trade credit tightened, and suppliers ran out of cash. For example, the continuity of the textile industry supply chain was impacted when the number of suppliers rapidly shrank from 22,099 in July 2008 to 6,262 in October 2008—a reduction of 72 percent.[1] As a result, composition of the supplier base varied, configurations of warehouses in relation to customers were altered, and inventory levels decreased throughout the supply chain. All this directly impacted existing business continuity strategies.

Though change surrounds us, what will not waiver are the expectations of others. Whether it's your customers, investors, business partners, or regulators, you're still accountable for providing value to the market and maintaining the ongoing entity during adverse times. In other words, there are no excuses for ignoring sound and proven risk management practices just because economic times are tough. And auditors, rating agencies, regulators, and other external parties that measure your organization's risk management practices can add fuel to the fire by offering a negative opinion that translates into a greater cost of capital or worse, negative press. Who wants to do business with a seemingly risky company?

To counteract the potential threat of obsolete or ineffective continuity risk management programs, organizations must move quickly and efficiently. Following are key questions that all organizations should consider regardless of the degree of volatility being faced.

Predisruption

- Are you actively engaged in the change as it occurs for the purpose of understanding what products and services are considered of greatest value?
  - Are these changes documented and has executive management validated them?
- Do you understand what the final configuration of flows, processes functions, and resources (people, technology, physical assets, and relationships) are as a result of change?
- Has the organization moved beyond continuity risk management that focuses on a facility and/or function to an approach that begins with value, flows, and processes?
- Have you established your continuity risk management priorities based on the products and services of greatest value?

The goal of business continuity risk is to align risk investments against that which could have the greatest impact to the value produced by the organization. This is an economic exercise, where you are trying to do the most with the least. In other words, there is a finite amount of available risk capital, time, resources, and management bandwidth. (Risconomic exercise as described in my book, *At Your Own Risk* [John Wiley & Sons, 2008]).

- Has your organization expanded the scope of its continuity planning activities to include the extended operation and third parties (i.e., from raw materials through supplies, logistics providers to the final customer)?
- Does your continuity mitigation strategy include the following:
  - As change occurs, whether it be at the strategic design layer (warehouses, factories, supplier locations, etc.) or the day-to-day operations (transportation, inventory management, production scheduling), it is critical that continuity and crisis planning take into consideration:
    - What is of greatest value (value segmentation/the priorities of your organization)?
    - What resources and processes are needed to support the creation, delivery, and servicing of value (process and resource mapping)?
    - What is the quantifiable and qualitative impact from loss of a critical resource according to value—revenue, asset, liquidity, strategic, brand/confidence, and compliance?
    - What are the required risk investments compared to potential impacts (risk financing/insurance, retention, retention with mitigation)?
    - Has the risk mitigation solution been validated (test, audit, simulate)?
    - Is the configuration/environment being monitored?
    - Are the risk solutions continuously assessed and optimized?
    - Have existing recovery, emergency, crisis, and IT disaster plans been updated regularly to reflect changes such as the consolidation of warehouses or the shutdown of a plant, elimination of suppliers, decreased inventory levels, or new transportation carriers?
- Do those organizations you rely on understand and practice your continuity expectations?

At Time of Disruption

- What steps should be considered when uncertainty becomes relevant and the organization's value becomes exposed? *The goal then becomes to minimize the financial and brand impact.*

- Utilizing the information from predisruption, what is the potential impact to the failed resources (revenue, liquidity, brand, compliance, and/or strategic)?
- Does your continuity and crisis management process contain the following:
  - Event identification—criteria for recognizing and responding to an event.
    - If determined, activate incident/emergency plans (emergency evacuation and life safety, product tampering, civil disturbance/terrorism, contractor emergency plans, etc.)
- Active crisis communications and management plan—the primary focus should be on ensuring the survivability of the organization by establishing a clear direction and communication with key stakeholders.
  - Containment—determine if desired impact thresholds and recovery times will be exceeded.
  - Escalation—predefined protocols and thresholds for escalating/promoting information and news flows in a timely, relevant, consistent, and accurate manner. Communication should be unobstructed among all stakeholders and there should be a clearly defined path for information to travel. In addition, there should be a person, or people, who can interpret the information, develop a response, and take action if necessary.
    - If determined, activate business and other relevant disaster recovery, restoration, and resumption plans.

Postdisruption

- After the event, conduct a group postmortem focusing on the following key questions:
  - What are the lessons learned?
  - How has the organization improved its risk mitigation and financing activities as a result of this event?
  - What problems were encountered?
  - Was your response effective?
  - Were you able to contain impact from the event?
    - If not, were you able to recover, restore, and resume normal operations?

What Is Risk Mitigation?

The concept of *mitigation*—reduction of risk to a manageable level—is central to your supply chain risk management program. This idea may be thought of as managing the risk parasite to a level where it can no longer continue to damage the body of your organization. Like an actual parasite, you may not be able to remove it, but you can neutralize its damaging effects.

Creating an intelligent and balanced mitigation policy is where your risk management program takes form, where it all comes together, and where all the organization's time, management attention, capital, and resources are spent. But remember, it must be action-based, specific, and practical. There is no benefit in bubbling the ocean. Organizations need to plan, design, implement, maintain, monitor, and improve their supply chain risk management in a cost-effective and nondisruptive (unobtrusive) way. A fundamentally sound supply chain risk management strategy prioritizes and allocates resources to what the organization considers its greatest value. The strategy is value central and organization neutral.

Building an Action Plan

Understanding the nature of risk is all well and good, but if that is as far as it goes, then organizations remain at risk. What good are a series of attractive, bound reports if there is nothing to act on? You need an action plan to see the task through. This is true even when your organization believes it cannot address risks outside of the immediate universe of a department or sector.

Many of the likely threats are, at first glance, far outside of your organization's control. Given this reality, do you just accept the premise that you have to live with these risks? No. You can and need to take steps to mitigate the threats. These mitigation steps can involve numerous action plans, including but not limited to:

- Diversification of suppliers and transportation routes and modes
- Shrinking the geographical size of the supply chain
- Improved communication, standards, and enforcement actions
- Changes in localized inventory programs to avoid a helpless unavailability of materials due to circumstances beyond your control

Remember, knowing *only* what can fail is failure itself. It's essential that your organization take steps to identify, analyze, evaluate, and measure, but at some point the organization must invest and execute risk solutions. What I find amazing in my years of meeting with dozens of organizations, and representing multiple industries, is the overwhelming number of internal and external risk assessments that have been performed; however, *no one has made the decision to take action.* You could be at greater risk, from a liability viewpoint, if you recognized the exposure and then neglected to take action. The key word here is *neglected* versus making a conscious decision to accept a specific risk. Those managing risk in the supply chain should have systems for capturing and escalating these risk decisions or, more to the point, for forcing a risk decision. The range of choices in response to any risk includes accept/retain, avoid, mitigate, transfer, or finance—but the choice has to be made. Second, a system for monitoring the action and ongoing exposure is essential to make sure the risk is managed in the desired way; this is especially important if you decide to mitigate a specific risk. Although multiple views may be brought to bear, supply chain risk must be viewed from one vantage point, and it involves a short list of two critical questions:

1. *Who is responsible for understanding and managing threats?*
   So often, organizations de-fund preventive measures because a risk has not been realized. This reliance on the old standard, based on budget constraints and the profit motive, is not only shortsighted, it is also a very real threat to your risk mitigation initiative. You need to identify not only functional methods for mitigating risk, but also to decide how to communicate the importance of these steps to the decision makers. If this step waits until a budget meeting, you have already lost because it will not be prioritized there. You have to end-run the pedantic budget process and appeal to a higher requirement, which frankly translates to organizational survival.
2. *How can my organization build the required attributes and change its traditional view of risk?*
   The key to avoiding or reducing risk in the new, interrelated world is to develop the intelligence and the flow of information—anticipating, avoiding through agility and flexibility, or reacting to warning signs, containing, and responding. The resiliency of your organization is going to be defined by how

effectively you are able to identify, seize, and build on these required attributes.

The Lay of the Mitigated Land

One of the greatest threats to your mitigation program is the concurrent existence of too many strategies, which are without a single driving force. This "constipation of initiatives" will kill you.

Boiling it down to its essence, applying the *lean* approach to risk mitigation, requires two very basic cutting back and clarification steps. These include:

1. *Do I know whom to contact in a crisis, ahead of time?*
   It doesn't do me any good if I have to figure this out after a crisis happens. I need to know how much it's going to impact me and my organization. There are six key factors I have to keep in mind: (1) information has to be readily available, (2) it must be current, timely, reliable, and accurate, (3) it must be tied into change management, that enlightened attitude that change is essential for progress and that change has to occur in a controlled, systematic way with predefined modeling, (4) any time a significant change is made to my organization, I must update my risk profile, (5) everything entering the process must be monitored and validated through testing, audit, simulation, modeling, and threat analysis, and (6) everyone in the organization has to understand and sign on to the program of *what* is needed, *why* it is a priority, *who* is going to do what, *how* it moves forward, and *where* action is going to occur.

   The challenges to this action-based approach include many obstacles, because you are going to propose that your organization revisit its basic management philosophy; that it change from profit incentive to a risk-reduction incentive (and convince management that these are really one and the same); and overlay risk management to every phase of the supply chain, risk assessment, and even the budget. Your biggest obstacles in trying to create a program of mitigation include:

   - Risk managers usually lack sufficient organizational clout to champion supply chain risk incentives, or even to have their ideas heard by the right people.

- Your organization, if typical, isn't fully aware of the best practices to manage end-to-end supply chain risk and, even worse, some managers just don't want to hear the bad news.
- Cross-functional supply chain processes make risk assessment and mitigation challenging, to say the least. Even the most basic idea of who has authority to mitigate a known risk may run into a complex resistance from others.
- Supply chain managers aren't motivated to focus on supply chain risk management; their emphasis has usually been on cost-cutting, defect-reduction, speed, and profitability; introducing risk throws all of that into secondary status.
- Lack of staff resources, not to mention time, budget, or even support from above for the added costs, dooms many risk management programs, even relatively easy mitigation ideas.
- Awareness on all levels or at least a belief in the threat itself is so often lacking that it becomes impossible to begin without also reeducating everyone to the reality of the range of actual threats.

2. *With these inhibiting factors in mind, you have to ask yourself: Has risk management failed?* Not necessarily. There are solutions, and these include a few basic ideas.[2]

   - *Educate the chain.* All supply chain partners have to be made aware of their role in ensuring safety and compliance on all applicable levels. Service level agreements (SLAs) that are part of the legal terms and conditions of procurement and service contracts should be used to help ensure compliance.
   - *Demand data collection excellence.* In many cases, the technical capabilities of suppliers—or lack thereof—can create severe constraints, which ultimately affect processing time, cost, and quality. These should be understood and planned for, capturing required data elements and required information through media in place, and then digitizing them as soon as possible.
   - *Institute documentation and communications consistency.* Documentation is critical to ensure that the correct packaging, storage, and handling procedures are consistently applied. This is both a quality and a safety concern.

- *Pay full attention to recall and destruction.* It is all-important to ensure that members of the extended supply chain know what to do if the product has been compromised and spoiled. This should be clearly outlined in SLAs between all players in the pharmaceutical supply chain, and internal controls should be built to ensure that the procedures are followed properly, including periodic quality audits.
- *Be obsessive in continuous monitoring.* Because of margin and market growth pressures, life sciences supply chains are more dynamic than ever before. Best-practice companies put in place data analysis processes and "human knowledge" collection procedures to spot specific red flags in their end-to-end supply chains. This should become the norm and should include definition, consistency, responsibility, impact, and event-driven discipline (meaning, taking action to ensure that, as a minimum, you are able to respond).

What Should You Be Worried About?

The guidelines provided in the previous section serve as an operations manual for approaching the problem but do not offer a solution. The actions you take determine how well you actually mitigate your risk. But even with all the preparation in the world, your mitigation-based action plan has to worry first about any range of risks that can be mitigated today, especially for a cost far below the cost resulting from a realized risk, and second, convincing your decision makers that your ideas are sensible, and trying to identify the risks you don't know about that could also be mitigated.

The action plan is critical. You need to begin with a specific action plan to mitigate the supply chain risk threat, involving the following steps:

- Recognize, anticipate, identify
  - Use intelligence, knowledge, experience, opinion, and monitoring to identify a range of risks that can and should be mitigated.
- Prepare
  - Apply planning, prioritizing, design, and strategy to develop specific mitigation plans.
- Support, endorse

- Rely on leadership, alignment, commitment, measurement, and making the business case; include the budgeting and comparative cost analysis to make your case to the financial interests within your organization, and remember, you make a good case when you demonstrate how mitigation is also profitable.
- Enable, integrate
  - Go to governance, policy, standards, organizational infrastructure, processes, protocols, tools, architecture, training, educating, and awareness, and recognize these as your primary mitigation resources.
- Balance, optimize, chose, identify options
  - Develop your action plan through prioritizing, modeling, pricing risk, measuring, transfer, avoidance/acceptance, reduction, mitigation, and alternate financing solutions,
- Validate, assure
  - Use assessing, testing, auditing, simulating, modeling, benchmarking, and measuring to educate others in your organization,

Also make distinctions about the steps in the process of putting mitigation into place. These steps include:

- During
  - Respond, intervene
  - Contain
  - Escalate
  - Measure
  - Prioritize
  - Resolve
- After
  - Recover
  - Resume
  - Restore
  - Adjust
  - Learn, critique, postmortem
  - Resolve
  - Measure
  - Profit
  - Improve
  - Act

Systemic Risk

The task is a big one. You need to break down risk into "bite-sized" challenges you can manage individually. Risks can be categorized in many ways. One that needs the greatest attention, notably as part of your organization's mitigation program, is systemic risk.

Back in the old days (pre-1980s), the term *systemic risk* did not refer to contagion of illiquidity within the financial sector alone. Back then, when the real economy was much more important than low-margin, unglamorous banking, it was understood that the really scary systemic risk was the risk of contagion of illiquidity from the financial sector to the real economy of trade in real goods and real services. If you think of it, every single non-cash commercial transaction requires the intermediation of banks on behalf of—at the very least—the buyer and the seller. If you lengthen the supply chain to producers, exporters, and importers and allow for agents along the way, the chain of banks involved becomes quite long and complex. When central bankers back in the old days argued that banks were special—and therefore demanded higher capital, strict limits on leverage, tight constraints on business activity, and superior integrity of management—it was because they appreciated the harm that a bank failure would have in undermining the supply chain for business in the real economy for real people causing real joblessness and real hunger if any bank along the chain should be unable to perform.

As the specialness of banks eroded with the decline of the real economy (and the migration globally of many of those real jobs making real goods and providing real added-value services to real people), the nature of systemic risk was adjusted to become self-referencing to the financial elite. Central bankers of the current generation only understand systemic risk as referring to contagion of illiquidity among financial institutions. They and we all are about to learn the lessons of the past anew. We are now starting to see the contagion effects of the current liquidity crisis feed through to the real economy. We are about to go back to the bad old days. Whether the zombie banks are kept on life support by the central banks and taxpayers of the world is highly relevant to whether the zombie bank executives pay themselves outsize bonuses and their zombie shareholders outsize dividends with taxpayer money. It appears sadly irrelevant whether the banks perform their function of intermediating credit and commercial transactions in the real economy along the supply chain. The bailout cash and executive and shareholder priorities do not seem to reach so far. The recent 93 percent collapse of the obscure Baltic Dry Index—an index of the cost of chartering bulk cargo vessels for goods like ore, cotton, grain, or similar dry tonnage—has caused a bit of a stir among the financial cognoscenti.

What is less discussed amid the alarm is the reason for the collapse of the index—the collapse of trade credit based on the venerable letter of credit. Letters of credit have financed trade for more than 400 years. They are considered one of the more stable and secure means of finance because the cargo secures the credit extended to import it. The letter of credit irrevocably advises an exporter and his bank that payment will be made by the importer's issuing bank if the proper documentation confirming a shipment is presented. This was seen as low risk because the issuing bank could seize and sell the cargo if its client defaulted after payment was made. Like so much else in this topsy-turvy financial crisis, however, the verities of the ages have been discarded in favor of new and unpleasant realities.

The combination of the global interbank lending freeze with the collapse of the speculative, leveraged commodity price bubble has undermined both the confidence of banks in the ability of a far-flung peer bank to pay an obligation when due and confidence in the value of the dry cargo as security for the credit if liquidated on default. The result is that those with goods to export and those with goods to import, no matter how worthy and well capitalized, are left standing quayside without bank financing for trade.

Adding to the difficulties, letters of credit are so short term that they become an easy target for scaling back credit as liquidity tightens around bank operations globally. Longer-term assets—like mortgage-backed securities, collateralized debt obligations (CDOs), and credit default swaps—can't be easily renegotiated, and banks are loathe to default to one another on them because of cross-default provisions. Short-term credit like trade finance can be cut with the flick of an executive wrist. Further adding to the difficulties, many bulk cargoes are financed in dollars. Non-U.S. banks have been progressively starved of dollar credit because U.S. banks hoarded it as the funding crisis intensified. Recent currency swaps between central banks should be seen in this light, noting the allocation of Federal Reserve dollar liquidity to key trading partners Brazil, Mexico, South Korea, and Singapore in particular.

Fixing this problem shouldn't be left to the Fed. They aren't going to make it a priority. Indeed, their determination to accelerate the payment of interest on reserves and then to raise that rate to match the Federal Funds target rate indicates that the Fed is likely to constrain trade finance liquidity rather than improve it. Furthermore, the Fed may be highly selective in its allocation of dollar liquidity abroad, prejudicing the economic prospects of a large part of the world that is either indifferent or hostile to the continuation of American dollar hegemony. If cargo trade stops, a whole lot of supply chain disruption starts. If the ore doesn't go to the refinery, there is no plate steel. If the plate steel doesn't get shipped, there is nothing to fabricate into components. If there are no components, there is nothing to assemble in the factory. If the factory closes the assembly line, there are no finished goods. If there are no finished goods, there is nothing to restock the shelves of the shops. If there is nothing in the shops, the consumers don't buy. If the consumers don't buy, the economy slows. Everyone along the supply chain should worry about their jobs. Many will lose their jobs sooner rather than later. If cargo trade stops, the wheat doesn't get exported. If the wheat doesn't get exported, the mill has nothing to grind into flour. If there is no flour, the bakeries and food processors can't produce bread and pasta and other foods. If there are no foods shipped from the bakeries and factories, there are no foods in the shops. If there are no foods in the shops, people go hungry. If people go hungry, their children go hungry. When children go hungry, people riot and governments fall.

Everyone along the supply chain should worry about their children going hungry. When that happens, everyone in governments should worry about the riots. Controlling access to trade finance determines who loses their jobs, whose children go hungry, who riots, which governments fall. Without dedicated focus on the issue of trade finance and liquidity from those in the emerging world most interested in sustaining the growth of recent years, little progress can be expected. Trade finance is rapidly communicating the stress on bank liquidity to the real economy. It presents a systemic risk much more frightening than the collapsing value of bits of paper traded electronically in London and New York. It could collapse the employment, the well being, and the political stability of most of the world's population. The World Trade Organization hosted a meeting on trade credit in Washington recently to highlight the rapid and accelerating deterioration in trade finance as an urgent priority for public policy.

Also, be aware that when things go wrong, they often do so in sets. For example, in 1944 when the Allies invaded Holland, they discovered too late that the infantry could not communicate with their comrades in Jeeps and other vehicles. Their communications gear was not coordinated. Replacement tubes didn't fit the sets. And the British paratroopers had landed 12 miles from their target bridge. The British suffered 80 percent casualties. A series of disasters doomed the invasion from the start, a tragic story told in Cornelius Ryan's *A Bridge Too Far* (Simon & Schuster, 1995). The object lesson: Any (or all) of the problems encountered could have been mitigated with better planning and with a more comprehensive action plan.

The final destination is known to create value in the market and to be profitable doing so. The road followed may be dark and winding, with many obstacles and forks along the way. But one thing is for sure: We know that we want to get to the final destination. We just need to be sure that we are looking out the window at the road ahead and not driving forward at 80 mph while using our rearview mirror for guidance.

> To properly address risk in a forward-looking manner, your organization will require sensors, listening posts, external sources, predictive and impact modeling, and, most of all, a far-reaching risk conscious culture. In other words, planning is one critical element, but it will have to be combined with a just-in-time supply chain risk management philosophy—one that is fast, low cost, and agile.

Notes

1. Panjiva, a company that collects and disseminates data on global suppliers and manufacturers, http://panjiva.com.
2. Marsh, Supply Chain Risk Management Group, http://global.marsh.com/index.php.

CHAPTER 10

Law #9: Financing

THE BEST POLICY IS KNOWING WHAT'S IN YOUR POLICY

Insurance: An ingenious modern game of chance in which the player is permitted to enjoy the comfortable conviction that he is beating the man who keeps the table.

—Ambrose Bierce (1842–1914), *The Devil's Dictionary*

Insurance: Plays a key role in the support of supply chain activity. It is just one method of dealing with risk so make sure you know what you are buying!

—Anonymous, *Insurance Industry Executive*

On May 12, 2008, an 8.0 magnitude earthquake shook China's Sichuan Province. Estimates put the number of dead at 88,000 and over 400,000 people missing. The earthquake damaged or destroyed millions of properties: homes, businesses, schools, hospitals, roads, and water systems.[1] Earthquake insurance, offered as an extension of more standard fire insurance coverage, quickly proved to be far less than adequate to cover the more than \$10 to \$15 billion in losses. The same estimates pegged insured losses at \$1 billion, a fraction of total damage. There are two important lessons to be drawn from this financial and social catastrophe. First, residential coverage is clearly not widespread enough to pay for losses. Second, a comparatively invisible type of loss, from business interruption (i.e., flow of goods versus direct property damage or stock), was far higher than physical damage losses. This affects both primary suppliers and second-tier providers. Even though insurance growth in China has been impressive, the problem remains. There is often too little coverage, high deductibles and co-pays, and a failure to recognize exposure among suppliers a primary provider relies on. This creates another potential single point of failure. As you might suspect, this problem is not unique to China. The threat is real and it is global. Financing risk exposure takes many forms; uninsured risks can be catastrophic if your organization has failed to ensure that its true exposures are adequately covered.

It may be that the hidden Achilles' heel in your organization is the one most widely understood (or assumed): the methods available to finance your risk exposure.

Insurance as a supply chain tool for managing risk is a crucial and important element of any program, and has been for centuries. In fact, for over 500 years, insurance has made logistics possible when it would otherwise have been too risky to take a chance on losses. For example, maritime insurance has always protected shipping from perils like piracy and sinking, which often meant a 100 percent loss to cargo. Today, many supply chain managers underestimate the role of insurance, assuming it is a simple or obvious solution to protect against known perils. But contrary to this widespread belief, insurance is complex and now is undergoing a massive change. The expansion of supply chains both geographically and technologically makes insurance more important than ever, but also more difficult to understand in context. It's a multifaceted problem with these potential component shortfalls:

- Insurable losses underprotected or not protected at all
- Insured coverage inadequate to cover the full extent of the loss
- Uninsurable losses that are assumed, incorrectly, to be covered
- Excluded perils assumed covered but, in fact, excluded in the policy terms

The rude awakening to insurance problems occurs most often through various classes of business insurance. However, in reviewing objectively your overall financing program through the supply chain lens, you are likely to discover that your organization has many strategies to address specific risks but is lacking one central program. For any supply chain risk manager, this intrinsic failure to understand the role of insurance in the larger scheme of supply chain can easily mislead top management into a false sense of security, the belief that "we are covered" when, in fact, the most serious threats may easily remain unaddressed—a single point of failure. The majority of today's insurance coverages address the loss of a resource (e.g., property) rather than the supply chain process flow of goods, services, and cash. The resource-based insurance approach presents complexity and makes it difficult when trying to overlay coverage through the supply chain lens.

Insurance costs more and provides less than in the past. This fact points to a crucial shortcoming in risk management. Too often, a distinction has not been made between insurable and uninsurable risks.

It should be noted that when I began writing this chapter I realized that I needed to enlist some of the industry's most experienced, licensed professionals. Their input and technical guidance proved invaluable, especially Nick Wildgoose, Supply Chain Global Manager, Zurich Global Corporate; Ben Tucker, Managing Director, Property Practice, and Paul McVey, Managing Director at Marsh, Property Claims.

Insurance and Its Role in Supply Chain Risk Management

> I buy insurance to smooth earnings, protect my balance sheet. I am satisfied with my investment when the cost of my premiums is equal to the return on claims.
>
> —CFO, Fortune 100 organization

As this book defines risk within the context of a supply chain, risk financing and insurance can be categorized in five dimensions, each of which has significant impacts on your organization. Examples of these are:

1. *Disruption of the supply of goods or services and inadequate coverage levels,* which causes a failure to satisfy a customer's requirements on time and exposes the organization. For example, liability policies are most likely to cover losses from bodily injury and property damages but often fail to address the threat from business disruption or from third-party claims. So disruptions often cost more than physical damages, but may be severely limited, subject to high deductions and co-pays, or altogether absent.
2. *Price volatility* may result in difficulties in passing on price changes and impact profits. Price volatility is impossible to calculate in the future, as we witnessed in 2008 and 2009 when energy and commodity prices soared and then rapidly declined.
3. *Poor quality* of products or services, either upstream or downstream, which impact on the customer's financial satisfaction and include future financial consequences.
4. *Reputation damage,* which arises from problems within the supply chain such as environmental threats. There is insurance for reputation risk; however, coverage is not broadly available and is expensive. Your risk management solution portfolio will be heavily weighted to risk mitigation (versus financing). Carrying out good supply chain risk mitigation practices can minimize your exposure.
5. *Unnamed perils (in the absences of physical damage).* In most policies, unnamed perils are not covered. For example, the 2009 Influenza A (H1N1) outbreak was probably not covered unless your policy includes a very specific clause specifying coverage for infectious or communicable disease outbreaks. Any supply chain manager needs to recognize that many threats arising from potential threats may be excluded from business interruption policies. Exhibit 10.1 illustrates a few of the many tradeoffs between coverage and cost that should be considered when purchasing insurance. Any current policy needs to be subjected to a thorough review, and new terms should be negotiated to ensure that the right risks are covered, and that deductible and co-pay limits are what you expect. In other words, you have to make sure you're getting what you think you're paying for. Many people are not.

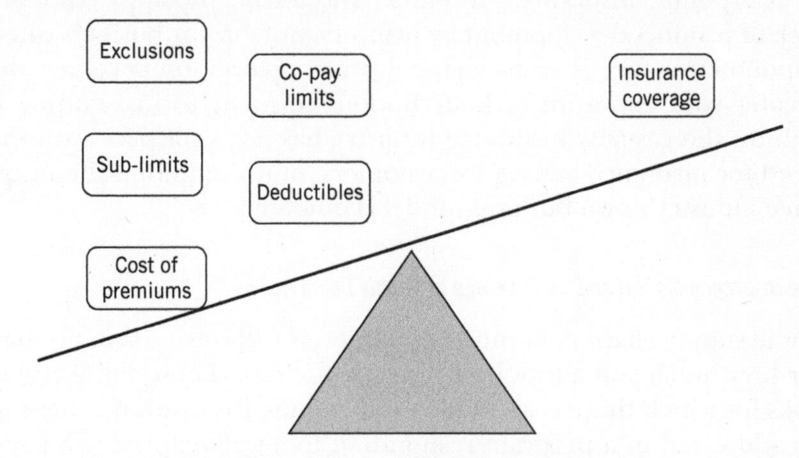

Exhibit 10.1 Considerations When Selecting Insurance

Background on Insurance in the Supply Chain Risk Area

A number of background factors come into play when considering the role of insurers with the supply chain:

1. *Supply chain risks pose an increasing threat to your organization.* This is unavoidable. However, it is important to examine and analyze exactly what is covered and to what limits. You may discover that operating from the assumption of complete coverage is a mistake. Supply chain risk may be easily excluded if losses are incurred away from primary suppliers, outside a specific geographic coverage region, or falling into the rather wide chasm of unnamed perils. For example, insurance is either limited or does not exist when trying to insure against nonperformance by a supplier, work stoppages, defective products, and most third-party threats.
2. *Corporate insurers operate in a shrinking marketplace,* meaning coverage has to become restrictive while costs continue to rise. So your premium cost may have been rising over the past few years, while your deductible and co-pay levels grow. And at the same time, the claims history of insurers may have led to revised exclusions in your existing renewal policies.

Corporate insurance customers should be unhappy with the lack of product development by insurers, notably for business interruption coverage. The more global your organization becomes, the greater your exposure to interruptions in many forms. Putting it bluntly, the casualty insurance industry has not kept pace with the need for insurance among its customers, in my opinion. The insurance industry's own business model is outdated.

The Insurance Market and Its Coverage of Supply Chain Risks

Some supply chain risks must remain even with insurance, no matter how much you adopt best practice policies. Those uninsurable risks for which there is an inadequate avenue for insurance have to be addressed in a program responding to a well-defined risk paradigm. In addition to uninsurable risks, you also need to address the need to finance unresolved risks. An uninsurable risk is either named as an exclusion or not named in a list of covered perils. In comparison, an unresolved risk is one that (1) the organization decides to live with because coverage is too expensive or comes with too-high deductibles and co-pays; (2) no one has ever considered or imagined; (3) is assumed to belong to someone else such as a first-tier or second-tier supplier or manufacturer; or (4) is considered too unlikely or remote to occur, even when its occurrence would be catastrophic. These risks cannot just be transferred; they have to be treated more realistically. Remember these key issues regarding business interruption and other forms of property and casualty insurance:

- You need an endorsement to covered orders by civil and military authorities.
- Policy requirements include the need for your organization to take reasonable measures to comply with applicable laws and regulations. This applies to anyone you think is covered, including suppliers who may not be under your direct control.
- You need to specifically identify a financing plan for unresolved risks, such as losses from contamination, mold, disease, and pollution.

Insurance solutions available in the marketplace are going to inevitably be less than adequate to cover your risks entirely.

But even so, your organization still needs to carry a level of coverage to protect against known catastrophic losses, at the very least. *Beware*; your client may require specific coverage and limits. Insurance companies assess this level of risk and ways to address it, as they recognize the needs of their customers for more coverage and of more creative variations. Within this, you need to coordinate supply chain solutions not only with your organization in mind, but including the requirements of your customers, internal audit processes, brokerage limits, and contracts, and the market's ability to underwrite risk. These are profound requirements and a complete assessment reveals that you cannot plan for or mitigate all of these risks with insurance. Even so, supply chain managers need to acknowledge that as a financing vehicle for risk management, insurance makes sense. You need to cover these threats with a financing vehicle, and as a protective product, insurance is probably your best way to manage risks. The question is whether enough of your risks are covered, whether they are covered adequately, and whether the ratio of cost to benefit makes sense.

Current Insurance Solutions and Their Limitations

Organizations recognize that they face increasing supply chain risks, following changes in the production and sourcing processes—for example, just-in-time production, single sourcing, and outsourcing, not to mention expanded global presence and reliance on second- and third-tier manufacturing. They are interested in the ways they can reduce risks through insurance and other mitigation avenues.

Business Interruption Insurance

This is one of the primary tools available to corporate customers in the area related to supply chain insurance; it typically covers loss of profit and continuing expenses as a result of physical damage to your premises as a standard level of protection; therefore, provides insurance coverage against events impacting your internal supply chain. Contingent business interruption (BI) insurance expands on this idea, protecting your loss of profit and continuing expenses following damage at a key third-party location (generally still subject to physical damage).

Current property policies still rely on complicated BI loss calculations and triggers that have not changed since the 1930s. Furthermore, global companies have to be prepared to carry more risks themselves, either on their own balance sheets or through a captive insurance company. For example, are you covered for acts of terrorism as defined by the Terrorism Risk Insurance Act (TRIA)?[2] This is only one example of the new forms of risk that is not even conceived of under traditional property and casualty coverage.

All of the major property insurers offer BI insurance as part of their property damage and machinery breakdown policies. More recent developments in the BI insurance market, such as agreed value solutions or contingent BI policies, are extensions or variations to the existing range of cover, but they remain outdated for the complex level of threats in the global marketplace. In other words, existing BI insurance is based on traditional, geographically limited models and has failed to recognize the complex nature of modern global business. Thus, "interruption" has a different meaning today than it had only a decade ago.

For today's risk manager, this simple reality has stark implications. Many global organizations continue to operate under the traditional management principles; they may have understood the universe of BI risk as it was understood in the 1970s or 1980s. But in a rapidly expanding, ever-more efficient global market, the old models have to be abandoned and a new evaluation and analysis demanded. Thus, interruption used to mean something relatively simple by modern standards. In fact, 30 or 40 years ago, no one imagined such interruption risks as terrorism, piracy, pandemic, or simple transportation risk based on global economics, politics, or trade restrictions.

Business interruption with agreed value settlements can be used where, for example, a product line is going to be discontinued because the production facility burns down. Here it would not make sense for the insurer to rebuild the plant to original specifications but not to allow for the building of a new plant, or to allow for the indemnity to be used for a different purpose altogether. This coverage has practical utility for some, but it does not address cases where an organization relies on a third-tier manufacturer who carries no insurance. In case of that plant burning down, the primary organization suffers business interruption but cannot get insurance for it.

Do your diligence; understand your upstream suppliers' position on risk financing and insurance. Trust but verify.

Even in cases where the basic BI coverage is adequate, competition in the marketplace has helped erode the premiums for contingent BI insurance to an extent that what was originally treated as a new policy type has deteriorated into an extension to standard cover, but with significant risks attached. In other words, risks are greater than ever but coverage remains fixed on traditional and outdated models.

The modern problem extends beyond the limits and exclusions of coverage. Current BI coverage is triggered by physical damage only, but there are a variety of other triggers that cause business interruption. Triggers such as suppliers' default, political risks, outsourced manufacturers' losses, and other failures in the supply chain, or simply the nonsupply of goods or services or the supply of insufficient or defective supplies, can have a devastating impact on profits. All of these are most likely not insurable under BI or under contingent BI solutions or agreed value covers. Because these threats cannot be protected by insurance, other solutions have to be brought into the equation, such as:

- Diversification of risk exposure through multiple supply chain reliance, which effectively means that a loss is not total because supply chain logistics can be continued through remaining unaffected chains.
- Contraction of the physical scope of the supply chain, a revolutionary idea that only a few years ago would have made no sense. This is accomplished when an organization changes its supply chain in several ways, including (1) working only with primary suppliers who can be monitored through audit, insured to the degree possible, and brought into the shared stakeholder team; (2) continued and expanded quality audits managed internally and imposed on first-tier—and sole-tier—suppliers; and (3) in the most extreme form of contraction, moving the supply chain closer to home and shortening the exposure links in the complex and extended chain.
- Cooperative efforts with other organizations to spread and share risk. (A model for this is the insurance industry, which widely reinsures its risks so that, in effect, the insurance

industry is a giant cooperative jointly managing risks.) This is distinct from diversification. A diversified risk is one where exposure is moved. A cooperative effort accepts the risk but shares it with other organizations with similar or identical stakeholders.

Trade Disruption Insurance

Trade disruption insurance is typically a form of advanced contingent BI insurance and addresses some of the problems in today's complex and global supply chain. Coverage includes property damage suffered by a direct supplier, transportation disruption due to weather, and insolvency of the direct supplier. Although it covers some of the triggers required by the organization, trade disruption insurance fails to protect the entire supply chain against a variety of triggers. Trade disruption insurance comprises elements of credit, marine, and political risks insurance added to the standard contingent BI cover available elsewhere in the marketplace. However, today's organization increasingly relies on direct suppliers who themselves outsource manufacturing, assembly, warehousing, and inventory functions to second-tier providers, often in other countries and at times unknown to the primary organizations. Trade disruption coverage is not applicable to this situation, meaning that a growing number of companies are exposed to significant risks today, even those carrying what they believe to be a comprehensive level of trade disruption insurance.

The supply manager needs to acknowledge that, at least at the moment, the insurance industry is not able to address the complexities of trade disruption threats as they exist in the real world. When evaluating the scope of your present coverage, remember to ask whether your policies extend beyond resources and also cover supply chain process flows (goods and services, as well as cash). Chances are you will find that you need to revamp your policies and take a hard look at what is protected and what is left out.

Because the majority of trade disruption policies specifically exclude acts of terrorism as a standard clause, any major event will cause catastrophic losses and lead to higher premium and broader exclusions. These exclusions may even extend to and include providing no coverage for specific countries or regions. So risk is more unpredictable whenever global business disruption becomes a likely risk to your supply chain. This problem points to required answers, including supply chain diversification, possibly even to contraction of its geographic scope. Sadly, this kind of tightening may also translate to shrinkage in capacity as well.

Mitigating the threat is going to require cooperation among industry, government, shipping, and logistics industries on a truly global scale. This cooperation will no doubt mean expanded definitions within trade pacts and treaties, asset segmentation by way of stakeholder collaboration, higher-level resiliency preparation, and, more than anything else, an increased level of risk consciousness on many levels. As one study observed in comparing the threats you face today with a global supply chain:

> While terrorism and natural disasters are different, they have several important features in common—uncertainty and wide variances in losses from one year to the next. Experts and decision makers face challenges in assessing the risks associated with these extreme events, developing strategies for reducing future losses, and facilitating the recovery process following a major disaster.[3]

Credit and Political Risks Insurance

Credit insurance covers the financial effects of a protracted default by the insured's customer. Political risk insurance protects financial interests against emerging markets risks. These represent specific coverages for corporate customers but only in specific circumstances. Coverage does not have the breadth of protection which most customers actually need. Any analysis of the range of threats you face related to credit and political circumstances point out how unprepared the insurance industry has been to address these threats realistically.

One attempt at mitigation of these risks has been the process of securitization. To transfer credit risks to the financial markets, exposures of different kinds (credit, political risk, surety, and suppliers' default) will have to be packaged in order to reach a critical mass to attract potential buyers, and to wrap undesirable exposures into healthy risk portfolios. This is a tall order. Given the problems in credit markets in 2008, it is a sure thing that insurers do not want to *extend* coverage in this area. If anything, they are now likely to run from it or to demand high premiums and unrealistically high deductibles just to provide any level of coverage. You may also discover that exclusions are so broad that the coverage itself is not adequate.

Supply Chain Finance Solutions Beyond Insurance

Banks have offered to transfer payment obligations, originally made to the individual suppliers, to their own balance sheet for a fee—in essence, a reverse factoring contract for the purchaser. In a sense, this represents a form of finance-based risk transfer and an alternative to the traditional insurance model. In the future, transfer payments may replace insurance as a more realistic method for addressing supply chain risks.

Both the company taking out such obligations as industry-based working capital funding as well as its direct (and indirect) suppliers will need to be vetted for financial strength and satisfactory payment history, which in turn may limit the scope for the product in relation to new suppliers and to complex supply chains. So an organization lacking its own financial strength or relying on manufacturing twice-removed in a developing country are going to have considerable difficulty qualifying for the basic capital provisions. This reality, among other causes, may eventually add to the growing momentum to eliminate second-tier reliance and contract supply chains—even in some cases meaning the entire supply chain is brought back to domestic operations exclusively. The trend toward financing outside of insurance does remove one area of risk from the supplier: the problem inherent in short-term guarantees when longer-term guarantees are necessary.

Marine Cargo and Goods in Transit Insurance Marine Cargo and Goods in Transit insurance typically covers physical loss or damage to goods during their transportation from a seller's warehouse to a buyer's warehouse, including intermediary storage. Other than a usual 10 percent uplift in the insured value to cover additional expenses in the event of a loss, Marine Cargo and Goods in Transit Insurance does not customarily cover any subsequent profit impact. Additionally, goods in transit often involve multicountry handling and processing of goods, and levels of coverage may restrict or exclude international commerce. If so, the coverage itself is of dubious value unless the greatest geographical risks are covered adequately. However, this is not always the case.

Shipments of expensive machinery such as turbines are scheduled to arrive at the construction site over a short time span to fit a project schedule, and if they fail to arrive because of a maritime peril the whole project can be delayed with subsequent costs. This coverage is commonly referred to as Delay in Start Up (DSU) insurance. However, as with all kinds of property and casualty protection, the devil is in the details. Delays due to some very real causes may be excluded, and secondary losses often are not included in the DSU policy coverage.

Loss of profits following an uninsured risk such as delay arising out of strikes or political risks or logistics infrastructure problems is not commonly available from cargo insurers. These exclusions only scratch the surface of the risk universe and further demonstrate how inadequate insurance is in addressing this risk universe. The principal legislation governing import/export cargo insurance is the English Marine Insurance Act 1906 (MIA).

In the MIA, marine insurance is defined in Section 7 as:

> A contract of marine insurance is a contract whereby the insurer undertakes to indemnify the assured, in manner and to the extent thereby agreed, against marine losses, that is to say, the losses incident to a marine adventure.

Section 8.1 of the MIA provides:

> A contract of marine insurance may, by its express terms, or by usage of trade, be extended so as to protect the assured against losses on inland waters or on any land risk which may be incidental to a sea voyage.

It is clear, therefore, that the MIA does not contemplate pure inland transit risks as part of its standard coverage (SC), where there is to be no sea voyage involved, nor does it contemplate air transport risks, whether international or otherwise. However, both inland transit and international and domestic air cargo risks are written as part of the marine line of business, and the principles of MIA continue to apply.

The Institute Cargo Clauses incorporate certain aspects of the MIA such as the requirement for insurable interest.

Supply Chain Insurance Customers' Wish List?

Research with a number of potential corporate insurance buyers has shown that:

- Customers would ideally like to see protection that kicks in when supply does not turn up, whatever the trigger; additionally, it may be desirable to include unknown risks but insurers are not likely to agree to an extension of possible losses; no insurer is going to agree to cover everything and anything, especially a threat not yet conceived, which is why the named perils clauses are comforting to property and casualty underwriters everywhere. Where does this leave the organization operating in an ever-expanding trade universe?
- When taking out insurance, the customer needs certainty: The insured will want to know what the indemnified amount will be if the supply does not turn up. Ironically, the most likely forms of loss are based on uncertainty, so this begs the question of how dependent your organization should be on a range of insurance protection. The only reasonable conclusion is to accept insurance as one of several means for financing threats, while also searching for alternatives for the portion that is underinsured or cannot be insured.
- Payment of indemnity will have to be made shortly after the event, not, as under current BI claims adjustment practice, following extensive forensic examination potentially years after the event. In today's rapidly evolving economy in which cash flow can make or break your organization's fortunes, the traditional insurance procedures are impractical. This is another aspect in which insurance has not kept pace with the practical requirements of the market.
- It would also be ideal for a number of customers to address the potential impacts of the internal supply chain within the organization and not to rely so heavily upon insurance. Because so many organizations depend on manufacturing processes in one location and then ship to other global locations, the wake-up call tells you that traditional insurance is not the whole answer; real risk mitigation demands a realistic

> analysis of what you need to do to diversify risk, better manage that risk through direct supplier controls, and accept some portion of risk that simply cannot be covered by insurance.

Given that products can be developed on this basis when they are coupled with risk assessment processes, this will certainly mean that the insurers are adding value to the operations of their customers. However, simply obtaining a range of insurance coverage under these older models is not going to address the most likely forms of risk you face.

Introducing Supply Chain Insurance: Approach and Challenges

The idea of developing products specifically to address modern threats is being actively considered by a number of insurers. A new product needs to be designed in such a way that it derives exposure limits, retentions, and the premium calculation parameters directly from the insured's profit and loss statement, but also in response to the realities of today's global markets—while also addressing the specific requirements of the modern supply chain and realistically addressing the threats faced within it. The coverage required is driven by profitability to the insurer, and understandably so; in some cases, profitability by business division is in play as well, notably in the consolidated world of financial institutions, where insurance is often found co-existing with banking, brokerage, investment analysis, mortgaging, investment, and many other segments. With its close link to the buyer's value drivers, gross profit, and eventually cash flow, the new design of insurance products will have to help protect value in the event of a major supply failure, including a range of possible ways that such losses may occur.

Compared to the current situation where many supply risks are uninsurable or simply not included in a list of known perils, a major supply failure has the potential to result in a reduction of the company's value through negative impact on its cash flow and profits. Insurers have historically been reluctant to offer realistic forms of protection because insufficient data has been available to reliably assess the financial risks that accompany the launch of a new supply chain insurance (SCI) product. The reduction in value suffered by a number of companies from a supply chain failure minus the price for SCI insurance represents the value added by such an insurance product.

Phrasing

The phrasing for a realistic and practical SCI product needs to serve two purposes:

1. To offer sufficient cover to ensure the insured is willing to buy the product
2. To protect the insurer so no unexpected losses are incurred

   Three approaches have been taken:

   1. *Named perils coverage.* When defining the perils—the triggers that allow a claim to be made under the policy—in advance the insurer has the security of reducing its exposure to incidents that were thought of at the outset. The insurer's risk engineering surveys can be directed specifically at those defined perils, although this may in turn restrict the scope of the surveys, missing risks that lie outside the defined scope and providing less value to the customer. The insured, however, might not buy in to such coverage as the supply chain may not be known well enough for an understanding of what incidents could lead to a breakage. In addition, the insured has the onus of proof with defined perils cover. This is a large problem because, again, *change* defines the very losses you need to cover, and unknown losses will never be included by insurers
   2. *All risks policy.* An all risks policy includes all possible scenarios from the outset and reduces the insurer's foreseeable risk through named, excluded perils. There are certain perils that could lead to huge aggregate losses in an insurance portfolio—such as pandemics or terrorism—which the insurer will have to exclude to protect its balance sheet. With an all risks policy, the insurer would have to prove that a loss is excluded under the policy if a notified loss is to be declined. Of course, this form of coverage will be quite expensive and involve substantial deductible and coinsurance clauses.
   3. *All risk and named perils combined policy.* In such a policy, underwriters recognize their ability to offer broad "all risk" coverage, which is the result of physical damage; and second, recognize that the insured also need coverage for

certain named perils which are not the result of physical damage. The named perils section of the policy permits the insurer to define the scope of the cover, permitting them to offer cover, which would not have been available even five years ago. The named perils cover can, for example, include coverage for such events as a pandemic, bankruptcy of a supplier, government-ordered recall of a supply, and power or utility service interruption. This type of contract is now available in the insurance market.

A corporate buyer would expect an insurance product that responded to its supply risk and one that was easy to handle in terms of claims. Added benefit is provided by a product designed to respond to all perils not specifically excluded, but a realistic analysis of cost versus benefit ultimately will determine whether this kind of coverage truly addresses the problem.

Only the all risks approach, not restricted to damage, political risk, or default is likely to meet organizational requirements by providing cover for the situation where deliveries simply do not turn up, whatever the reason. The insurance clause of the wording responds when expected supplies do not arrive on the insured's premises at the agreed time.

Definitions would need to help clarify the cover: the nonarrival of supplied goods and services, and the resulting effects on the gross profit of the insured.

Exclusions from All Risk Contracts

Exclusions allow the insurer to avoid foreseeable and undesirable losses; they also help the insurer to reduce vulnerability in respect of potentially catastrophic events. The following list covers a couple of examples that could have detrimental effect on an entire insurer portfolio (upon individual review, by insured, some of these exclusions could be lifted subject to satisfactory underwriting assessment):

- *Pandemics.* Insurers would want to avoid a scenario where exports from Asia, for example, are stopped due to a continental epidemic. However, if an epidemic only breaks out in a single location and a single production entity is affected, insurers should consider covering such exposures.

- *Political risks.* Russia has shown how Europe, in particular, can be affected by political actions against individual trading partners.

Risk Assessment

To underwrite a new line of business is a formidable task. Reliable claims data are not available for the new product. However, in the case of BI insurance, claims data may be used from the outset to develop future loss assumptions. A full assessment of the compatibility of such data—available in most major insurance companies—and collection of further data would have to be incorporated as part of the overall process.

Loss Experience

Loss experience is a very valuable tool for the insurer if consistently monitored over the last five or more years, and as long as the supply chain structure has not changed during that time. As ever, the action taken by the affected company following instances of supply failure also gives strong indications as to the robustness of its continuity plan in respect of supplies. As a marketing tool and extension of policy terms, favorable loss experience modification to premium costs provides an inducement to organizations taking part in this coverage.

Three examples of the areas to be considered by the insurer in looking at providing insurance for a customer are:

1. *Supplier default.* One trigger regularly mentioned by corporate insurance customers as an area of concern is the default of a direct or indirect supplier. This became particularly important in 2009 due to the global credit crunch. Default statistics provide a good overview of how risky a supplier's industry sector is, but simple data on the number of defaults not related to the size of the defaulted company or debts outstanding leaves a requirement for more comprehensive evaluation.
2. *Supply patterns.* Insurers may see a regular supply as higher risk because the likelihood of a supply failure is higher with a higher number of events. Large, single deliveries, however, pose a higher risk to the customer's balance sheet, representing a higher loss potential or impact.

3. *Suppliers' suppliers.* Supply failures are often caused by delays in the supplier's own supply chain. These are most commonly defined as tiers of supply. Tier 1 suppliers are traditionally where the customer has focused its efforts, but organizations in this position need to be aware that issues can arise lower down the supply chain, such as tier 2.

Pricing

The pricing of an advanced supply chain insurance product would consist of two components: a calculation model to determine the limit requirements and a risk premium factor to be applied to the limits a customer buys. The risk premium would have to be based on the likelihood of supply failure, based on risk assessment, and also taking into account country (political and other), industry (default), natural catastrophe risk, and so on.

Claims Handling

Claims handling would be a key component for both the customer and the insurer. Corporate buyers would want to have relative certainty as to what amount the insurer is going to pay, and when. Where the indemnity is set at the outset, the claims handler only needs to assess the validity of the insured's claim that profits have been lost following reduction or failure in supply. The rating tool provides the limit bought and a similar formula will determine the indemnity in the case of nonsupply. The insured would have to provide evidence that its business was interrupted, and to what degree. The insurer would need to ensure that it was paying the correct amount for genuine claims; in most countries this is known as a proxy for indemnity. The underwriting of claims would be a major component and cost element for the insurer; this would be especially true if perils covered included secondary losses beyond the initial and tangible claim.

Subrogation

If individual suppliers are at fault for a supply failure, insurers would want to reserve their rights to subrogation. The insured, therefore, would have to transfer its contractual rights to the insurer, which often causes unforeseen problems. The insurer may want to participate in successful contractual penalty claims made by the insured against the suppliers.

Corporate Customer Benefits Arising from Supply Chain Insurance

1. *Reserves.* A new insurance product may result in a reduction of the ratio of uninsurable risks, and as a result part of these reserves could be released.

   In cases where the opportunity cost for the released reserve (cost of capital) is significantly higher than the cost for insurance, SCI provides added value to the insured. The challenge for the chief financial officer is how to accurately compute the reduction of financial risk in monetary terms. Yet another challenge is to convince the underwriting portion of the insurance industry to explore this possibility.
2. *BI assessment expenses.* Business interruption risks need to be assessed as to compliance and effectiveness of the applicable business continuity plans. The underwriting assessment for SCI will take away some of the work or cost required by the business continuity management team so that there is a small additional cost benefit for the purchase of the insurance product.
3. *Detailed knowledge of exposures.* The insurer will bring in risk engineers and other specialists to map supply chains and to assess the likelihood and financial impact of an incident where this work has not already been performed by the insured. If they had previously been undertaken by the corporate customer it will still provide an outside view on exposure calculations. This assumes, of course, that insurers would be able to gear up their internal staff to quickly develop a supply chain risk management expertise necessary to make a fair evaluation.
4. *Possible increase in value for business as a whole.* How would financial markets react to the news that corporate customers have to buy protection for their supply chains? Insurance coverage usually protects value rather than increasing it. With SCI, however, analysts may welcome the fact that the board of a company considers buying coverage for previously uninsurable balance sheet risks at a time when the public focuses increasingly on risks, particularly to supply chains and their sustainability. It is certainly an area that is increasingly being

looked at by analysts and rating agencies. This could also involve the appropriate use of captives to optimize shareholder value.

In addition to the hard benefits listed above, there are soft factors that may influence the purchaser's decision:

- *Peace of mind.* The chief financial officer and risk management team can be sure they have done everything they can to protect the balance sheet. One important aspect of the insured's financial risks has been turned into a known and finite expense.
- *Benchmarking* of supply chain risk practices through comparison against the requirements set by the insurer or other external party such as the broker.

Conclusions

A number of corporate insurers have identified Supply Chain Insurance as a possible answer to the increasing challenges in terms of supply chain risk faced by their corporate customers. According to a leading insurer's internal research, many large organizations believe that current business interruption and other insurance arrangements do not fully suit their needs. Insurance expenditure on business interruption insurance where it is focused on property damage is widely seen by insureds as a cost to purchase protection as a commodity, albeit it is limited to its known tangible value. Any new products that are introduced by insurer should look at how they add value to the undertakings of the insured in order to be successful.

What Does the Future Hold?

Supply Chain Insurance products may become established in the marketplace, and the increasing demand from customers is making this very likely. The specialized skills that insurers and their broker partners have developed in pricing risk for many areas of business activity will be able to add considerable value to their customers. Other insurance products in the market might disappear or be cannibalized. There is also likely to be a number of links established with existing marine insurance and other products to provide customers with appropriate overall cover.

The need for insurance-based risk strategies requires that any and all forms of property and casualty insurance be included in the mix of financing solutions. Still, the challenges remain, and transforming the insurance industry to respond to modern financing requirements is going to demand effort and cooperation. Today, insurance may actually aggravate risk exposure, if only because your organization's executives take comfort in having coverage—while failing to understand why risk exposure continues to grow.

Here's a riddle: What protective measure makes the situation worse instead of improving it? The answer is insurance. Specifically, insurance worsens your risk exposure when times are tough, especially regarding trade credit. For example, when margins tighten not only for you but also for suppliers, manufacturers, and transportation resources, premiums go through the roof and levels of covered risks decline, or coverage you once assumed easy to find is now unavailable. A simple reality: Insurers will not offer coverage for potential claims they cannot afford. This problem comes up after expensive natural disasters (check rates for homeowners in the Gulf Coast if you want an example). It also comes up when international trade becomes a low-margin, high-risk, multifaceted, and complex series of far-reaching supply chains. This is the situation that many organizations find themselves in today.

In fact, the supply chain you deal with involves not only your suppliers and segments; today, the larger supply chain involves every organization as well as governments, national organizations (EU, OPEC, etc.), and political/economic interests (this includes not only recognized political factions but those in power and out of power, terrorists, pirates, and more).

As far as the trade credit problem is concerned, it may currently be an invisible risk, but if you have any involvement with international movement of materials, it will become a very real risk in the future. Companies may face the risk that one or more of their key customers will not be able to pay their trade debt. Bankruptcy as a business strategy, leveraged buyouts, fraud, civil unrest, domestic and international developments, and natural disasters—these are just some of the exposures that will impact a customer's ability to pay. Unfortunately, these practices have become more frequent with the downturn of the global economy in 2008 and 2009. Trade credit insurance can help protect companies from the harmful effects of buyer insolvency or slow payment.

One way to address this is through an expanded resource network. For example, Marsh's Trade Credit Practice specializes in developing solutions tailored to clients' specific credit exposures. The company maintains an extensive international network of credit insurance offices, so clients have ready access to local experts. This internal knowledge about international markets also enables Marsh to advise on the source and type of coverage that is going to be most suitable for a particular situation. In addition, Marsh works with underwriters to expand market capacity and develop improved trade credit products. With trade credit insurance in place, companies can extend more credit to creditworthy customers while reducing the risk of nonpayment, thereby promoting safe sales expansion. Favorable bank financing can be more easily obtained, assigning the insured's accounts receivable as collateral.

If your organization faces trade credit-based risk, you need to establish a similar network or, cheaper and easier, get yourself linked into an existing network program. But what exactly is appropriate coverage going to include? Trade credit coverage may extend to insuring up to 95 percent of a specified loss. Foreign exchange transfer risk, where the buyer is unable to make payment in contract currency due to the imposition of local currency controls, is included as a covered loss, which will be increasingly appealing if world currency volatility worsens in the future. Some political risks, such as import/export license cancellation or embargo, can also be included in a trade credit policy. Credit insurance can also protect against domestic insolvency, or mitigate the risk of a client failing to pay in a timely fashion.

The policy structure varies from a single- or multiple-buyer basis, covering domestic sales, foreign sales, or all sales combined. Most trade credit programs insure short-term (less than 180-day payment terms) trade receivables and are structured on a multiple-buyer format, insuring a broad spectrum of risk.

Risks may range from a company's largest domestic exposure. Multiple-buyer policies may cover sales periods of one to two years. The underwriting market includes government-supported export credit agencies (ECAs) and a host of private U.S. and European commercial insurance companies.

Many organizations rely on insurance to resolve supply chain exposure. Trade disruption, business interruption, contingent business interruption, marine and cargo, and other well-known

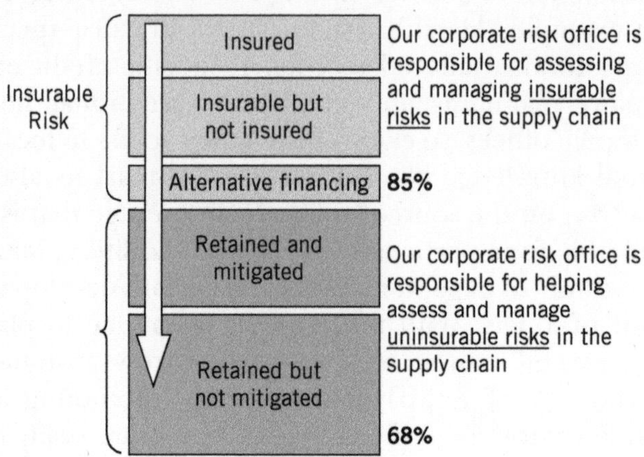

Exhibit 10.2 Insurable Risks

insurance programs are in place for most organizations. But this range of specific coverage often falls short of providing the safety net that your organization probably needs to properly manage the broad risk impact. You need to analyze the shortcomings, common mistakes, misinterpretations, limitations, and flawed assumptions when relying on insurance to finance and transfer your organization's supply chain risk. Your awareness level is the key; it is a safe bet that most of the decision makers in your organization have only scratched the surface of their awareness of risk, and of the insurance requirements you need currently to finance those risks.

An analysis of insurable risks and how they are financed, transferred, or accepted tells the story (see Exhibit 10.2). The big question you have to ask (and convince others to ask as well) is: Does the current structure of risk financing adequately protect my organization?

The Invisibility Factor

Many risks are invisible, if only because they have not yet come to life. The risk parasite is often dormant within the organization's body. Ironically, this is made worse when the organization finances the risk through insurance. There is a widespread assumption (and it is false) that insuring a threat eliminates it. Insurance coverage has been out of sight, out of mind. Suppliers beyond the first tier, likewise, are out of sight, out of mind. Outsourcing, manufacturing, logistics once delegated—all are out of sight, out of mind.

For example: In 2003, eight states and one Canadian province were blacked out simultaneously, affecting 50 million people. Even though power was restored in less than 24 hours, the cost to the U.S. economy was between $6 billion and $30 billion. Obviously, the longer a blackout, the more it costs and not all of the commercial losses are going to be recovered through insurance. Even so, this kind of threat is both expensive and invisible. No one anticipates a blackout and, of course, no one plans for it. Emergency response is likely to improve in many ways when companies use past experiences to better deal with the identical problem in the future. But the problem remains. This improved emergency response is based on past threats and not on future ones; those remain invisible.

Some forms of preparedness (like exit routes for employees when operating in the dark, first aid availability within a building or warehouse, or a well-thought-out communications strategy) are important preparedness steps. But they do not address the invisible issues that are going to be suffered in the next event, whether a blackout, a pandemic, or an assault on your IT assets.

Insurance issues are separate and beyond the matters that can be planned for. If you know the enemy is going to drop bombs on your city every night, you learn to cope by going underground in subway stations or backyard bomb shelters. But that is as far as your planning can see.

In planning for the insurance-related responses to a disaster, several important planning features should be incorporated as part of your broadly based risk management strategy. These include:

- Forensic accounting services, used to evaluate and articulate claims as a matter of preparing to actually place a claim with your insurer. These services are also useful in the event that your claim or a part of it is challenged and moves to the legal arena.
- Claims consultation, a process for managing claims documentation, facilitating timely payments, and associating complex claims with equally complex policy clauses.
- Mass-tort and liability consultation, the process of organizing to participate in what may of necessity become a widespread lawsuit. For example, in the 2003 blackout, it was only a few days after the blackout when a class-action lawsuit was filed. This raises yet another possible realm of risk exposure: What if

your organization is named as defendant in a lawsuit resulting from an invisible loss? How can you prepare to mitigate exposure by reducing the threat?

If you expect suppliers, employees, even customers to take action and responsibility, you have not addressed the risk. For example, you want suppliers to behave in a certain way—to create and maintain a button-down environment—but this doesn't just happen on its own; suppliers, like everyone else, need incentives.

Specifically, how should the range of supply chain risk be managed and what key questions should you be asking? For example: Isn't buying BI/CBI insurance enough? Why is this common assumption flawed and what can you do to change it? As the examples in the preceding pages have pointed out, there is a good probability that your BI/CBI insurance is far from adequate for the range of risks your organization believes it has been protected against. You are likely to need to review existing policies and identify the steps needed to further finance your threats beyond insurance.

When you have created risk transfer with an insurance product, you also have an expectation that it will pick up your risk of loss, and this assumption is usually 100 percent right. The property and casualty world has something called an "all risk" contract. Clients think they have the all risk contract, but in fact they have only paid for a cheaper version with specified losses; anything not listed is not covered. So often, the question comes up: "Why am I not covered after 50 years of paying premiums?"

The questions you need to ask in your organization are: Did you buy a proper product for my exposure? What is that product supposed to do? Many policies are just coverage for large losses, the catastrophic type with typical deductibles and small claims limits. For example, an increasingly popular loss demonstrates the problem. Your insurer may carry as high as a $200 million retention limit for environmental contracts, whereas policyholders are expected to pay up to $50 million in premiums each year.

It comes down to making the right match instead of throwing money away on insurance you don't really need, or insurance that doesn't give you the coverage you think you're getting. What are you trying to achieve and what are you trying to cover? What analysis has been performed internally, if any, to determine whether you're getting the protection you think you have? What is your tolerance for pain? How much is that parasite hurting your insides?

Typically, analysts don't look at coverage; they look at protection that you carry and pay for. Do you have a mechanism of recouping some of the financial impact you will suffer above and beyond your coverage? More to the point, has anyone even asked this question before? One of the great dangers of insurance is that organizations merely assume they are protected because they have a policy. You might not have given adequate attention and concern to the multiple tiers of risk you face overall.

A View from the Insurer's Side

How do insurance carriers look at aggregate supply chain exposure in a defined geographic area or for a specific incident? This is a big question, but the answer is not clear to most risk managers. Underwriters are not really focused on this question about supply chain risk in the aggregate, but are focused instead on specific kinds of losses, the cost/coverage relationship of an insurance policy, and questions of deductible levels and premium costs. The moral of this story: The insurer's underwriting question is always going to come down to: How much is a client going to absorb, what are waiting periods (no liability under policy for 45 days, etc.), supplements, and time frames?

An insurance underwriter tries to narrow coverage to specific events and in a policy that is not providing all loss coverage, your organization might be in for a rude awakening. Not only are many catastrophic losses excluded, but you may have been paying high-level premiums for many years but not getting enough protection. As what the insurance company refers to as "the insured," your organization needs to embark on a crash course of internal education. Your insurer has all of the information you need, but sadly does not provide it unless asked (or demanded) to do so.

An example of the less than tangible facts about insurance: Product recall coverage is tough to underwrite and involves potentially extreme cash flow issues and reputation risk. Consequently, it is also very expensive to buy. AIG, Ace, and others say they write such products, but in the real world these are not economically feasible to purchase. Trading dollars, you can buy product recall protection with specific limits and coverage for named hazards, but it's going to cost you a lot. The economics hurt it. This is also true for any type of insurance in which the total scope of loss cannot be known in advance, or when the known loss levels are too high for the insurer to carry, so limits are placed on the maximum payout. As a result, you end up with expensive coverage and a high deductible, with exorbitant premiums—and your losses are only partly covered.

Anytime you put your supply chain risk under insurance, you face another kind of risk, one that may come up only when you put in a claim. For example, the underwriter might argue that you misrepresented the level of risk. This is a way to minimize the insurer's claims exposure, and it will arise particularly when a single insurer has retained the full coverage liability (or when retention limits are unrealistically high and the company has been unwilling to enter any reinsurance agreements that share the larger risks).

What are the three questions every supply chain manager should be asking management to think about?

1. *Have we taken a realistic look at the depth and breath of our coverage?* If something goes horribly wrong, do we have a risk transfer product that funds us enough to keep us (and our suppliers) on our feet? Can we go to another third party to help maintain business in the worst-case scenario?
2. *What is the outcome if "x" happens; what are we facing with our suppliers?* On this question, you cannot spend enough time talking to people on the ground. Raising the question of unthinkable threats is essential before you can know whether your combination of insurance, transfer, and acceptance is correct.
3. *Does the organization understand what loss control our suppliers are taking?* More to the point, what is our liability if they are not protected? Your organization may risk not only losing a key supplier, but losing customers as well, when insurance coverage does not provide the blanket of protection you need. With second-tier manufacturing in the mix, the potential exposure may be even more significant than you think at first glance.

Another big factor is how remote your supply chain has become. Now you not only are unsure about whether or not your suppliers have the right kind of insurance, you are dealing with people you may have never met. So many executives are still operating on a model at least a generation out of touch. In the past, you knew your suppliers personally, they were local, and you had a long-standing relationship with them. Now you are dealing with the unknown on many levels—not only the remoteness and uncertainty of supplier operations and second-tier reliance, but even the basic question: Is my organization's liability protected adequately through supplier-initiated insurance? You probably don't know.

An increased number of offerings in contingency business interruption coverage include expanded supply chain risks, such as the risks associated with denial of port access, blockage of ingress and egress at business sites, curtailment from a named supplier, and failure of public utilities. Does your company rely on international shipment and, if so, do you carry these kinds of contingencies? Are levels of coverage adequate given the volume of materials you ship? How about deductibles and claims limits? Run an analysis of the worst-case scenario and then decide whether you are truly covered.

Remember one key point about this issue: You are probably underinsured and the coverage you are paying may not cover your losses. At the very least, it is essential to understand the distinctions between insurable and uninsurable risks. Many of your losses will also be uninsurable, so you need to identify ways that the risk management process can be adjusted to protect against these losses. Anyone who relies too much on insurance for these threats is underinsured and needs to take another look. Be aware of the differences between resource coverage and supply chain process coverage. This could be one of the weakest links of exposure in your supply chain.

Notes

1. United Nations Children's Fund (UNICEF), May 11, 2009, www.reliefweb.int/rw/rwb.nsf/db900sid/EGUA-7RXN96/$File/full_report.pdf.
2. The Terrorism Risk Insurance Act (TRIA) is a United States federal law signed into law by President George W. Bush on November 26, 2002. The Act created a federal "backstop" for insurance claims related to acts of terrorism. The Act is intended as a temporary measure to allow time for the insurance industry to develop their own solutions and products to insure against acts of terrorism. The Act was set to expire December 31, 2005, then extended for another two years by legislation in December 2005, making the new expiry date December 31, 2007. On Dec. 26, 2007, the Act was again extended under the Terrorism Risk Insurance Program Reauthorization Act, which extends the Terrorism Risk Insurance Act through Dec. 31, 2014. Other sources include the US Treasury Web Site, http://www.treas.gov/offices/domestic-finance/financial-institution/terrorism-insurance/; and the National Association of Insurance Commissioners's, http://www.naic.org/topics/topic_tria.htm; and Ben Tucker (Marsh).
3. "Managing Large-Scale Risks in a New Era of Catastrophes," Wharton School of the University of Pennsylvania, March, 2008; preface and executive summary.

CHAPTER 11

Law #10: Manage the Risk as You Manage Your Own

YOUR SUPPLY CHAINS ARE ALL INTERDEPENDENT BUT UNIQUE

> I was driving to work one morning, going on a different route than usual to avoid an exceptionally heavy traffic flow. At a four-way stop, I looked both ways and, after the obligatory full stop, I proceeded into the intersection. And then it happened. A car came out of nowhere, nicked my front bumper, and spun my car about 90 degrees. No one was injured, but the damage to both cars was more than $10,000. It was the other driver's fault (she was on her cell phone and didn't see the stop sign), and I'm certain that her next insurance bill went way up.
>
> At the time, a number of thoughts raced through my head. If only I had gone the usual way the accident wouldn't have happened. The paperwork and the tow to the body shop took hours, not to mention getting a rental, rescheduling missed meetings, and the strain on my mind. It all happened because I took a different route. Didn't it?

Supply chains work like that. Relatively minor decisions or events outside of anyone's control drastically alter everything that follows. If I had taken my usual route, something far worse could have transpired, and then I'd be kicking myself for not taking a different route. In other words, we don't really have control over everything, or, in some cases, anything. All we can do is plan ahead to reduce the damage or, in the world of risk management, minimize the likelihood of threats and mitigate vulnerabilities. That's why we rely on stop signs and traffic rules, as well as solidly built cars, air bags, and seat belts. All of these are designed to reduce fatalities and serious injuries when we imperfect humans make mistakes and have accidents. And just as the other driver's carelessness ruined my day as well as hers, all of the actions we take in the next five minutes have the potential to affect other people. This is the human supply chain and we are all parts of it.

Throughout this book, I have emphasized some very specific aspects of supply chain risk that are common to all organizations (although I must admit I was a bit frustrated since I only had enough room to scratch the surface). The same observations apply to each of us as individuals, and how we behave as people adds up to a collective string of behaviors we exhibit as members of organizations. Our free will determines the actions we take or avoid intentionally, but free will can only go so far. Beyond free will are the arbitrary and random occurrences that strike without warning. Anyone can find himself in a bank as a hold-up occurs, or on the road when a bridge collapses, or working for a company that gets acquired and dissolved. These things are beyond our control. This is why we have to function within our personal supply chains with a degree of appropriate risk awareness. If the activity inside of a bank seems odd, we should not enter but rather phone the police. If you see the roadway ahead swaying and buckling, it makes no sense to keep driving forward. And you want to keep your resume up to date, not to mention maintaining a network of good contacts in case your career comes to an unexpected bump in the road.

The point here is an important one: We all live with risk. It is not a vague matter affecting your company but not you. Risk doesn't exist at a distant port or in a warehouse in another country; it is everywhere. However, risk is manifested in a unique way for every industry, geography, organization, and individual. Remember the quote "If you've seen one supply chain, you've seen one supply chain." In some industries, achieving 98 percent risk tolerance is considered acceptable, and that's okay. But if we apply that risk tolerance to the U.S. airline industry, then we would have 1,740 flights falling out of the sky every day (2 percent of 87,000 daily U.S. flights). The point is that risk tolerances vary, and so does the makeup of the industry and its impacts on others. If you apply the rules of organizational supply chains to your own behavior, you reduce your own risks and you also reduce the risks to the organization of which you are a part.

Questioning Old Assumptions

I want to repeat a question I asked in the very first section of this book, in the Laws of the Laws. What if the premise on which your organization is built is no longer valid? The point I wanted to make when I first posed this question is not that it is a troubling idea, but that it is not asked often enough. The same thing applies to you personally. We humans do, indeed, need to continually evaluate and reevaluate our premises, the assumptions on which we operate, and the beliefs that drive our activities. The lessons you can learn from asking this question have a profound series of ramifications, not only within your organization but in your life, too.

We all operate without stopping to think about the basic needs we all have. There are three: food, energy, and shelter. Everything else falls somewhere within one of these three essentials. From the organizational and societal point of view, we can express these as commodities (agriculture and forestry, oil and gas, or construction and housing, for example). But this tends to put these in an impersonal venue when, in reality, we need all of these things on a daily basis. You need to feed yourself and your family, protect them from the cold, and provide them with shelter. You rely on interdependent supply chains to bring these basic needs to your community or front door. Everything else you need is an outgrowth of these three essentials. Your personal supply chain is rudimentary in its most primitive form, but we all complicate our own supply chains by adding in a series of *wants* on top of the *needs* that define the supply and demand elements. We don't have customers other than our own families and employers, but we certainly do have suppliers, and we rely heavily on materials, logistics, financing, and mitigation—in other words, the organizational supply chain is a highly organized version of our personal supply chain.

So in our quest to continue the supply chain of food, energy, and shelter, what risk parasites do we face? I am not going to try to list them because we are all aware of what would happen if any of the necessities in our lives were to come to a halt. On a personal level, risk is not meaningless nor should it be ignored, as it has been by so many people on the organizational level. But there is a danger. Just as organizational risk has lost its association as a negative or even as a threat, it has become easy for us as individuals to ignore or forget the supply chain risks we all face. My purpose in emphasizing this danger is not to trouble you, but to make the point I have been stressing throughout this book: You can mitigate and eliminate risk only by (1) being aware of it, (2) measuring its impacts, (3) recognizing the course of events, materials and information, (4) deciding what steps have to be taken today to avoid future exposure, and (5) constantly monitoring it.

The risk parasite that is simply everywhere is best managed on a personal level in precisely the same way it is handled organizationally. So the object lessons in this book apply to our basic needs supply chain of the three essential commodities: food, energy, and shelter. An organization may recognize that it has to provide product to its customers, ensure the movement of materials through suppliers and a logistics chain, and provide warehousing, retail space, and offices. These are the organizational versions of the three basic needs: food (materials and product), energy (logistics), and housing (facilities and operations).

The risk parasite functions for individuals as it does for organizations, manifesting itself at each and every single point of failure. On a drive to work, every four-way stop represents a hazard, and every other car on the road is a potential single point of failure. The risk is everywhere and is an attribute of your supply chain. This is why it makes no sense to punish ourselves for not taking a different route on a particular morning. We could avoid a specific *incident* but we cannot avoid the *risk* itself. The best you can hope for is to be aware of your personal risk parasite in the same way you're aware of your organization's risk parasite, and take steps to mitigate or avoid its effects. This is why we wear seat belts, avoid using our cell phones while driving, and buy cars that have been impact tested and come with reinforced construction and air bags.

Important Questions to Keep in Mind

In the Laws of the Laws chapter, I proposed a series of four questions every organization should ask. I now ask you to apply them on a personal level. The questions are:

1. *How do I create value and significance and what role does my personal supply chain play in that process?* Can I visualize my risks,

and understand and measure their impacts? This is a huge question, because when you ask it, you are examining your entire life and purpose.

2. *How do other people in my life (family, friends, employer, co-workers—my personal stakeholders) view and define my supply chain risk, if at all?* In other words, what expectations do others assume or impose on me? How do they measure success and failure when it comes to managing risk? Asking this question forces us to define how we interact with others; it can be a troubling question to ask, though, because it may reveal realities we don't want to deal with. But if you are to have any prospects of defeating your risk parasite, you have to know the score with your own personal stakeholders.
3. *What impact do my own actions, abilities, and motives have on protecting the essential needs (food, energy, shelter)?* This question can manifest in several forms. The responsible working head of households needs to ensure a continuing income stream to protect the family and its well-being and a destructive behavior can be devastating, so an alcoholic or someone with a gambling addiction will either get help and avoid disaster or destroy the entire supply chain as a consequence. The *impact* of our behavior certainly exists within the organization, but it also co-exists in every aspect of our lives. And it has the potential of being either a positive or a negative factor.
4. *Who is responsible for managing my personal supply chain risk?* Some people tend to think they have to do everything themselves and cannot rely on others; on the far end of the spectrum, some people assume someone else will step in and take care of everything. The truth lies in between. We are individually responsible for identifying all of our single points of failure, but we also rely on our stakeholders to do their part.

If you are able to think about and address these important points, then you will be in better shape than most people. Identifying the context for solution, overlaid with the practical limitations of cultural, social, and personal limitations, is the best way to improve chances for success. It really all comes down to how well you understand the components of your personal supply chain (and its risk parasites, stakeholders, and shared responsibilities) that determines how well you—like your organization—can manage and better understand your own single points of failure.

Personal Laws of the Laws

This book has been premised on the observation that a series of specific operating laws apply to the supply chain. These consist of customers, suppliers, materials, logistics, financing, and mitigation. But all of the supply chain aspects also operate within the constraints of four Laws of the Laws, and this applies to your personal supply chain as well.

The four Laws of the Laws are:

Law of the Laws #1. Everyone, without exception, is part of a supply chain. This is true for organizations and for individuals. There are no safe havens where this law does not apply, and I challenge anyone to describe a situation exempt from this law.

Law of the Laws #2. No risk strategy is a substitute for bad decisions and a lack of risk consciousness. You can, for example, buy a car with the best safety rating and features, but this doesn't mean it is okay to ignore traffic rules. The strategy itself is a necessary and orderly part of how we operate, but diligence and the selection of good decisions is an attribute of a high level of risk consciousness. A point I have emphasized throughout this book is that the higher your risk consciousness, the better your chances for effective management of the supply chain, both organizationally and individually.

Law of the Laws #3. It's all in the details. This may seem at first glance to be a rather cynical rule, but in fact it is a profound observation. If you have read through the many case histories and examples presented in previous chapters, one recurring theme is evident: The successful and effective instances when supply chain risk was reduced required close attention to the details.

Law of the Laws #4. People always operate from self-interest. I think this is probably the most important Law of the Laws. You cannot expect others to suffer losses to protect you, and by the same argument, you are always operating with your basic requirements in mind, on behalf of yourself and your families (primary stakeholders). So the pursuit of food, energy, and shelter is at the heart of self-interest and it cannot be avoided. However, even while operating out of self-interest, you can still be an enlightened stakeholder in the broader supply chains of which you are a part (these include your family, employer, friends, and even fellow drivers sharing the road). In fact, recognizing the presence of self-interest makes you a better and more informed stakeholder in all of the supply chains to which you belong, for several reasons:

- You are aware of not only your own self-interest but everyone else's as well.
- Knowing that self-interest is always present makes you better equipped to look out for and mitigate risks.
- Many of the potholes you face can be anticipated and avoided once you accept the reality of personal self-interest.

The unavoidable reality of the globally connected supply chain means that single points of failure are found everywhere and not just within organizations. All of the troubling aspects of supply chain risk that we face are better managed by awareness and cooperation with other stakeholders. This is the most important point of all. Risk does not exist in isolation or elsewhere in our personal or organizational lives. We cannot escape it, but we can manage and mitigate it.

The degree to which you can manage risk ultimately determines how well you identify single points of failure and then pinpoint the steps you can take today to avoid dangers in the future. No one wants to have a fender bender at the stop sign, but it happens. So relying on diligence and awareness as well as on seat belts and air bags points the way to avoiding fatalities when risk happens, and looking both ways will avoid most accidents. These are supply chain words to live by.

Index

A

A Bridge Too Far, 247
Abraxis Pharmaceutical Products (APP), 191
Ace Group, 275
Acer, 176
AEY Inc., 152
AIG, 48, 275
Alcoa, 10–11, 188
Alien, 9–10
All risks and exclusions, 264, 265–268
Allianz SE, 160
Amazon.com, 123
AMD, 190
AMR Research, 125
Apache Energy, 10–11
APEC economies, 211
Apollo 13 disaster, 61–62
Apple Computer, 135
Arm & Hammer, 217
At Your Own Risk, 38, 174, 205, 235
Atradius NV, 158
Audits and enforcement standards, 138
Avian flu, 75–79, 115–116
Avon Products, 164–165

B

Bacon, Kevin, 79
BAE Systems North America, 66–68
Bartol, Craig, 177
Batilla Group, 176
Baxter Labs, 11, 191
Best Buy, 190–191, 215
Big Three (auto companies), 152, 158
Black Death, 173–174, 196–197
Black Friday, 123
BMW, 156–157
Boeing, 188
BP, 176
Brown, Gordon, 194
Bullwhip effect, 56
Bush, George W., 82
Business Alliance for Secure Commerce (BASC), 220–221
Business interruption insurance (BI), 255–258

C

Cadbury Schweppes, 11, 144
Campbell's, 150–151
Cargill, 110, 178
Cargo theft, 203–205
Carmakers Trade Association (France) (CCFA), 127
Carrefour SA, 189
Carroll, Lewis, 37
Centre of Research on the Epidemiology of Disasters, 112
Change, 43–48, 54–56, 66, 184–186, 234–237
Changzhou Scientific Protein Laboratories (SPL), 191, 193
Chappell, Michael, 190, 194
Chavez, Hugo, 109–110
Chen Jianjun, 193
CHEP USA, 203
Chinese Dairy Association, 143–144
Church & Dwight, 217
Cisco, 88, 118–119, 135, 176, 189
Clear line of sight, 23, 162–163
Coca-Cola, 11, 132
Colella, Amy, 123

Collaborative effort (manufacturing), 181–186
Collateralized debt obligations (CDOs), 45, 245
Common language, 164–165
Corporate Responsibility (CR), 176
Credit insurance, 159–161, 259–260
Credit Suisse, 192
CSX Transportation, 208–209
Cui Huifel, 193
Customers, 124–141

D

Darden Restaurants, 88
Dell Computer, 189
Delta Consulting Group, 229–230
Demand-based strategy, 127–132
Department of Defense, 69–70
Deverticalization and deglobalization, 218
Diablo Canyon 2 reactor, 17
Disaster recovery plans, 139–140
Dow Chemical Company, 175
Dreamliner jet, 188

E

Eastman Kodak, 126, 132–133
Emerson Electric Company, 176
Enterprise resource planning (ERP), 42
Ericsson, 19
Eschenbach, Andrew von, 191
Euler Hermes SA, 160
Export credit agencies (ECAs), 271
Exposure diversification, 136–137
ExxonMobil, 11

F

Federal Emergency Management Agency (FEMA), 208
Federal Reserve, 245–246
Financing issues, 158–159
Fisher-Price, 56
Folgers Coffee, 209
Fonterra Co-operative Group Ltd., 11, 55, 144, 176
Food and Drug Administration (FDA), 63, 94, 98, 190, 192
Ford Motor Company, 15, 110, 152
Frederick, Shannon, 59
Friedman, Thomas, 104

G

Gazprom, 11, 201–202
General Electric, 176
General Mills, 178
General Motors, 11
Glass Steagall Act, 46
Global 500 organizations, 168
Golden Temple of Oregon, 124
Goods in transit insurance, 260–263
Government Accountability Office (GAO), 191
Gross domestic product (GDP), 78, 211
Gustav (Hurricane), 209

H

Hamilton, William, 37
Harley-Davidson, 88
Heinz, 144
Heparin, 191–193
Hewlett-Packard,
Hytek, 31–32

I

IBM, 45, 52, 176, 189
Imperial Sugar, 177–178
Industrial Revolution, 173–174, 196
Innovation chain, 134
Insurable risks, 272
Insurance
  all risks and exclusions, 264, 265–268
  business interruption (BI), 255–258
  credit, 159–161, 259–260
  goods in transit, 260–263
  loss experience, 266–267
  Marine Cargo Insurance, 260–263
Marine Insurance Act of 1906 (MIA), 261–262
  named perils, 264
  risks (insurable), 272
  securitization, 259–260

solutions and limitations, 255–263
subrogation, 267–268
Intel, 11, 18–19, 190
Internal education, 138–139
International Maritime Bureau (IMB), 205–206
Invisibility factor, 272–275
Irwin, James, 79, 116
Ivan (Hurricane), 121

J

Jidoka, 15–16, 23, 156
Johnson & Johnson, 121, 176
Joocie's Grape Juice, 93–99

K

Kadam, Rajeev, 13
Katrina (Hurricane), 121, 208–210
Kentucky Fried Chicken, 144
Knowledge base, 138–139
Koala, 144

L

Laws of the Laws
advice from, 100
basic, 26
details, 227
explained, 12–13
indirect threats and, 27
key questions, 282–283
listed, 14
personal, 284–285
supply chain, 145–146
valid premise, 281
Lee Der, 55
Linyl Melyuan Seasoning Company, 192
Lipton Tea, 144
Liu Jian, 193
Lockheed Martin, 195
Logistics flow, 202, 212–216
London Metals Exchange, 209
Loss experience, 266–267
Lotte Group, 144
Lovell, Jim, 61–62
LVMH Moét Hennessy, 176

M

Marine Cargo Insurance, 260–263
Marine Insurance Act of 1906 (MIA), 261–262
Market and client factors, 135–136
Marsh & McLennan, 57, 229, 271
Mattel, 11, 56, 178–180
Mazda, 206–207
McKinsey Group, 57
Melamine poisoning, 11, 69, 143–144
Mengnlu-Arla, 144
Merkel, Angela, 194
Microsoft, 11, 123, 135
Mitigation, 238–247
Mucha, Gary, 66–69
Murphy, Bob, 227–229

N

Nader, Francois, 59
Nadler, David, 229
Named perils, 264
Nantong Koulong, 193
Nargis (Cyclone), 112
National Association of Corporate Directors, 59
National Cargo Security Council, 204
NATO, 201–202
Neiman Marcus, 135
Nike, 31–33, 35–36, 135, 169, 176–177
Nixon, Richard, 126
Nokia, 19–20, 135, 189
Nongovernmental organizations (NGOs), 46, 174
Nordenberg, Dale, 192
NPS Pharmaceutical, 59

O

Oklahoma! 139
Olam International Ltd., 13
Olympic Games, 35, 137–138
OPEC, 270
Organizational genome, 105–106
OSHA, 178

P

Park 'n Shop, 144
PCS Nitrogen, 108

Pentium FDIV bug, 18–19
Pepsico, 156
Petróleos Mexicanos, 11
PG&E Corporation, 17
Piggly Wiggly, 178
Piracy, 205–208
Policy structure chart, 150
Political Risks Insurance, 259–260
Prescription Drug Marketing Act, 63
Proctor & Gamble, 81, 176, 209
Product theft, 219
Production (critical), 186–197

R

Ranta, Paul, 176–177
Red queen hypothesis, 37
Resiliency management, 234–237
Rio Tinto, 10–11, 176
Risconomic exercise, 235
Risk and risk management
  accountability, 45–46
  action plan, 108–112
  aggregate exposure, 46–47, 57, 59
  aligned priorities, 68
  assessment, 266
  assumptions, 53
  awareness, 49, 92–99
  big production, 175–178
  conscious culture, 104, 112
  continuous change, 46–47
  defined, 13–14
  evaluation criteria, 168
  execution gap, 66
  expectations, 64–65
  external evaluation failure, 47
  geographic, 57
  impacts, 26–27
  increased by sourcing strategies, 154–165
  intelligent supply chain, 229–233
  kingdom (keys to), 102–105
  lessons learned, 44
  logistics, 200–203
  long-term, 24–26
  low frequency, high impact, 51
  misaligned priorities, 67
  mitigation, 74, 238–247
  mob mentality, 46
  multiplier effect, 176
  overlay, 43
  paradigm, 66–71
  parts and the whole, 22–24
  piracy, 205–208
  price, 48
  prioritization, 22, 50
  role-based, 58
  selling to third parties, 48
  set downstream, 70
  sourcing policy, 147–152
  systemic, 44–45, 244–247
  transactional, 51
  transfer policies, 48
  triggers, 34
  unexpected, 51
  universal dimension, 93
  universe of events, 34
  visibility and transparency, 45
  wake-up call, 39–43
Risk parasite
  consciousness, 18–20
  described, 10
  destruction of, 61–62
  dormant, 272–273
  drivers, 39
  evolving, 37
  examples, 11
  expanding, 37–38
  factory to customer, 186–187
  management, 282
  new breed of, 40
  strategies, 18–20
  universe of events that trigger, 34
Rita (Hurricane), 209
Roche, 79, 115–117, 124–125
Rockwell Automation, 227–229, 230
Roudier, Francois, 127
Rubicon Resources LLC, 88
Ruihia, 193
Ryan, Cornelius, 247

S

Saks Fifth Avenue, 125–126
Sanlu Group, 11, 55, 143

Scientific Protein Laboratories, 191–192
Seconds from Disaster, 28
Secret Service, 82
Securitization, 259–260
Shell Oil, 176
Shenzhen Hepalink, 191
Single point of failure syndrome, 47, 110, 147, 203, 212–216, 226, 251
Six Sigma, 26, 68, 141–142
Sourcing strategies, 154–165
Srinivasan, Mandyam M., 121–122
Starbucks, 144
Streamlined, 121–122
Strunce, David, 191, 193
Subrogation, 267–268
Suppliers, taking up the cause of, 163
Supply chain
- activities (risk), 62–63, 73
- awareness, 16–17
- bullwhip effect, 56
- concentration, 58
- consist, 41
- decentralized, 37–38
- DNA, 87–89, 90–91
- driven force, 125
- energy, 80
- everyone is part of, 14–18
- extended, 101–102
- failure, 151–154
- finance solutions, 260–262
- flows, 134
- food, 20, 89
- global, 44, 135
- information flow, 216–218
- initiatives, 111
- insurance, 250–269
- moving target, 58
- offensive practices, 135
- overlay chart, 231
- positive and negative impacts, 140–141
- processes and subprocesses, 233
- production capacity, 117, 119
- profitable, 41
- proper scope, 190, 194
- pull and push, 120
- risk intelligent, 229–233
- risk management program, 144–154
- risk overlay, 12, 100
- risk paradigm, 63, 70, 81–82
- risk programs, 66
- slave to demand, 117
- strategy, 161–162
- supplier as part of, 164–165
- sustainable, 40–41
- universe, 122

Swine Flu (H1N1), 75–79, 115–117, 252
Szwast, Scott, 57, 133–134

T

Tamiflu, 79, 115, 124–125
Target, 81, 88, 215
Terrorism Risk Insurance Act (TRIA), 256
Tesco, 88, 135, 189
Through the Looking Glass, 37
Tiffany's, 88
Titanic, 48–49, 53
Toyota, 11, 15–16, 23, 81, 176
Trade Disruption Insurance, 258–259
Tragedy of the Commons, 22
Transfer and sharing plans, 137–138
Trust (suppliers) but verify, 165–170
TSMC, 190
Tylenol, 121

U

U.S. Customs, 88
UMC, 190
Unilever, 144, 176
Union Carbide, 175
United Parcel Service, 57, 133–134

V

Viatsoy, 144
Visteon Corporation, 152
Volatility in demand cycles, 132–135

W

Wal-Mart, 11, 55, 59, 88–89, 123, 135, 178, 189, 212, 215
Warehouse theft, 203–205

Wellcome, 144
Weng Shengfu, 192
Williams, Doug, 195
World Bank, 78
World Health Organization (WHO), 115–116
World Is Flat, 104
World Trade Center, 136–137
World Trade Organization (WTO), 194–195, 246–247

X

Xbox, 123

Y

YouTube, 175

Z

Zheng Xiaoyu, 69
Zhu Jinlan, 193
Zurich Financial Services, 48